The German Way of War

The German Way of War

A Lesson in Tactical Management

Jaap Jan Brouwer

PEN & SWORD
HISTORY

AN IMPRINT OF PEN & SWORD BOOKS LTD.
YORKSHIRE - PHILADELPHIA

First published in 2017 by Uitgeverij Aspekt as *Auftragstatik en het Pruisische/Duitse leger 1850-1945*

First published in Great Britain in 2021 and
reprinted in this format in 2024 by
Pen & Sword Military
An imprint of
Pen & Sword Books Ltd
Yorkshire - Philadelphia

Copyright © Jaap Jan Brouwer, 2021, 2024

ISBN 9781526797179

Printed and bound in England
By CPI (UK) Ltd.

Pen & Sword Books Limited incorporates the imprints of Archaeology,
Atlas, Aviation, Battleground, Digital, Discovery, Family History, Fiction,
History, Local, Local History, Maritime, Military, Military Classics, Politics,
Select, Transport, True Crime, After the Battle, Air World, Claymore Press,
Frontline Publishing, Leo Cooper, Remember When, Seaforth Publishing,
The Praetorian Press, Wharncliffe Books, Wharncliffe Local History,
Wharncliffe Transport, Wharncliffe True Crime and White Owl.

For a complete list of Pen & Sword titles please contact

PEN & SWORD BOOKS LIMITED
47 Church Street, Barnsley, South Yorkshire, S70 2AS, England
E-mail: enquiries@pen-and-sword.co.uk
Website: www.pen-and-sword.co.uk

or

PEN AND SWORD BOOKS
1950 Lawrence Rd, Havertown, PA 19083, USA
E-mail: uspen-and-sword@casematepublishers.com
Website: www.penandswordbooks.com

Contents

Foreword

A great deal has been written about the Second World War, and the authors are almost always historians or former officers. It is therefore remarkable that a management consultant has ventured into this area. The author describes the military organizations from the perspective of his profession and comes to interesting conclusions. Why did the German armies achieve such astonishing successes when they were very much in the minority in numbers of tanks and men? And how were they capable of such achievements despite conducting a war on multiple fronts?

The key to the successes of the German Army was its modern combat doctrine and leadership style. This doctrine, in which tanks played a central role, was ingrained at all levels of the organization. If in the chaos of the fighting the connection between fighting units and the command centre was lost, German units continued to fight on their own initiative, while their Allied counterparts often did not know what to do. German commanders were trained to critically assess any situation, and were allowed to deviate from the orders given and use their own initiative if the situation so required. They had learned that battles could deteriorate quickly into chaos and that they had to act fast to utilize all possibilities. This was not a culture of '*Befehl ist Befehl*' [orders are orders], but of modern, flexible leadership.

After the Second World War, the Dutch Army initially focused on the British Army, later on the American. We adopted the American doctrine and its hierarchical style of leadership. Detailed planning and preparation in advance in combination with rigid implementation was the norm. Officers were not expected to deviate from orders given without their commander's permission. In non-operational circumstances, one tried to avoid future errors by the constant adjustment of rules. In fact, this was far removed from the military's core competence, namely being able to deal with the uncertainties of the battlefield. Dealing with uncertainties is difficult for everyone involved, and people must therefore be trained in it time and again. This also means that mistakes must be accepted and that one must dare to learn from them. People who don't make mistakes don't exist.

FOREWORD

In recent years we can find in US management books interesting ideas and theories about modern leadership. It is suggested that these are new insights, but this ignores the fact that the German Army developed a management concept in the period between the two world wars that answers many current questions in the field of management and organization. It is therefore interesting to learn something of this management concept: it was not only based on academic theory, but also tested in the hard practice of the battlefield and proved to be extremely successful. Because there are many similarities in the functioning of companies and the armed forces, this book is recommended both for officers of the armed forces and for managers in the business world!

Lieutenant General H. A. Couzy (1940-2019),
former Commander-in-Chief of the Royal Netherlands Army

Acknowledgements

This book can be seen as a compilation the insights I have gained in recent years studying the American, British and especially German Army in the period from 1850 to 1945. These organizations have fascinated me from my childhood, and I am very pleased that both the literature and my practice as a management consultant still offer new perspectives on them almost every day. Learning is an ongoing process in this area, and that is perhaps one of the most interesting dimensions of history. I have tried to translate my fascination into a logical and consistent story that on the one hand offers a clear analytical framework and on the other hand deals sufficiently with the reality of the battlefield. I received support from Major Ruud Veen, officer of the Royal Netherlands Army, with regard to the latter. He is responsible for the chapter on the fighting at Overloon in 1944. This chapter offers a nice illustration of the theory that precedes it. Special thanks also go to Eric Roncke who, with his erudite interpretation of history and culture, demonstrated that on the one hand reality is more complex than we think, but on the other hand that it shows greater coherence than we initially see. In addition, a word of thanks to my wife Loes and our children Michiel, Cathelijne and Sophie, who were witness to the emergence of this and all my other books on military organizations. They have given me the time and space to dive into books and magazines, whether on holiday or not, and have been kind enough to listen to all my stories.

While every effort has been made to trace the copyright holders of illustrations which are not otherwise credited, the publishers and I apologize for any inadvertent omissions.

References in the text are to the bibliography and are expressed thus: 15:294, where the first is the source's number in the list, and the second is the page number.

CHAPTER ONE

Introduction: Defeat as a Basis for Learning

In 1806, the Prussians suffered a painful defeat by Napoleon's armies at the Battle of Jena (there were actually two battles, one at Jena and one at Auerstadt). To give an impression of the magnitude of the battle and the effects of the ensuing defeat, the French deployed 121,000 men and the Prussians 117,000, with resultant losses of 12,000 and 38,000 respectively. This defeat had a profound impact. While Prussia lost large parts of its territory and inhabitants to France, perhaps more importantly the loss underlined the need for reform of both the army and the feudal state of Prussia. Reformers such as Scharnhorst, Gneisenau and Clausewitz had fought at Jena, and in the following years they laid the foundations for much needed reforms and sparked the transformation of Prussia into a modern state. Under the leadership of this renewed Prussia, France would eventually be expelled from German territory. It was the starting point of the leading role that Germany would come to play in Europe, a role that it still plays today.

After Jena, contrary to common practice in other armies at the time, the Prussians evaluated in detail the reasons for their defeat. They came to the conclusion that the battlefield was 'a chaos'. We can imagine this when we consider the sheer number of people fighting in a relatively small area. The Prussians concluded that this chaos doomed every attempt at centralized command and control, since the time lag between messages from the front to the commanders and back again was so great that they were only applicable to the situation of a couple of hours earlier.

The Prussians concluded, in fact, that the battlefield was so complex and unpredictable that using detailed plans and orders actually put them at a serious disadvantage: after the first shots had been fired, plans and orders were immediately irrelevant and did not reflect the reality of battle. Moreover, a commander actually wants his soldiers to react positively to unexpected situations in real time, rather than having to wait for orders.

Troops must learn to deal with these situations and the chaos of the battlefield themselves. Very significantly, it is this very chaos that creates the ideal environment for troops to seize the advantage, provided that they have been trained to respond to opportunities. Therefore, if there is no chaos, you must create it to unbalance your opponent. This view was, and is, contrary to that of most army organizations which, then and now, attempt to control the battlefield and the course of the fighting. This Prussian analysis formed the basis of *Auftragstaktik*, a command concept with highly decentralized decision-making and ample room for initiative.

The evolution of what we now call *Auftragstaktik* started in 1812, when the rules for infantry were adjusted based on the above analysis; the classic rigid combat formation was replaced by a more flexible one, with units directly under divisional commanders who were given more room to use their own initiative and freedom of thought and action. However, at lower levels in the organization, manoeuvring with large formations of soldiers as one group remained commonplace.

It was a technological change in the middle of the nineteenth century that forced everyone to fundamentally rethink battlefield operations, when the classic musket was replaced by the breech-loading rifle. The speed of fire of the latter and the range at which this fire was effective made manoeuvring in larger formations on the battlefield far more dangerous. This marked the onset of major changes in the way infantry operated and can be regarded as one of the decisive arguments used by the Prussian Army in introducing *Auftragstaktik* in both depth and breadth in its organization. The Wars of German Unification of 1864 against Denmark, 1866 against Austria and 1870–71 against France confirmed that technological development, not only of weapon systems but also, for example, of the telegraph, had definitively undermined prevailing doctrines and tactics. These new weapons and technologies forced military organizations to split existing formations into ever-smaller units and spread these over an ever-wider area. Army commanders, corps commanders and the commanders of divisions and regiments could no longer physically overlook and control their units, and were thus forced to drastically devolve decision-making to lower echelons. However, the results could be disastrous, as these lower levels of command were not always able to cope with these new responsibilities. It was clear that it was necessary to develop a new command concept that, on the one hand, placed responsibilities and decision-making capabilities lower in the organization while, on the other, guaranteed that the commanders of these units would not take counter-productive decisions.

Helmuth von Moltke, Chief of the *General Stab* (General Staff) from 1857 to 1888, played a decisive role in the development of *Auftragstaktik* and can be seen as the spiritual father of this new command concept. From him came the dictum, 'No plan survives the first contact with the enemy'. Von Moltke was a diligent student of Frederick the Great's campaigns and philosophy, and of military history in general.

'No plan survives the first contact with the enemy.'
Von Moltke, Chief of Staff, Prussian Army, 1857–87

When he attended the annual *Kriegsspiele* (war games) of the *General Stab* in 1858 he was not yet famous; his victories in three wars were in the future. However, he was upset by the slurry of paper and the degree of detail in the orders, because he knew that in war there was no time for such nonsense. In his review of the *Kriegsspiele* he stated that 'as a rule an order should only contain what the subordinate for the achievement of his goals cannot determine on his own'; in other words everything else must be left to the discretion of the commander on the spot. In the following decades under von Moltke's leadership, the Prussians developed a new command concept for their armies, a concept eventually known as *Auftragstaktik*: *Führen durch Aufträge* (leading by assignment).

Auftragstaktik, the British way
The British also had a form of decentralized decision making, but in their case based on the inherent hierarchy of their class society. Members of the upper classes could buy an officer's commission without necessarily knowing anything about war. In practice, this was not a problem, since they gave orders to their 'best men' i.e. the professional officers who commanded their companies and who in turn depended on non-commissioned officers (NCOs). These NCOs were professionals who led their units, often consisting of mercenaries, with regard to the limits of the ruling doctrine. These could be adapted because the doctrines differed; for example, that of Hessian soldiers was different from that of Spanish mercenaries.

Auftragstaktik did not evolve without controversy, and the years after 1871 were characterized by a struggle between the 'moderates' and the 'hard-liners'. The first were the adopters of *Auftragstaktik* who wanted to decentralize decision-making to the lower echelons and preferred independently operating units. The latter were those who wanted to keep command and control centralized, particularly as more modern weapons threatened to disrupt the traditional ways in which troops were controlled. Hard-liners were contemptuous of *Auftragstaktik* because, in their eyes, it would undermine discipline and thereby put the entire military command and control system at risk. However, its development continued and *Auftragstaktik* eventually gained a permanent position in the thinking of the imperial army. In 1888 the term was first recorded in the Exerzier-Reglement für die Infanterie der Königliche Preussischen Armee (exercise regulations for the infantry of the Royal Prussian Army).

The American Civil War (1861–5)

The American Civil War was in every sense a terrible war, with more than 750,000 soldiers and probably as many civilians killed. European military observers were shocked by the way in which both parties fought. On the American battlefields new weapon technologies collided with what were the often archaic tactics of both sides. The observers noted that:

- Cavalry without infantry in a supporting role was used to carry out meaningless charges at enemy lines
- Guns were dispersed across the units, so there was no central fire control, each gun firing at its own discretion
- Bayonets were used as weapons and not, as on the European continent, as deterrents or a means to threaten the opponent's units until one or the other gave way and beat a retreat. Mobs of men fought each other with bayonets, resulting in large numbers of wounded and killed

Possibly the worst feature was that lines of infantry faced each other in 'classical' formations but fired using modern rifles. As a result,

---

row after row of men was hit and fell dead or wounded, only to be replaced by fresh ranks. This resulted in mass slaughter, particularly when the Northerners started using the first rapid-fire repeating rifles.

These observations clearly indicated the consequences if armies did not adapt their doctrine and tactics to new technological realities. They underlined the need for European armies to look for new command and control concepts.

The fact that no plan survives the first contact with the enemy does not mean that plans should not exist. In fact, the opposite is true: planning is a necessary element in war. The reality is that account should always be taken of the need for improvisation by those operating in the front line, where planning and reality meet; in other words, between the command and control system and the harsh reality of the battlefield. Soldiers and local commanders need professional leeway to put formal plans aside when reality requires. This is the nucleus of *Auftragstaktik*: decision-making wherever an ever-changing reality is most manifest. Von Moltke and others realized that the army leadership was not omniscient. They understood that the complexity of the battlefield necessitated a style of leadership that left room for independent thinking by officers and their men. Thus they placed 'thinking' and 'acting' at the right level within *Auftragstaktik*: the level of soldiers and their officers in the front line.

This was in contrast to *Befehlstaktik*, where 'thinking' and 'acting' were strictly divided and men only had to follow precise orders. In *Befehlstaktik*, 'thinking' is done by planners at the top of the organization (general staff, army and divisional staff) and 'acting' is delegated to the troops in the field. This separation of 'thinking' and 'acting' makes troops dependent on orders from above and results in extended reaction times in an ever-changing environment.

As a consequence, *Auftragstaktik* made a clear distinction between the *what* and the *how* questions. An order should clearly describe what should be accomplished, for example to take an ultimate target such as a bridge or a hill. How the target should be won was left, however, to the discretion of the commander in the field. This created room for flexibility on the part of the troops in the field. Put another way, there was no 'one best way' laid down in a plan, as *Befehlstaktik* might try to do, but rather 'many roads leading to Rome'. As a result, the commander and his soldiers in the field could choose the one they wanted to use.

Decentralization in the genes

This new command concept is in the German DNA. Germany as a nation state has had a relatively short existence, only since 1871. The area we now know as Germany comprised for centuries a colourful collection of cities, principalities and kingdoms, totalling more than three hundred entities, each with its own characteristics and legal status. There was no central power, so that all these cities and sovereign states, while having to co-exist and cooperate with each other, also had to learn to stand up for themselves and take their own decisions. In other words, this made for an optimal form of decentralization and individuality.

Until 1806 this combination had formed the Holy Roman Empire, not a state in the modern sense of the word but a political association of worldly or ecclesiastical entities directly or indirectly subject to the Roman-German emperor. Until the Battle at Jena in 1806 this sovereign was almost always the oldest man in the Habsburg dynasty. In addition to this political and administrative reality, the Germans had, as a result of the arrival of Protestantism in 1517, also disconnected themselves from the most centralist organization of that period, the Roman Catholic Church. Luther, in his book *Von der Freiheit einer Christenmenschen* (On the Freedom of a Christian Man) laid the responsibility for the interpretation of faith on the individual and not the leadership of the Church. This was an early and remarkable form of decentralization of responsibilities in which one took faith in one's own hands, thereby confirming the strong German tradition of self-reliance.

In this way, the Prussian Army and its successors, the Kaiser Heer, Reichswehr and the Heer as part of the Wehrmacht, were primarily guided by targets and not by the way these targets should be reached. However, it should be remembered that this was in part embedded in the prevailing *doctrine*, the standard approach for certain situations. This doctrine was nothing more than a basis for further elaboration and allowed for all kind of variations. Although *Auftragstaktik* was not a licence to act entirely at one's own discretion, it greatly enhanced the freedom of decision-making at the lower levels of command.

1.1 Auftragstaktik and battlefield performance

A closer examination of *Auftragstaktik* produces a surprisingly different image of the Prussian and later German Army to the one familiar from books and movies. The authoritative military historian Martin van Creveld rightly points out:

> Contrary to the widely held clichés about 'blind obedience' or *Kadavergehorsamkeit* [zombie obedience] and Prussian discipline, the German Army had, at least from the time of Moltke the Elder, emphasized the crucial importance of individual initiative and responsibility, even at the lowest levels.

There are many ways in which a war can be won or lost. With the fundamental willingness to grant subordinates the freedom to act at their own discretion, and with confidence in their professionalism, the Prussians made a quantum leap in thinking about the way a military organization should be managed. They introduced a new paradigm that none of their future adversaries recognized, let alone understood.

In recent decades, Hollywood has created an inaccurate impression of the German soldier by depicting him as a brainless, mechanical creature with stereotypical behaviour, led by unscrupulous officers who do not hesitate to send their men to a certain death. This is a false representation of reality, as the Americans were well aware. Both during and after the Second World War they conducted extensive research into the psychological and sociological dimensions of the Wehrmacht and its modus operandi. In reality, the reverse of the Hollywood version was true. The Americans, or more broadly the Allies, with their bureaucratic planning and rigid operational methods, frequently suffered in confrontations with the more flexible and efficient German forces. As Colonel Trevor Dupuy points out in his book *A Genius for War*:

> The record shows that the Germans consistently outfought the far more numerous Allied armies that eventually defeated them . . .

On a man for man basis the German ground soldiers consistently inflicted casualties at about a 50 per cent higher rate than they incurred from the opposing British and American troops <u>under all circumstances</u>. This was true when they were attacking and when they were defending, when they had a local numerical superiority and when, as was usually the case, they were outnumbered, when they had air superiority and when they did not, when they won and when they lost.

This was true even when the Wehrmacht had seen better days and possibly 80 per cent of Germans divisions (arguably the best ones) were fighting in the east, since the Germans saw the Soviets as the real danger. As a footnote, the higher casualty rate inflicted on the Allies in the Second World War still remained relatively meagre compared with the battlefield performance of the German Army on the Western Front in the Great War. This was an astonishing 225 per cent; in other words, for every German soldier killed or wounded, 2.25 Allied soldiers fell.

Splendid ignorance: relative battlefield performance in the Great War

Battlefield performance and, in particular, relative battlefield performance is an indication of the efficiency of military units. To demonstrate this we might compare two equally strong soccer teams. Two teams of eleven play against each other and, because they are equal in numbers, you might expect that the number of goals they score will approximately balance, although one of them may win in the end. However, you would also expect that if one of the teams has fifteen players, this will be reflected in the final score. If this is not the case, the team with more players has recorded a lower field performance than the other. This can be translated into military organizations in terms of deaths and injuries, and in this way you can calculate what is termed the *absolute battlefield performance*. If you then take into consideration other factors, for example that one party is fighting from a defensive position, you can calculate what is termed the *relative battlefield performance*.

We know from Dupuy's calculations that the relative battlefield performance of the Wehrmacht in the last year of the war in the west was 50 per cent higher than that of the Allies. This is already pretty remarkable, taking into account that 80 per cent of the Wehrmacht was fighting on the Eastern Front, often deploying their best units there.

The battlefield performance of the combatants in the First World War is particularly interesting, as initially there was a fairly even balance in men and materiel between the two sides. When calculating performance, however, we must be aware of the fact that while our focus is usually and primarily on the Western Front, we often ignore the fact that the Germans made at least as great an effort in the east. What has been termed 'The Forgotten War' cost the lives of hundreds of thousands of Germans and Austrians and several million Russians and was the spark that ignited the Russian revolution. It was only after March 1918 that the Germans were able to deploy their troops from the Eastern to the Western Front. Because this war in the east is mostly not taken into account, the differences in numbers of deaths and soldiers involved between the combatants are not really surprising at first sight. There were 13.5 million Germans under arms of whom 1.8 million were killed, 5.7 million Britons with 510,000 killed in France (of a total of 743,000) and 7.9 million Frenchmen with 1.3 million killed. So on the Allied side 1.8 million British and French were killed. In addition, 100,000 Americans were killed from a total of 1 million deployed. Therefore, at first glance, if we compare these figures, there seems to be an even balance, with 1.8 million Germans killed from a force of 13.5 million, and 1.8 million British and French from a force of 13.6 million, without taking the Americans into account.

However, as discussed, the 13.5 million Germans fought on two fronts and, although the exact distribution is unclear, most sources assume the numbers on each were more or less equal. The number of German casualties on the Eastern Front amounted to between 400,000 and 800,000; for the purpose of this calculation, let us call it about 600,000. If we then position about one third of the total number of German troops, namely 4.5 million, on the Eastern Front, a figure lower than mentioned by the sources, this distribution has a dramatic effect on the absolute battlefield performance in the west. Compared with 1.2 million (1.8 million minus 600,000) Germans killed in the west from a force of now 9 million Germans, 13.6 million Allies still counted a loss of 1.8 million killed. Therefore, had the Germans been able to deploy the same number of troops as the Allies, the latter's casualties would have been 13.6/9 or 1.51 times 1.8 million; in other words, 2.7 million killed. This, when compared with the 1.2 million Germans killed, gives a ratio of 2.7/1.2 or 225 per cent, in other words 2.25 Allied soldiers killed for each German. In such a situation with so many more men, the Germans would probably have killed even more Allies and arguably won the war. Furthermore, as the Germans launched more, and larger, offensives than their adversaries, so their *relative* battlefield performance was even higher.

If we pursue a scenario in which half of the German Army fought in the east, one that is very likely according to some sources, the battlefield performance escalates dramatically. In this scenario 6.75 million German soldiers fight 13.6 million Allied soldiers, a formula that gives a very clear result: 13.6/6.75 or 2.1 times 1.8 million killed results in 3.78 million Allied soldiers killed versus 1.2 million Germans, a battlefield performance of more than 300 per cent.

The Americans are not taken into account in these figures. During their relatively short period at the front, of little over a year, they lost 10 per cent of their men. The British reached this percentage after some four years of war, the French somewhat earlier. This meant that the Americans had a very low battlefield performance; in other words, they were slaughtered.

In the latter stages of the Second World War the Germans had a relative battlefield performance of 150 per cent, and it is clear that in the earlier years their relative performance was much higher. For instance, at the first encounter between US and German troops in 1943, at Kasserine, the relative battlefield performance was a staggering 500 per cent in favour of the German units involved; for every German soldier injured or killed, five Americans were killed or wounded. This forced the Americans to fundamentally revise their doctrine.

The conclusion must be that only serious mismanagement on the Allied side can explain the difference in relative battlefield performance. These figures are seldom seen in history books because most authors focus on the victors, who tend to write them. Moreover, historians are generally poor mathematicians. In this book we will try to discover why the Prussian/German Army had a much higher battlefield performance and what role *Auftragstaktik* played in this.

1.2 In search of excellence

To get a grip of the phenomenon of *Auftragstaktik* we can use a 'light' version of the well-known management consultant's '7-S' model from Peters and Waterman. The pair published this model in 1984 in their book *In Search of Excellence* and, while some might argue that the model is dated, it is still extensively used today because of its comprehensiveness and strongly analytical character. The model analyzes an organization from seven different angles, each of which starts with an 'S', hence the name. These are:

- Strategy
- Structure
- Systems
- Staff
- Style of leadership and operating
- Skills
- Shared values

An added dimension of the 7-S model is the combination of the 'hard' elements of the organization (strategy, structure, systems) and 'soft' elements (staff, style, skills and shared values). The idea behind the model is that all these elements within an organization are interrelated and influence each other. As a consequence, changing one of the elements will lead to changes in the others. Ideally, the elements should be developed in conjunction with each other on the basis of a shared vision of the organization.

In Search of Excellence: Peters and Waterman
The model of Peters and Waterman was based on a study of success factors in sixty-four organizations. Their research showed that successful organizations keep things simple: a simple structure, simple strategies, simple communications, and so on. Such organizations have the following characteristics:

- Strong action and task-oriented
- Simple structure with limited staff departments
- Constant and intensive contact with customers
- Increased productivity through investing in people
- A high degree of autonomy for various departments to make full use of their entrepreneurship
- Strong emphasis on what the company stands for (its core values)
- Focus on the things the company is good at
- Being at the same time flexible and rigid: hard on achieving targets and accountability, but giving freedom on how to reach these goals

As we will see, this reads much like the guiding principles of the Prussian/German Army; or put in another way, the organizations researched by Peters and Waterman all share the characteristics of the Prussian/German Army.

The model does not require much adjustment in order to be applied to military organizations. It is more a question of which 'S' the different topics should be ranked under. The main change compared with the original model can be found in the first S, namely 'Strategy'. In using the model for military organizations, this translates into three elements:

- The 'Mission of the Army'
- The resulting 'Vision of the Organization' and the command concept, for example that of the German Army, *Auftragstaktik*
- The 'Doctrine': the more or less 'Standard Operating Procedures' on the battlefield

INTRODUCTION

The Mission represents the higher ambitions of the military organization, which may seek to operate on a global level or solely defend the homeland. These different missions require totally different organizations and become apparent in the vision through which the organization and the command concept are built. Ideally, the vision and command concept is translated into principles that should apply to all the other categories of 'S'. In this way, the vision and command concept is consistently translated through the depth and the breadth of the organization. The doctrine is, in turn, reflected in the Standard Operating Procedures: how to engage opponents in different situations, whether to attack after an artillery bombardment, to carry out diversionary actions, try a pincer movement, deploy tanks, and so on.

Figure 1: The model of Peters and Waterman translated to military organizations

Element	Relevant topics
Strategy	Mission and vision Command concept Doctrine, with standard operating procedures, etc.
Structure	The structure the army, divisions, battalions, etc. The distribution of responsibilities and decision-making power over the various levels of authority in the organization The decision-making structure The cooperation between the various elements, such as divisions and battalions Logistics Staff Speed of action and agility Evaluation and learning system Knowledge system
Systems	The communication and deliberation structure Feedforward and feedback systems
Staff	Overall vision of what is expected from men The recruitment of men Training and development programme Teams and team performance The psychological and social dimensions of individuals and groups Group building and group cohesion

Skills	Requirements in knowledge, skills and attitude Incorporation of skills in training and development programmes Adaptability of skills and development programmes to new situations
Style	Overall vision on leadership The recruitment of officers and NCOs Training and development program of officers and NCOs Promotion system and requirements for promotion Power and authority in relation to subordinates Professionalism Trust Discipline Respect
Shared values	Community sense Morale

The aim of this book is to arrive at a clear view of the way armies have been organized and to explain the higher battlefield performance of the German Army. We relate German, British and American points of view to each other and to the way things worked out in practice, using a large number of case studies from the battlefield by way of illustration. In this way, we intend to tackle both theory and practice.

We hope that by the end of the book the reader will agree with the famous Dutch footballer Johan Cruyff, when he said, 'You can only see it when you understand it.'

CHAPTER TWO

Command Concept

In this chapter we will discuss the mission, vision and command concepts of the various armies. For example, what command concept did they use, and was this elaborated logically and consistently and translated into all elements of the organization? We examine whether the command concept met the requirements of the reality of the battlefield and how it worked in practice. We also look at the preconditions of what we call 'the concert of battle': issues that should be taken into account when confronting the enemy.

2.1 Introduction

As we have seen, the Germans, or more accurately, the Prussians, developed their doctrine as a result of their battlefield experiences of the 1800s and introduced *Auftragstaktik, Führen durch Aufträge* later that same century. This was in sharp contrast to their previous *Befehlstaktik*. The latter amounted to a command concept based on plans and orders from above, whereas *Auftragstaktik* meant that goals were clearly formulated ('what should we have achieved and when?') but the path to them was largely to be decided at a commander's own discretion ('how are we going to achieve these goals'). Regarding the latter, there was of course a framework, the so-called doctrine, as an important binding element. This separation of 'what' and 'how' resulted in a flexible organization with appreciable delegation of responsibilities and powers, permitting a high degree of self-regulation and flexibility. In other words, within *Auftragstaktik* the emphasis was on the mission that had to be achieved jointly (mission orientation, not order orientation). In accordance with this approach, operational units were given a very high degree of independence instead of having to frequently conform to detailed plans. They were also expected to have a high degree of flexibility so that they could respond quickly to the opportunities and threats of the battlefield. This was important, especially given the formula that Impact = Speed × Mass: the faster one acts, the more impact one has, but also the less mass one needs. However, in a centralized decision-making system, there is a greater time lag between action and reaction, and therefore you need much more mass to settle battles to your advantage, a concept we shall examine in the following chapters. Within the further elaboration of *Auftragstaktik* by the Prussians and Germans we can distinguish a number of other core elements in addition to the strong degree of decentralization, namely:

- An emphasis on the team and creating social cohesion within teams, whereby we can actually rank any type of combat unit among teams
- An emphasis on collaboration between teams
- An emphasis on the leadership qualities of the officers and non-commissioned officers, the latter being regarded as the most important level of management

One of the remarkable features of the concept was the emphasis on the combination of independence of and cooperation between fighting units. The Prussians were able to combine these into a powerful concept that was best expressed in what were termed *Kampfgruppen*. We will elaborate on this in Chapter 3.

During the Austro-Prussian war of 1866 and the German-French war of 1870–71, *Auftragstaktik* delivered convincing results, although these wars particularly demonstrated the need to properly train the lower echelons to deal with their new responsibilities and powers.

2.2 The First World War

The First World War differed completely from earlier wars. *Auftragstaktik* did not emerge fully in the west, since the armies became stuck in mud of the trenches, and the extremely static character of trench warfare offered no room for the type of flexible warfare that the Germans had in mind. In the east, however, the war had a very dynamic character. After a slow and sluggish start under General Prittwitz, the war gathered momentum as Ludendorff and Hindenburg took command and increasingly fought along the lines of *Auftragstaktik*. Ludendorff and Hindenburg, unlike von Prittwitz, were capable of combining new technologies with the concept of *Auftragstaktik*, and this resulted in very successful and characteristic deep penetrations and broad pincer movements of a type that would be repeated on the Eastern Front in 1941 and 1942.

In the west, the greatest challenge of trench warfare was not to force a breakthrough in the front, but how to exploit the resulting gap. This was because, even if the front was breached, the infantry and artillery had difficulty in making progress across the muddy terrain, with the result that attacks tended, both literally and metaphorically, to 'bleed to death'. The development of the tank was one of the answers to this problem, and they could often guarantee that an attack could be carried through. However, it would take a long time before tanks were sufficiently reliable technically. Until that time, the infantry bore the brunt of forcing breakthroughs and consolidating positions in newly conquered territory.

While the British and French still routinely forced their infantry 'over the top' in massive frontal attacks, with resultant appalling losses, the Germans carefully studied the question of how to break through defensive lines. This resulted eventually in a new offensive doctrine, the *Hutiertaktik*, named after the commander-in-chief of the German Eighth Army in Russia in 1917, General Oskar von Hutier.

The Supreme Command of the German Army had given Hutier the task of testing a newly developed tactic in order to break the stalemate around Riga, a city that had successfully withstood a siege for two years. To everybody's surprise the new tactic worked so well that Riga fell in two days. From that moment on *Hutiertaktik* became the official name of the new tactic. (15:172/173 and 41:2–5)

While the British invested in technology i.e. tanks, the Germans invested in people and used specially trained and heavily armoured units, the *Stosstruppen* (storm troops), implement *Hutiertaktik*. These units were small and operated independently, infiltrating the enemy lines at specific places (*Schwerpunkte*: focal points) in no-man's-land. They were then able to move into the hinterland to cut lines of communication and destroy enemy artillery positions. The *Stosstruppen* were trained to fight in small independent groups and to exploit opportunities. In fact, *Hutiertaktik* demanded, even more than *Auftragstaktik*, independent thinking on the part of operating units, as men had to make decisions on the basis of their own judgment. (2:191)

Another new offensive doctrine, *Angriff im Stellungskrieg* (attack in trench warfare), had close ties with the concept of *Auftragstaktik*. Within a general framework, commanders and men were given the opportunity to find their own way of dealing with situations without awaiting orders from, or intervention by, higher echelons. In addition to *Hutiertaktik*, the Germans also developed further defensive tactics to create 'elasticity in depth'. These required appreciable initiative and creativity from commanders in the field, at the level of junior officers, who often had to take major decisions in fast-changing situations without consulting their superiors. Importantly, this was not just conceptual; as might be expected of the German Army, officers and men were very thoroughly familiarized with this new way of offensive and defensive warfare through an extensive training programme.

The German Army was the only force that responded to the limitations and possibilities of the First World War battlefields by adjusting its doctrine, as well as the training and competencies of its officers. Furthermore, it delegated decision-making powers to the lowest level in the organization, that of the team in the front line. (45:205/206)

In this way the Germans seamlessly applied their doctrine to the reality of battle in the west, a theatre of war where every ambition to develop some degree of central control had long been abandoned. In the hell of trench warfare another type of soldier was born, one who in response to the horrors of the battlefield had become creative and independent. They were also well prepared. The German NCOs, or *Feldwebels*, who were responsible for the basic training of recruits, had the task of making the training as realistic as possible, so that soldiers were already accustomed to the disorientating violence of war and, importantly, would avoid immediate panic. For example, they learnt how to survive in small groups in no-man's-land without guidance and without external discipline. Their own morale and their own assessment of the situation helped them survive. This type of soldier needed a completely different method of control, insofar as any was needed. (32:149)

2.3 Changing the game

Probably the best description of the new German tactics in the First World War comes not from an official account, but from the novel *Questa Storia* (This Story) by the well-known Italian author Alessandro Baricco. It is set in 1917 on the northern Italian front, where the Austrians and Italians had confronted each other in a three-year stalemate. In the novel a company surgeon explains to the main character of the book what had happened two days earlier at

Caporetto, where the stalemate had ended as the whole front collapsed within eight hours after the deployment of German *Stosstruppe* units. More than 300,000 Italians were taken prisoner, while a further 300,000 fled:

> He explained to me the two laws of assault that, according to the war manuals, had to be observed with every attacking manoeuvre. The first was as old as the art of fighting and decreed that you had to conquer the highest points, from which you could dominate the terrain. More than a strategic principle, it was a fundamental principle that was confirmed time and time again by fortresses all over the world, situated as they were at a height from which every human movement could be monitored. The second rule, which was undeniably logical, pointed to the need to advance in a compact formation, on the widest possible front, so that you did not run the risk of losing units up front which would be doomed if separated from the rest of your men; first they would become separated from supply and then they would irrevocably be surrounded. From a geometric point of view, there was no denying the logic of this reasoning. They were rules that the Germans knew all too well, and you could even say that they had actively contributed to drafting them. But on 24 October 1917 they attacked with the help of a strategy that could be summarized as follows: ignore the rules and do the opposite. Without paying attention to the highest points, they advanced through the valley below, where the defences were weaker and the defenders less watchful. And they did so in small assault units, which had been given an unthinkable command: penetrate the enemy lines and do not stop, thus losing all contact with the main force and having to decide movements and actions independently. The idea was to penetrate the enemy lines like termites gaining access wherever the wood is softest. They would then dig into the inside of the enemy lines until they reached the highest points, and these, without even being conquered, would automatically collapse. That was exactly what happened.

This is the most expressive description of *Hutiertaktik*, performed in this case by *Stosstruppen*, that we know. It gives a true picture of the way in which the Prussian/German Army had learned to operate: ignoring the existing rules and relying on the ingenuity and perseverance of independent units and the individual soldier. *Hutiertaktik* was therefore a true game-changer. Its psychological effects were also considerable: as Baricco writes, 'Nobody could understand what was happening when that German officer emerged from the clouds behind us with a revolver in his hand after he had climbed up from the valley below with four or five of his men.' The Italian troops, 268 in total, surrendered; they could not cope with the fact that the rules of the game had changed: the enemy was always meant to be in front, in lines on the other side, not behind them.

The deployment of *Stosstruppen* provided the Germans with important insights into how independent units (including individuals) could function in extreme situations without falling into complete disorder. Training and the development of a sense of security and confidence were the keys to success. However, although the new *Hutiertaktik* led to local successes in 1918, it could not counter the strategic reality, demonstrated by the growing material supremacy of the Allied side, which eventually led to the German surrender later that year. After the First World War, the Germans, just as they did after their defeat at Jena in 1806, thoroughly evaluated their combat performance, and this again led to new insights that were translated into practice in the years between the two world wars.

The British Army: misled by its own success

The British Army in this period was a truly imperial body that had successfully kept the British Empire under control. The wars that the British had waged were, apart from the First World War, what might be termed 'low intensity conflicts' or 'small wars': in other words, mostly local affairs. As a result, at the opening of the Second World War, the British Army lacked any kind of common vision or doctrine. Its forces were scattered around the globe and had often adapted themselves to local conditions, thereby making the development of an overall vision or doctrine possibly even counter-productive. As we will see, the responsibility for developing any level of vision and doctrine, as well as any necessary associated training, was undertaken by individual regiments. Given the type of local war that the British were accustomed to fighting, an overall concept was regarded as only of limited use for the British Army as a whole.

The British had considered the First World War to be an extremely 'costly trip' to the European continent and, still protected by a strong navy, they did not intend to be drawn into a European war for a second time. The First World War had confirmed the mission of the British Army, which remained focused on the Empire. It was felt that the concepts and tactics developed over the centuries were still very effective in the Empire, so that even if they did not work that well in the European theatre, this did not seem to disturb the British. As a result, the British experience of the First World War did not lead to in-depth evaluation, a fundamental rethinking of or changes to the doctrine, tactics, structure, recruitment, selection, training and leadership models of its armed forces. This was underlined by Britain's status as one of war's victors, a position further reinforced to some extent by the structure of British society. The British higher officer class in general had led a reasonably relaxed life behind the front lines; death and injury were left to the junior officers and lower classes.

It should be noted, however, that the British were considerably more cautious about the lives of their troops than the French and eventually developed the tank to break the deadlock on the Western Front. The fact that the British had emerged as victors from the First World War strengthened their view that their doctrine and organization were adequate and thus suited to any future war on the continent. They played down the successes of *Hutiertaktik* and the *Stosstruppen* by attributing them to elite units, just as they later attributed the successes of the Germans in the Second World War to elite Panzer units. They did not realize that *Hutiertaktik*, combined with new thinking on management and organization, was to become standard in the Reichswehr in the period between the two world wars, and that the quality and professionalism of the German soldier was founded on the versatile, widely applicable and well thought out philosophy of *Auftragstaktik*. Not only did the British not understand this philosophy, they paid little attention to it, even after the Second World War. This proved to be a costly miscalculation.

The great step forward made by the Germans between the world wars was the welding together of the aforementioned doctrine of tactical offensive with the flexibility and firepower of tanks, accompanied by mechanized and armoured infantry. The Germans perfected these models of operation into a powerful single attack doctrine, that of the tank offensive. The combination of tanks with halftracks carrying *Panzergrenadiere* (armoured infantry) created breakthroughs that could be exploited with success. Infantry with anti-tank weapons protected advancing armour and entrenched themselves on conquered terrain in strategic positions. An additional and very important difference to the tactics of the First World War was that the offensive no longer focused on the disabling of the enemy artillery, hitherto the 'prime target', but on disabling what is termed his 'C3I' capacity (Command, Control, Communications and Intelligence). This capacity can be regarded as the brain and nervous system, and if it can be damaged or destroyed, an enemy will often collapses. It should not be overlooked, however, that all armies of the period, whether French, British, Soviet or German, were looking for a 'silver bullet' in the field of tank deployment. It was just that the Germans were fortunate that a number of concepts and ideas came together at the right time, a good fortune that resulted in what became called Blitzkrieg, a tactic now known all too well.

2.4 The philosophy of chaos

It must be understood that the Germans approached the concept of waging war from a fundamentally different philosophical position to their opponents. Almost all other armies faced by the Germans in the wars of the nineteenth and twentieth century saw it as their main challenge to win control of the battlefield. They tried to gain a hold on the intricate choreography of battle and to direct it along the lines planned by centralized command and control structures. This bowed to the natural instinct to control one's environment and mould it according to preconceived ideas. From this point of view, the strategist feels most at home facing a linear and static front, which can be attacked at pre-selected points with a previously calculated number of people and resources. For the Allies in the First and Second World Wars, the ideal battle was a mathematical exercise in which the correct tonnage of shells and an optimal mix of units would physically shatter the enemy at one certain point of the front. However, the more chaotic, fluid and dark the battle, the more the Allies lost their grip on events, and this sometimes led to panic. As a result of the centralized command structure followed to a greater or lesser degree by all Allied commanders, subordinates would often ask their commanding officer, 'What should I do?' in situations that offered them opportunities. The responses were often inadequate or passive, because commanders were unfamiliar with the realities of the battlefield.

The Germans, however, accepted chaos as a natural part of warfare and learned to live with it. They often used precisely this confusion and uncertainty ('the fog of war') to gain the initiative on the battlefield, while deliberately unbalancing their opponents by creating as much chaos as possible. By delegating responsibilities and decision-making power to the lowest echelons, they made it possible for individual commanders to find their own way of reaching predefined goals within an agreed framework. This mobile, fluid, non-linear battlefield was the environment in which the German philosophy and the German Army thrived best. When this philosophy came to full effect in the form of Blitzkrieg during the Second World War, its characteristic elements comprised the following: infiltrations; short, intensive bombardments of communication centres; surprise attacks in the most unexpected places, isolating the opponent's strongpoints; and the unexpected appearance of mobile tank units in the enemy hinterland which destroyed his logistical and communication structure. (55:51–2)

It is also interesting to observe that this non-linear way of fighting continually gave the Allies the impression that they were greatly outnumbered; in reality, the reverse was usually the case. The Germans maintained this delusion wherever they could: units that were deployed in the morning on one side of the front suddenly appeared in other places in the afternoon. In fact, the Allies were always well in the majority, even more so as they tried to follow Montgomery's rule of thumb that a ratio of 3:1 in favour was a reasonable basis for success. A good example of this was the Allied landing at Anzio on 22 January 1944. Although there was some opposition to the landing, as at Salerno in 1943, the Allies met little initial resistance, with the exception of a number of attacks by the Luftwaffe. The Allied units at the beach were, however, pinned down by the 71st Infantry *Abteilung* (more or less a battalion) and the *Aufklärungs* (reconnaissance) *Abteilung* from the 29th Panzer Division, who were on leave in the area from Monte Cassino: a total of a few hundred men. The Germans, using the tactics described above, gave the landing troops the impression that they were confronting a major fighting force. As a result, the inexperienced Americans gave way to the almost automatic reflex to dig in on the beach, bringing the offensive to an immediate standstill.

Stopped in their tracks: the landings at Anzio

By midnight, 36,000 soldiers and 3,200 vehicles had already landed on the beaches at Anzio. The Allied losses amounted to thirteen dead and ninety-seven wounded, while about two hundred Germans had been taken prisoner. The Allies broadly succeeded in advancing 3km and in some places 5km inland and conquered the harbour of Anzio, before halting their offensive and digging in. The ultimate goal of this operation had been either to lure German troops away from their southern winter front, or to use the weakness in the areas behind the German lines to advance south and attack the Germans from the rear – a flanking movement in the true sense of the expression. What the American General Lucas did, however, was to pump more people and materiel into the small bridgehead and reinforce his defences by digging foxholes. Yet Rome was only 50km away and, since a reconnaissance unit had travelled unopposed to the city shortly after the landings, circled the Colosseum and returned without problems, Lucas could have arguably taken the capital the same day. This missed opportunity led to protracted and pointless fighting and lengthened the struggle for Italy.

The Allies had no real answer to the Germans' flexible operating units, which had learned to cope with chaos. Often they reacted passively and characterized their own actions as 'sluggish' or 'lacklustre' and the attitude of their officers as an 'almost timid operational and tactical command'.

2.5 The tank offensive in reality

The German command concept appeals most to the imagination through its tank offensives, which represented Blitzkrieg in its truest form. The Germans realized that no opponent could have the upper hand all along the front; therefore, as a result of the lessons learnt and experiences gained in the First World War, they concentrated their forces at a single point, termed the *Schwerpunkt*. This was not a new invention, but rather a centuries-old trademark of German tactics. The Romans described it as one of the main characteristics of the way German tribes fought, whereby the force of their attack was focused on one point of the Roman cohort, resulting all too often in its disintegration. As Field Marshal Paul von Hindenburg would declare, 'An operation without a focus is like a man without character.'

As the *Schwerpunkt* was the weakest point of the enemy's defensive line, this was the ideal attack route and offered a good opportunity for artillery support. (2:37) A tank offensive (in fact, any type of offensive operation) could be concentrated on this part of the front. The ultimate goal of the tank offensive was not the front itself but way beyond the front line, in the enemy's hinterland. Following *Auftragstaktik*, the tanks were tasked to progress as far and as fast as they could behind enemy lines. Individual commanders were given appreciable discretion to manoeuvre their forces and to act according to their own insight, as long as the set goals were reached. (14:139)

A tank offensive could be divided in three phases:

- The infiltration phase
- The breakthrough phase
- The pursuit phase

The infiltration phase
This phase was opened by a preparatory artillery bombardment and bombing by the Luftwaffe, while tanks were concentrated at the *Schwerpunkt*. The tank attack itself took place in two successive waves or two parallel groups. The mission of the first wave was to break through the enemy lines, eliminate his artillery positions as soon as possible and then push deeper into the enemy hinterland. The tanks would be accompanied by infantry, the *Panzergrenadiere*, in their *Sonderkraftfahrzeuge* (Sd.Kfz.) armoured half-track vehicles, whose task was to silence enemy anti-tank guns. In line with the army's tactical doctrine, the tanks of the first wave left the clearing of any pockets of resistance to the second wave. It is interesting to note that the full mechanization of the German infantry commenced as late as 1941 and only reached its peak in 1944, before which much of the infantry followed the tanks on foot or in trucks. This was because the priority for German industry had been the production of tanks rather than armoured half-tracks.

Panzergrenadiere in Roman times

The combination of cavalry and infantry was already being used in Roman times by Germanic tribes, in the form of a combination of riders and foot soldiers. In this variant of what is termed *Verbundene Waffen* (see below), a rider was armed with shield, spear and axe, and his partner, a warrior armed with a shield and spear, would hang from the horse's mane. Together the pair made a formidable combination, as described by Caesar in his commentaries on the Gallic War, *De Bello Gallico*. In the same book, Caesar highlights the structure of the Germanic forces. This comprised a core of professional warriors surrounded by tribal members who were conscripted. According to Caesar, these units were as good as the professional Roman legions. This surprising phenomenon was also seen in the Second World War, for example in 1944 near Arnhem, where German units consisting of raw recruits under professional leadership proved to be as good as and often better than their British counterparts, many of whom were from elite units.

The firepower and the speed of this form of attack often broke the resistance of the enemy, after which the Panzer units could quickly push further to reach their strategic targets far behind the front line. The gap they had made in the front allowed the second wave of tanks and infantry to conquer positions, with the aim of maintaining the breach, protecting the flanks and communication lines, cleaning up pockets of resistance and taking specific strategic positions. They were supported by anti-tank units, which fought off counter-attacks by enemy tanks. (51:42)

The ultimate goal was to give the attack's third wave as much freedom of action as possible. The third wave had to overpower the enemy's 'C3I' command structure, while remaining as intact as possible in order to inflict as much damage as it could on the enemy. (2:54)

The breakthrough phase

Once the opponent's C3I capacity was eliminated, his organization generally collapsed, and coordinated resistance was no longer possible. In the terminology of the Germans, this was the 'breakthrough phase'. In the vacuum thus created, the German armoured troops, with their abundant

C3I capacity, were able to advance deep into the enemy hinterland, leaving the advancing infantry to deal with any pockets of resistance that might remain behind the first waves of attack. (54:206) In reality, the enemy's command structure had frequently collapsed much earlier, because the appearance of German tanks behind the lines had a crippling effect on their opponents' morale.

The pursuit phase

This phase started the moment the enemy began to pull back in any numbers or simply retreated en masse. The goal of this phase was to prevent the regrouping of the enemy forces by continuing to pursue them relentlessly. German troops, supported by the Luftwaffe, tried to cut off the retreating enemy by swift manoeuvres and ever-deeper penetration of areas behind the front. The ultimate goal was to neutralize all opposition (2:41), preferably by a pincer movement and ensuing encirclement, which would lead to the ultimate destruction of the enemy forces.

The destruction of the enemy's C3I capacity, when compared to traditional models of battlefield confrontation with their focus on destruction of the opponent's troops (*Vernichtungsgedanke*), was an effective and fast way to deal with the enemy at a relatively low cost in casualties for both sides. (54:206) It was thus not about the destruction of people and equipment per se, as in the First World War, but the deprivation of the opponent's ability to use them. Speed and mobility (*Beweglichkeit* and *Bewegungskrieg*) and the creation of chaos comprised the core of the tank offensive, the use of such tactics proving the superior training and leadership of the German armoured troops. When all these elements came together, characterized by an almost unstoppable advance, the phenomenon of Blitzkrieg was born. The German armoured troops had in fact managed what may be termed 'the choreography of the tank offensive' in a manner that was, and remains, unique.

An important innovation in the Second World War as compared to the First was the use of armoured halftracks, the *Sonderkraftfahrzeuge*, notably the Sd.Kfz. *250* and *251* and their variants. These vehicles made it possible for the *Panzergrenadiere* to keep pace with the tanks, even in difficult terrain, thus removing the main reason for the failure of tank offensives, namely the separation of tanks and infantry. Maintaining contact was vital, as the latter had to protect the tanks with anti-tank guns as well as overwhelm the anti-tank guns of the enemy and other pockets of resistance.

If, for some reason, the half-tracks could not keep up with the tanks, the attack halted until such time as it could be resumed. The half-tracks not only protected the soldiers against enemy fire but were capable of off-road operation in areas where good infrastructure was lacking. (2:54)

2.6 Reconnaissance in force

One of the features of these tank offensives was reconnaissance in force. The Germans attached a much higher value to information collection by exploration than their opponents. At the outset, separate reconnaissance units were established and trained and, as the Germans believed in fighting if necessary to gain information, these units were not only very mobile and well equipped, they were also heavily armed.

Each division had such a reconnaissance battalion, the *Aufklärungs-Abteilung*, whose task it was not only to collect information but also to respond to any opportunities that arose during an armed reconnaissance. The *Aufklärungs-Abteilung* was often the most mechanized and heavily armed unit of a division and therefore able to serve as a strategic reserve for the less motorized divisions. (14:137) In addition to collecting general information on such features as the enemy's artillery positions, the reconnaissance had to provide information on any weaknesses in the enemy lines that could be used to identify a *Schwerpunkt*. The reconnaissance units scanned the enemy front in a fluid movement in search of such weaknesses.

Because of their considerable firepower and aggressive posture, which often led to intense skirmishes, actions by reconnaissance units were frequently believed to be major attacks. This would cause the enemy to respond with counter-fire, troop movements, radio traffic and the like, all of which could be analyzed by the Germans to provide useful information for possible follow-up actions. Once a *Schwerpunkt* was located, the reconnaissance unit would contact the divisional commander. The commander could then start the attack by putting his tank units in place, while also instructing the reconnaissance unit to continue its activities and force a breakthrough. In this way, exploratory actions could suddenly morph into a regular attack with much greater tactical implications. Reconnaissance units were therefore a serious factor that an opponent had to take into account at all times.

In not only tank offensives, but everything the Germans undertook, the formula $I = S \times M$ occupied a central place. Impact = Speed × Mass often proved that even units of small size could have a major impact on the course of a battle, provided they were able to act quickly. For that reason the Germans wanted to keep the time lag between observing enemy movements and responding to them as short as possible. *Auftragstaktik*, with its decentralized decision making and short intervals between perception and action, focused on this, and concepts as *Beweglichkeit* (mobility) gave solidity to it.

The equation also applies in reverse: the longer it takes to make a decision and plan actions, i.e. Speed is reduced, the more Mass you need to force a breakthrough, i.e. achieve Impact. This downside is well exemplified by the Allies, with Montgomery the key figure, since they were masters at stretching out the time lag. As a consequence, they needed disproportionately more mass and thus more men and materiel to force a successful impact.

The framing of Landser Fritz and GI Joe

One of the interesting developments after the Second World War was that the German Army, its individual soldiers (*Landser*, or Private, Fritz) and officers were continually typecast as mindless beings who blindly followed orders and were thus regularly surprised by the Allies. Further traits depicted included unreliability, unprofessionalism and cowardice, with the relationship between officers and men being shown as cold and heavy-handed, the former demanding the impossible of the latter. American soldiers, however, were often portrayed as a sociable bunch who talked openly with each other, listened to suggestions and radiated a real 'can-do' mentality. The relationship with their officers was shown as friendly and casual, with informal behaviour the norm.

However, in the forthcoming chapters we will discover that much of the stereotypical behaviour attributed to the Germans was precisely the behaviour that was, in reality, displayed by Allies. The attitude of American officers, the carelessness with which soldiers were deployed, the behaviour of the Allies in making the same mistakes again and again, the exclusion of newcomers (thereby reducing their chances of survival at the front), the sluggishness of decision-making, the generals who were never seen at the front and who fought battles from far behind the lines, bad staff work and bad planning; these were all variants of behaviour shown by the Allies. In psychological terms, therefore, this 'framing' is just a projection: a transference of your own weaknesses and failures on to your opponent.

Movies and series such as *Saving Private Ryan* and *Band of Brothers* in fact contribute to a negative image of the Americans themselves. For example, in the first version of *Saving Private Ryan*, on more than one occasion German prisoners of war are shown being executed. They are, of course, by definition the 'bad guys', but the shooting of prisoners of war, even Germans, remains a serious war crime. In later versions these executions were removed. The same applies to *Band of Brothers*; a scene where one of the Americans empties his machine gun into a group of German prisoners of war disappeared completely from later versions, with only the vaguest suggestion that such an incident might have occurred. Also the scene in which the commander, Winters, executes in cold blood a young German soldier who has clearly surrendered has become less explicit in later versions.

A break with this policy of avoiding any negative depiction of the typical American 'GI Joe' can be seen in the recent film *Fury*. What is arguably an all-time low is reached when a tank commander, played by Brad Pitt, forces a newly-arrived crew member to execute a German PoW in order to prove himself. In earlier films this might have been presented as justified, but to modern audiences the act does not exactly enhance the image of the American soldier in his role as keeper of the moral high ground. We can, however, assume that such situations were rare occurrences on the front in the west, since in reality reason would have ultimately prevailed between officers and men. Such reason was based on the knowledge that, in these situations, there is a great degree of reciprocity: if you do this to your opponent, he will do it to you.

2.7 Cooperation as a weapon

The success of Blitzkrieg was based on a three-dimensional collaboration between the various army components and the air force, both in the mobile and hectic conflict of an attack and in following the initial breakthrough. The principle of *Verbundene Waffen* (combined arms) played an important role. This required the different parts of the army (tanks, infantry and artillery) to be able to operate together seamlessly in order to act as the integrated multifunctional combat units required by the concept. In other words, cooperation between these different parts of the army had to be smooth at all times, regardless of traditional boundaries and perceptions.

There was great emphasis on joint training and exercises, so that intensive and optimal cooperation at all times would become natural in combat situations. We will delve deeper into this in the next chapter, when we describe the phenomenon of the *Kampfgruppen* or 'Combat Groups'.

Innovation the German way

The German Army was driven by innovation, not only in terms of management and organization, but also in hardware. The concept of research is in the German genes and it was combined with the rapid testing, adaptation and implementation of new technologies. Some of this can be illustrated by the following:

- Tank types were constantly adapted to the changing demands of the battlefield, producing many variants
- New tanks were developed quickly: the Army chiefs worked closely with chief engineers of manufacturers, interviewing experienced tank crew and the crews of anti-tank units right up at the front to draw up inventories of what was needed. In modern parlance one would speak of co-creation and co-design
- Guns, both artillery and anti-tank, were mechanized in all kinds of variants
- The Germans introduced uniforms in camouflaged colours and with spot patterns
- The Germans were the first to deploy paratroopers in great numbers to force breakthroughs, as at Eben Emael and on Crete
- Aerodynamics: all aerodynamics after the Second World War were based on German design and technology that had led to an enormous volume of inspiring designs by 1945. For example, 'Stealth' bombers are still based on Horten's designs, as is the Space Shuttle

---

- Jet engines: after the Second World War these were heavily influenced by German design and technology which, when combined with aerodynamics, led to the development of many types of operational jet fighters
- Helicopters: the Germans had the first operational helicopter
- Infrared: the Germans introduced 'hunter-killer' teams, in which half-track vehicles with infrared floodlights illuminated the field for Panther tanks equipped with night vision equipment.

All the above developments were characterized by a very limited 'time to market': the technology was quickly made available for the battlefield. It is also interesting to note that Albert Speer, in his position as head of the *Reichsministerium für Bewaffnung und Munition* (Ministry of Armaments and Munitions), could be found at the front at least one week a month, talking with tank crews, engineers, *Panzergrenadiere* and so on. The central question was always what was needed and whether the current materiel met requirements and lived up to expectations. His visits led to a continuous flow of directions to manufacturers for improvements, adjustments, and so on.

An interesting but not yet investigated phenomenon is the effect of open innovation in wartime: in May 1944 the German government suspended patent law, and companies were allowed to use each other's patents for a reasonable fee. This provided a historically unprecedented impetus to innovation that had a beneficial effect on the German industry for decades after the war.

After the Second World War, the Allies, in turn, showed a keen interest in German knowledge and technology. Through Operations Unicorn and Paperclip Germany was stripped of its knowledge and technologies in a highly professional manner. Operation Paperclip focused on scientists, of whom more than 1,600 were ultimately recruited to continue their work in the United States and Great Britain. The best known of this group was of course the rocket scientist, Wernher von Braun.

Unicorn focused on the dismantling of research laboratories and production facilities that were of interest to the winners. For example, the world's largest wind tunnel in the Ötz Valley in Tyrol fell into French hands. This grand prize in the eyes of the Allies was dismantled and transported by thirteen trains to Modane in the French Alps, where it was rebuilt and, to this day, provides services to the aviation industry.

The British in turn dismantled the Hermann Göring aviation research institute in Volkenrode and rebuilt it at Farnborough. There, after studying the German materiel, chief engineers Morgan and Davis of Farnborough Aviation Research Establishment came to a upsetting conclusion: 'We realised within a matter of minutes that our entire aircraft development programme was already out of date.' For example, the principle of the 'swept wing', necessary to achieve high speeds with jet aircraft, was completely unknown to them. The British 'T-Force' was responsible for securing interesting objects and people at the request of British companies, ranging from machine factories to perfume makers, and had the power to arrest and hold competing German entrepreneurs to extract essential knowledge about products and production processes, and to dismantle installations and R&D facilities. By the beginning of 1947 this technology transfer had become so great that the Foreign Office was afraid it would seriously hamper the reconstruction of Germany and insisted that it be stopped, a process that was completed on 30 June 1947.[1] The value of the intellectual property that found its way to the Allies has been estimated at 3,500 billion euros (at current values), without taking into account the turnover and profit that could be achieved with this knowledge and technology which, logically, must amount to a multiple of this figure.

2.8 The British doctrine

While the Germans had a clear command concept originating from the mid-nineteenth century, this was lacking on the British and the American side. For example, according to the Allies in both the First and Second World Wars, the ideal battle was a mathematical exercise in which the

---

[1] 'How T-Force abducted Germany's best brains for Britain', Guardian, 29 August 2007.

correct tonnage of explosive and an optimal mix of units at a certain point of the front would inevitably shatter the enemy.

In order to obtain an idea of the origins of British tactical doctrine in the Second World War, we will consider the experiences of the British before and during the First. Prior to the latter, the British doctrine was based mainly on the experience gained in relatively small-scale colonial wars, which led to the neglect of planning any system of operation in larger formations. What might be termed the 'morality of battle' was seen as an important prerequisite for success. This was expressed in the Infantry Training Manual issued in 1914 by the British General Staff as, 'To close with the enemy, cost what it may'; while General Sir William Robertson, the Director of Training for the British Army at the beginning of 1914, also proposed that 'interference with the desire of the troops to push into fight at all costs' should be avoided at all times. The idea behind these principles was that a future war would be short and a decisive victory soon attained. However, as the Great War progressed and the size of the British Army on the Continent increased, the high command increasingly fell back on solutions from the past: in other words, they 'applied old principles to new conditions'. The result was that the predominant tactic of the First World War comprised an introductory artillery bombardment followed by a massed infantry attack with the bayonet. As the attack had to be seen through, whatever the cost, the key to success when meeting resistance was to deploy ever increasing numbers of men and materiel until the enemy front broke. (59:16) This resulted in very large numbers of casualties and a correspondingly low battlefield performance, as discussed previously.

After the First World War, the British, Americans and French, as victors, felt disinclined to fundamentally analyze the experience of the four years of fighting. As a result, existing battle concepts were not further developed, neither were any new strategies identified. It was some fifteen years after the First World War that a report, 'Notes on certain lessons of the Great War', was prepared by the British which analyzed ways of working at the operational level. The report concluded that surprise was an important element missing on the British side and that the British had acted too predictably in many situations. It was suggested that future commanders had to take the initiative, and the usefulness of prolonged artillery bombardments was also questioned, as they gave away the element of surprise and destroyed the ground so much that it was virtually impossible for attacking troops subsequently to negotiate it. Surprisingly, the solution was sought in the decentralization of the artillery, arguably the best weapon on the British side, so that local commanders could make use of it. Although this seemed a logical solution, the end result was that the British, for example in North Africa, operated in a fragmented manner and with insufficient cooperation, to the extent that they were unable to mass-concentrate their artillery on defined points of the front. Montgomery would ultimately reverse this development and emphasize the importance of artillery in forcing a breakthrough. (27:21–2)

More generally, when analyzing the battles in North Africa, those that lend themselves to a meaningful analysis reveal that the personal experiences and views of the commander, for example Auchinleck or Montgomery, were all-important and had a great effect on the organizational and command structure, the type of leadership, the planning of actions and the manner of fighting. This only contributed to confusion on the British side, as local commanders did not always know how to act in certain situations. Moreover, ideas were seldom well thought-out or tested enough in practice to be meaningful and effective.

Until the arrival of Montgomery, these ever-changing personal ideas, concepts and innovations formed the basis of the British doctrine. This was in stark contrast to the German Army, in which there were established institutions and agencies which carried out evaluation, introduced new methodologies and developed and implemented new organizational structures.

Unique case or standard operating procedure?
Due to the lack of a generally accepted vision and command concept, case histories are important in reconstructing the British way of operating. This is one such case.

The problem the British faced was that German tank guns had a longer range than theirs, and this case describes how British tanks and 25-pounder howitzers cooperated closely to stop a German tank attack. Part of the artillery was set up in front of the British tanks and fired at the German tanks at long range. When the latter had approached to 1,000m, the artillery was quickly coupled to towing vehicles and withdrawn. Another section of the artillery, placed behind the British tanks, covered the retreat of the forward

---

artillery by firing at the German tanks. When the latter were close enough, the British tanks in turn attacked the German tanks from the flank and, in cooperation with the artillery, succeeded in halting the German attack. (43:102) Because this model of operation is not described anywhere else, it is not possible to determine whether this type of cooperation between tanks and artillery was at the personal initiative of the local commander, or whether it was part of a broader tactical doctrine. Such relatively well-documented examples are rare, so it remains to be seen whether this was indeed part of a tactical doctrine or the result of an interesting personal initiative. Generally, besides the 'fog of war', the British 'fog of organization' also played a role.

A lively discussion was held between the two world wars regarding the deployment of tanks in a future conflict. Although individuals such as General Fuller and Sir Basil Liddell Hart encouraged further thought, with their publications on the lessons to be learnt from the First World War, including on mechanized warfare, this did not lead to a widely accepted doctrine on the deployment of tanks. (27:13) We will return to this point later. As a result, there was no clear concept of how to break through enemy lines at the start of the Second World War. The modus operandi of the British remained similar to that of the First World War: in other words, following an artillery bombardment, troops would attack on a broad front in the hope that the artillery had sufficiently undermined the enemy's positions. This was despite the fact that, by the end of the previous war, the British had already experimented with tactics similar to Germany's and thus had access to knowledge and experience of a different way of operating.

Lord Carver, a junior officer during the Second World War and later Commander-in-Chief of the British Army, recognized the weak points in British doctrine:

Our real weakness is our failure to develop a doctrine for a concentrated attack with tanks, artillery and infantry on a limited part of the front. Again and again our tanks attacked on a broad front, with the momentum of the attack immediately disappearing when the front line was stopped by enemy tanks or anti-tank guns. When artillery was involved in the attack, it kept itself busy with firing on enemy positions, after which the next row of tanks pulled up to meet the same fate. Infantry played no role in this; it served only to occupy objects after they had been conquered by the tanks. (42:112)

This sort of tactical manoeuvre had not changed substantially by the end of the Second World War. Due to the lack of a generally accepted command concept from which a clearly derived tactical doctrine might have evolved, we will have to depend on case histories to reconstruct the British way of operating. As each overall commander was able to interpret it in his own way, this could vary greatly from situation to situation.

2.9 Time for a change: the arrival of Montgomery

It was Montgomery who first reconsidered a number of fundamental issues concerning command concept and tactical doctrine. During the Tripoli tactical meetings of 15–17 February 1943 he attempted to formulate a common approach. The purpose of the talks was: 'To see how we stand; to get a solid framework or base which will serve as a background to everything we do; to check up on things that really matter when we go battle fighting; to examine the technique of certain more important types of operations; to disseminate knowledge amongst ourselves.'

Montgomery understood that the generally poorly-trained British troops and officers only functioned well under central management and coordination and within a clear and detailed planning framework. Therefore, starting at both the strategic and tactical levels, and in order to ensure his approach to command was reflected in both, he largely ignored the views of the various factions by appointing his protégés to key positions. In so doing, he was able to elevate his personal doctrine to become that of the 21st Army Group, the most powerful British combat unit of the war years.

Montgomery's view of management

Montgomery formulated the following views on the management of the battlefield:

- There must be clear basic principles formulated that need to be elaborated in detail in the form of a Master Plan

---

- The Master Plan must be drawn up by the commander of the Army Group and not by his staff
- The Master Plan must allocate resources to targets. The Master Plan details successive troop movements during the battle
- Air superiority must first be obtained before sea and land actions can take place
- The supreme command must be able to group and regroup units, depending on the situation
- Forces must be deployed concentrated under the central leadership of the commander of the Army Group
- Firepower goes beyond the use of lives and tanks. Artillery fire must be centralized and concentrated according to the needs of the Army Group commander (16:26–7)

The above is not so much a detailed and balanced doctrine, but rather an outline of Montgomery's view on management of the battlefield. The centralization of power and the emphasis on plans stand out. It functioned in practice as an obligatory testing framework for the actions that took place under Montgomery as commander. It is unclear whether, and to what extent, Montgomery's ideas were further elaborated into a more balanced concept and found a place in units other than those under his command.

Montgomery is generally described in the literature as a commander with negative character traits. Most importantly, however, he was apparently able to use these negative traits to his advantage. As Sir John Hackett put it:

His great talent for leadership was shown in the way he managed to exploit even the negative sides of his character to positive ends: his egotism, his ambition, his ruthlessness, which at times bordered on spitefulness, were all used when necessary to get people thoroughly worked up and then steer their fury and energy into the right channels . . . he would never allow himself to think that a mistake could have been made in his circle for which he was not himself responsible. (25:309)

However, perhaps most significantly, the British simply had no other commander with Montgomery's appeal and who could count on Churchill's unconditional support.

Montgomery also realized that, in many respects, the British Army lacked the qualities of the German Army, and he did not want to fight in the same way as Rommel, his direct opponent. Therefore, instead of attempting to match Rommel's use of battlefield mobility that comprised wide-ranging manoeuvres with independent units to attain goals deep behind enemy lines, Montgomery concentrated on building a solid and static defence line, leading to relatively static battles and frontal attacks. Units had to be deployed under central command and control, with superiority in men and materiel necessary in order to guarantee victory. This was a way of fighting that best suited British abilities. (51:209. 42:119. 59:24, 39. 63:129) As a result, Montgomery left no room for individual initiative, because the British Army simply could not cope with this, tending rather to disintegrate into small groups that ended up fighting their own battles. He therefore created a strong centralist command and control system in which units were expected to adhere strictly to the plan he and his staff had drawn up. In other words, *Befehlstaktik*: a rigid way of war in which operations were to be carried out entirely along the lines of the plan, a command style that, however obsolete, suited the British Army well.

Vision of leadership
Montgomery described his vision of leadership in his memoirs as follows:

> One of the first responsibilities of a Commander-in-Chief is to create what I have called 'atmosphere' as a state of mind in which his staff, his subordinate commanders, and his troops will live and work and fight. His armies must know what he wants; they must know the very fundamentals of his policy; and they must be given firm guidance and a clear lead. Inspiration and guidance must come from above and permeate the whole force. If this happens all concerned will go ahead on the lines laid down, the force will acquire balance and cohesion, and the results will be evident in battle . . . In addition to 'atmosphere' there are two basic requirements for generalship. The first is to create the fighting machine and forge the weapons to his own liking. This involves a profound knowledge of the conduct

of war, and of training. The second is to create an organization at headquarters, which will enable the weapon to be wielded properly. The fighting machine must be set into motion, at the appropriate time, that it can develop its maximum power rapidly. The troops must be launched into battle in a way which promises the best prospects of success – and the troops must know this. The 'stage-management' of the battle must be first class. (43:20–1)

The reason for these views was that the British Army did not have a shared vision of leadership. Montgomery gave expression to the desired basic competences of this leadership in the Army. His experiences in the First World War had also taught him how vulnerable troops could feel, hence his emphasis on creating trust:

But in those days I came to realize the importance of the soldier knowing that behind him were commanders, in their several grades, who cared for him. The general who looks after his men and cares for their lives, and wins battles with a minimum of losses, will have their confidence. All soldiers follow a successful general. (43:23)

Montgomery also believed that communication was of great importance:

Sometimes I spoke to large numbers from the bonnet of a jeep, sometimes I spoke to just a few men by the roadside or in a gun pit. I would also address them less directly by means of written messages at important phases in the campaign or before a battle. These talks and messages fostered the will to win and helped to weld the whole force into a fighting team which was certain of victory. (43:23)

On the other hand, after the start of a battle Montgomery would retreat to his caravan to await results and, due to his slow response to developments on the battlefield, eventually acquired the nickname of the 'North African tortoise', or 'Montgomery Africanus'. To some extent this was not unjustified; at times his centralist style of leadership created lengthy lead times, which further emphasized the M of Mass in the formula Impact = Speed × Mass. Only by using extremely large numbers of personnel and much equipment were Montgomery and, more broadly, the Allies, able to take the initiative.

El Alamein showed that Montgomery had fully mastered these aspects. In a broader context, El Alamein was a good example of the type of warfare in which the Allies would prove to be successful for the rest of the war: the use of overwhelming numbers of men and quantities of materiel, combined with a classic method of warfare based on detailed plans and with little room for personal initiative. Yet, despite all the criticism of Montgomery's character, he was arguably the right man at the right time. As a commander who managed to make the necessary decisions in order to get the British Army on track again, he was a change-manager of distinction.

Irrespective of the above, a strong feature of the British was that, once they had manoeuvred themselves into a stationary position, or 'dug themselves a classic trench', they were unyielding and never gave up, no matter how hopeless their position. However, when in the course of the war the tide turned and they had to take the initiative, they continually struggled to find an organizational concept that exploited the possibilities of motorization, mechanization (i.e. tanks) and cooperation with the air force. All too often they fell back on old First World War tactics of a classic artillery bombardment followed by the advance of infantry accompanied by tanks. This is the greatest criticism that one can level at Montgomery: following his success at El Alamein he was unable or unwilling to develop a new command concept more aligned with current requirements. Although by the beginning of 1944 he had elaborated on the necessary theoretical considerations to do this, he failed to make them widely known, to appoint commanders who understood what he meant or to adapt training manuals and training. In effect, however, this was something that exceeded his actual powers and would have required a real effort from the wider British high command over a long period of time and with far-reaching consequences. As a result, Montgomery's views were merely noted, which meant that for the rest of the war the British used infantry tactics that did not suit the actual situation on the contemporary battlefield but were copied from the First World War, such as tanks serving only to support the infantry.

2.10 The Allied doctrine: Befehlstaktik and brute force

After the disastrous battle of Kasserine the Americans were forced to copy Montgomery's doctrine. As we shall discuss later, they had no alternative.

War therefore became a mathematical exercise, based on the assumption that the Germans could only be overcome by overwhelming superiority in materiel and numbers.

Kasserine

This battle in North Africa marked the first direct confrontation between Americans and Germans. Between 14 and 18 February 1943 their armies fought for control of the Kasserine pass, a battle finally won by the Germans, although the Americans prevented a full German breakthrough to the hinterland. The Americans were shocked by their losses at Kasserine, these totalling more than 10,000 men. The Germans lost 2,000 men, giving them an absolute battlefield performance of 500 per cent. However, as the Americans had deployed more men and were in defensive positions, the Germans' relative battlefield performance was even higher. Furthermore, the relative effectiveness of the Germans was all the more notable because, for the most part, their troops were not Rommel's veterans but recently flown-in men without much combat experience. The failure of the Americans was down to a combination of inability to improvise, bad leadership, poorly trained personnel and the lack of a clear doctrine. The Americans realized that this way of fighting would inevitably lead to politically unacceptable losses and were therefore willing to conform to the views of Montgomery, who was only too happy to be seen as the senior partner in the relationship. However, since Montgomery stuck to his views as the war progressed, tensions arose with the Americans, not at least because, unlike the British, the Americans did learn and adapted their tactics.

Working with rigid plans often led to the complete paralysis of fighting units and thus the whole front. The Allies were not able to take advantage of opportunities when they arose, since they were required to wait for new orders or a new plan and did not dare to go beyond the last predetermined element of the overall strategy. For example, they were not capable of emulating the German trademark tactic of using tanks to perform the classic breakthrough behind the front, because they lacked the necessary technological and organizational background. They were also unable to carry out pincer movements and major encirclements, or to stage a chase. This led to embarrassing scenes such as the weak pursuit of Rommel's units after the battle of El Alamein. An extremely cautious Montgomery allowed Rommel time and space to withdraw in an orderly fashion and even occasionally to carry out cheeky counter-attacks with the few operational tanks he still had.

The Allies thus fought the rest of the war on the basis of this systematic doctrine. Their units were required to stick to predetermined plans, goals and routes of approach, with limited freedom to act on personal initiative, thus ignoring every aspect of *Bewegungskrieg*. As a result, they did not develop an offensive doctrine in which, for example, tanks were able to play an important role. Instead of pinning down the enemy with artillery in order to give themselves room to move, Allied troops manoeuvred to find the enemy and then called in aerial and artillery firepower to try to destroy his positions and everything in the neighbourhood. (16:385) As John Ellis put it in *Brute Force*, 'American infantry tended to transpose the doctrine of fire and manoeuvre into one of manoeuvre and fire.'

'Brute force' in the true sense of the word led to the senseless destruction of the monastery of Monte Cassino in Italy and the city of the same name, as well as the large number of deaths among the civilian population in, for example, Normandy. Estimates of the number of civilian deaths caused by what has been called the 'indiscriminate bombing and shelling' of the Allies in Normandy varies between 20,000 and 50,000. The actual numbers are still unclear, because of the absence of a thorough investigation until recently. Whole villages and cities, such as Caen, were wiped out by Allied bombing. As a result, it is little wonder that the Allies were not always welcomed as liberators. The use of 'brute force' and the consequences this had for the civilian population, in both fatalities and damage to buildings and infrastructure, should not be underestimated.[2]

---

[2] Jean Quellien, a prominent French D-Day historian put it this way: 'There is definitely a feeling among the local population that the suffering of French civilians was not sufficiently taken into account . . . When one looks at testimonies in 1944 and 1945, the sense of anger was very clear. One finds phrases such as, "Oh, the bastards!".' Such expressions completely disappeared

2.11 The reality of the battlefield: Sicily 1943 and Normandy 1944

The consequences of these different command concepts are well exemplified by the reality of particular battlefields. A good example from 1943 was the hesitancy on the Allied side during Operation Husky in Sicily. After their landings on the night of 9/10 July, the Allies were clearly in the ascendancy, and the Germans and Italians were forced to retreat into an increasingly small pocket of the island. When it became clear as July progressed that the position of the Germans had become untenable, it took ten days for Montgomery to draw up a plan for a follow-up offensive. When that plan, Operation Hardgate, was finally put into action on 1 August, the Germans had had ample time to prepare for the evacuation of their units in an orderly and organized way. As a result, while the Allies believed they were progressing as a result of sound planning and tactics, in reality the Germans were simply conducting a series of successful rearguard actions to cover an orderly evacuation of Sicily, an operation that was carried out with complete success. (16:318)

The Germans succeeded in transferring almost 40,000 troops, 10,000 vehicles, 47 tanks, 94 artillery pieces, 2,000 tons of ammunition and fuel and 15,000 tons of other supplies to mainland Italy between 11 and

---

over the years as it is politically incorrect to speak them openly, but when you talk to people privately, a certain number definitely still have a problem with it ... Even though it is not easy to express for the simple reason that the bombings were carried out by Allied forces who liberated Normandy.'

Caen fell victim to a number of major air strikes. During the first attack, on 6 June, American bombers attempted to destroy the bridges over the Orne, but they missed their targets altogether and flattened parts of the centre, killing around 600 civilians. When Montgomery failed to capture Caen the same day, it was included on the list of Norman cities that had to be razed to the ground by Bomber Command to prevent German reinforcements reaching the coast. The total number of civilian casualties on D-Day was around 3,000, about the same as the number of Allied soldiers who died on the beaches of Normandy. 'The soldiers' deaths are often talked about; rarely the civilians,' says Quellien. Halifax and Lancaster bombers bombed Caen again on 7 July to drive a wedge into the German front. A total of 2,000 inhabitants were killed.

17 August. The exercise involved four experienced divisions plus their staff and completely intact command structures. Only 20 per cent of their nominal numbers were killed or taken prisoner. The rescued units were subsequently able to give the Allies an extremely hard time in their progress up the mainland of Italy.

In retrospect, it is surprising that the Allies had made no plans during the preparation of Operation Husky to cut off this obvious escape route. Once they had realized that the Germans were preparing an evacuation to the mainland, they were seemingly unable to act speedily enough to draw up plans for a coordinated deployment of the army, navy and air force. For example, the Royal Navy, which could deploy a wide range of ships, made no attempt to disrupt the steady flow of vessels between Sicily and the mainland, while the Allied air force commanders said they could not spare any more planes because of the bombing campaign against Rome. The Germans were astonished that the Allies had not used their air superiority to greater effect. (16:318)

Guadalcanal

Organizational paralysis was also a structural problem on the American side. This is exemplified by the events on Guadalcanal in the Pacific, where the battle won by the Americans eventually fizzled out. After American units had successfully surrounded the Japanese in a corner of the island, the surviving Japanese succeeded in retreating to the beach in an orderly fashion. On the night of 1 February 1943, 5,000 Japanese troops were evacuated by well-concealed landing craft to nineteen destroyers, which lay only 700m from the coast. This failed to prompt any action on the American side. The same happened on 5 and 7 February, with again no attempt to intercept the vessels. In all, 13,000 men were evacuated under the eyes of the Americans without any losses on the Japanese side. (16:462)

Another example of the paralyzing effect of inflexible planning is shown by the Battle of Falaise in August 1944, the largest battle following the Allied landings in Normandy in June, and by the Germans' subsequent retreat.

...ory

...ise is seen as one of the most important encircling ...y ... Allies in the Second World War. However, it should arguably be described as 'an encircling attempt', because the victors eventually found only destroyed German materiel in the area surrendered to them: 688 tanks and pieces of mechanized artillery and more than 1,000 artillery pieces. In terms of manpower, the German units had already largely left the battlefield.

The essential point is that the Falaise Gap was not properly closed until 18 August, and in these precious extra days the Germans managed to extricate thousands of men. Twenty-six divisions, nine panzer, two parachute and fifteen infantry, were involved in the Falaise battles, but of these only one, the 77th Infantry, was permanently eliminated. To be sure, many of these divisions were reduced to a shadow of their former selves. Three had to be pulled out of the line immediately and sent to the rear to reform. But the rest, six panzer, one parachute and four infantry divisions, albeit no more than weak battlegroups, absorbed their replacements on the move and where necessary fought stubborn rear-guard actions all the way back to the Siegfried Line or into Holland. More important still, almost all of the divisions that were withdrawn to the rear had important cadres of NCOs, junior officers and headquarters staff still intact. Thus exactly as with Tenth and Fourteenth Army in Italy only two months previously, they retained a nucleus of experience and expertise to provide real military stiffening to the mass of replacements they now had to absorb. These replacements moreover, were absorbed remarkably quickly and all of these divisions returned to the line as more than adequate fighting formations, within a few months. (16:391–2)

It was of more than of symbolic importance that German higher headquarters for the most part escaped the envelopment, as the Allies were to learn when these headquarters demonstrated the remarkable rapidity with which they could reconstitute divisions and corps around themselves. The survival of the cadres and headquarters influenced the whole German conception of the battle, with much benefit to German morale apart from the practical utility in repairing shattered formations. (16:392)

This example also shows the speed with which German units were able to rebuild combat formations around the core of the surviving cadre. As Field Marshal Harold Alexander, the British Supreme Commander of the Allied Forces Headquarters, wrote in 1944:

> The enemy is quicker than we are at regrouping his forces, quicker at thinning out on a defensive front to provide troops to close gaps at decisive points, quicker in effecting reliefs, quicker at mounting attacks and counter-attacks, and above all quicker at reaching decisions at the battlefield. By comparison, our methods are often slow and cumbersome, and this applies to all troops, both British and American.

Because of their centralized command structure, all Allied commanders had, to a greater or lesser extent, to deal directly with subordinates who were unable to exploit unexpected opportunities or deal with unexpected situations. By contrast, at Kharkov in 1943, the German Waffen SS Field Officer, Joachim Peiper, adopted a radically different approach.

Joachim Peiper's armoured ambulances

During and after the battle for Stalingrad, the Germans transported entire divisions by train from Western Europe to the east in order to fill gaps and build new lines of defence. One of the most spectacular 'power projections' was the deployment in February 1943 of the 2nd SS Panzer Corps, comprising the SS Division Das Reich and SS Division Hohenstaufen, under Paul Hausser. Their goal was Kharkov and the stabilization of the front by forming a defensive line. The objective was to prevent a further advance of Soviet units to the west after the fall of Stalingrad and to guide as many German units as possible to safety through a 'no-man's-land' of several hundred kilometers.

Immediately after their arrival by rail the end of January 1943, the 2nd Corps had spread across the snow-covered plains to make contact with the troops of the 298th and 320th Infantry Divisions and guide them to safety. The latter had been retreating in small groups towards Kharkov following the Battle of Stalingrad, and during this

---

harsh journey many were captured by Soviet units. In some cases, German prisoners of war were liberated by Waffen SS reconnaissance units, who attacked Soviet positions deep in the hinterland. Units of the SS Leibstandarte Adolf Hitler Division succeeded in forcing a temporary corridor for the survivors of the 320th Division, but this was cut on 12 February. Surrounded, and with 1,500 wounded in their ranks, they had to be pulled out as soon as possible. A *Kampfgruppe*, led by SS-Sturmbahnführer Joachim Peiper, at that time the commander of the 2nd Panzer Grenadiere Battalion, which was equipped with half-tracks, was ordered to save these units. Peiper's battalion, strengthened with a unit of StuG (Sturmgeschütz) III Armoured Fighting Vehicles and sixty ambulances, managed to punch a hole in the Soviet lines, destroy several Soviet tanks and advance almost 50km behind the Soviet lines to find the remains of the division.

After the wounded had been loaded into the ambulances, Peiper's forces and the remaining men from the rescued divisions discovered that Soviet troops had cut their retreat by destroying the only bridge over the river Udy. The Waffen SS unit attacked the Soviets and, after heavy fighting at close quarters, managed to retake the bridge and repair it provisionally. Although the column of ambulances was able to cross to the German lines on the safe bank of the river, the heavy StuGs and halftracks could not, requiring Peiper to seek other ways to cross. After a reconnaissance behind Soviet lines, another crossing point was discovered, enabling Peiper to return with his units and escort the rescued infantrymen back to the safe lines of the Division. Peiper's losses were limited to a few dozen dead and wounded. This incident is thus a beautiful illustration of *Auftragstaktik*, the doctrine of deep penetration in the hinterland, and the use of a *Kampfgruppe*, as well as the leadership, courage, decision-making power, perseverance and determination of all those involved.

On the Allied side, Patton was one of the commanders who tried in vain to escape a rigid model of warfare, although it is questionable whether he would have had any chance of success in a real confrontation with German armoured units, as he lacked the type of troops, materiel or tactical doctrine to take on such a confrontation and survive. Where he and his staff did excel was in the movement of large numbers of people and materiel in a short time. Examples of this were his advance to the Seine and the Meuse in August 1944 and the repositioning of his units during the Ardennes offensive in December that year.

> The historical material superiority of the Americans had led them to a display a marked tendency to underestimate the importance of surprise, manoeuvre and improvisation.
>
> Franz Halder, German Chief of Staff

Normandy also saw examples of Allied units failing to seize the opportunities offered to them. For example, German positions were so weakened after Operation Cobra, the outbreak of the Allies from the bridgehead of Normandy in the period from 25 July to 4 August, that General Elfeldt, commander of the LXXXIV Corps, feared that his lines could collapse at any moment, to be followed deep penetration and encirclement of his force by the enemy. The Americans, however, instead of continuing their successful offensive in an easterly direction in order to finish the job, broke off fighting for unclear reasons in order to turn west for the siege of Lorient and Brest with their port facilities.

Elfeldt declared after the war:

> This surrender of the initiative is one of the most colossally stupid decisions of the war. The American troops of the First Army on my front were not tactically at all clever. They failed to seize opportunities: in particular they missed several chances of cutting off the whole of my corps. (16:385)

Eventually, the American armoured units were permitted greater discretion, and Patton, with his newly arrived Third Army, was allowed to advance to the east. His march was impressive. He left Avranches on 5 August and reached the Seine on 20 August and the Maas on 1 September, 450km in twenty-five days. This distance might be seen as similar to those frequently achieved earlier in the war by the Germans. However, Patton's advance was through territory that had long been abandoned by the Germans, who remained at a distance, with the exception of a few rearguard actions. At no time did the Germans feel the threat of an encirclement or the cutting of their main escape routes by Patton, whose drive east was seen by some as more of a 'triumphal procession than an actual military offensive'. (16:386)

Logistics and traffic-handling were undoubtedly special achievements by Patton but had little to do with the classic tank offensive that was the hallmark of the German panzer divisions. Omar Bradley, Patton's commander-in-chief, wrote in his autobiography:

> Without meaning to distract from his extraordinary achievements, Patton's great and dramatic gains, beginning in Sicily and continuing through Brittany and across the Seine at Mantes, Melun and Troyes had been made against little or no opposition. Until now Patton had not really had a serious fight on his hands. (16:386)

Therefore Patton was never involved in any kind of mobile armoured battle with the Germans, a fact often overlooked. Furthermore, the Germans he was chasing were in fact retreating in an orderly fashion without fear of encirclement.

The above also shows that mobile offensive operations are very different from a simple pursuit. An offensive requires attacks that break an enemy, whom the attacking army then attempts to encircle, destroy or capture. Attacking forces also have to deal with rearguard actions and consider means by which obstacles to the offensive can be bypassed or overcome. This was never mastered by the Allies, and this made it possible for German units time and again to withdraw and regroup in an orderly and organized manner.

On the road to Paris and beyond

After the Battle of Falaise, the Germans retreated towards Belgium, the Netherlands and Germany itself, during which time the Allies were once again given the opportunity to cut off and encircle German units before they reached the Seine. On 21 August, units of Patton's Third Army managed to establish a bridgehead over the Seine at Mantes.

Exploitation of this bridgehead down the east bank of the river Seine offered enormous opportunities and the Germans believed

---

that they were so weak on the east bank that this manoeuvre might well have assured the entrapment of the remains of Army Group B in a worse debacle than the Falaise pocket. The allies, however, preferred to try and close the trap by wheeling down the west bank, relying on the speed of their advance and their firepower to close off any crossing points used by the Germans. However, mobility was not their strongest suit, whilst their track record in applying fire power, especially aerial, to the interdiction of ferry routes was not encouraging.

The attempts to keep the Germans from transferring units across the Seine proved remarkably ineffective. The result was no surprise.

In the first five days of mass crossings, between 20 and 24 August, the German employed ferries (there were 60 between Elbeuf and the sea), pontoon bridges and improvised rafts, and even swimming, by which means 25,000 vehicles were ferried to the east bank. Further major crossings took place on the 26th and 27th, at the end of which over 300,000 men were also across. Once again, almost all the higher headquarters escaped. (16:397)

2.12 The absence of an American doctrine

One of the major problems on the American side can be clearly discerned as a result of the strategies and tactics described in the previous sections: here too an unequivocal doctrine was missing. Before the Second World War, American strategists had mainly depended on French and German sources. They translated these for their own use, but new and pertinent insights and opinions were seldom formulated. Although one apparent advantage to this methodology was that inspiration could be drawn from a variety of viewpoints and ideas, the major disadvantage was that the plethora of information could be confusing and even contradictory. The Americans were particularly fond of studying the Prussian and German Army, whose operations and battles were regularly analyzed and replayed, an approach reinforced by regular exchange visits in the interwar period between the staff officers of the two countries. This was reinforced by the fact that their armies were of similar size during this period, since the

Versailles Treaty restricted the German Army, while budgetary constraints limited the American. Visiting Germans were not much impressed by West Point and other American military institutes, a subject we discuss later, but a visit to the Ford factories was a regular part of the trip and confirmed their image of the production potential that the United States had already shown in the First World War, a capability that was certainly recognized during the subsequent conflict. It became apparent that while in Germany 'out-of-the-box' thinking was encouraged, to the extent that young officers like Heinz Guderian (an early pioneer and advocate of Blitzkrieg) might even risk their careers to develop new tank tactics and weapons, such initiatives in America were successfully repressed by the establishment.

It was also the case that when the US Army decided to use the Prussian/German Army as a source of inspiration, its officers, due to their own upbringing and long-held cultural prejudices, failed to appreciate the background to or nuances of German methods. (48:37) A good example can be seen in the Americans' fixation with the German General Staff. They completely overlooked the most important and successful characteristics of the German officer system, such as its advanced recruitment, selection and training structure and the promotion system linked with them. Consequently, they simply copied the apparent structure of the General Staff but then allowed that copy to run down, amidst stifling bureaucracy and factional struggles, to the extent that it failed to match the more effective German model.

> The discussion about an ongoing revolution in command philosophy, the Auftragstaktik, completely escaped the attention of visiting American officers, as did other important traits that made the German officer corps the efficient group it was. (48:40)

In other words, the concept of *Auftragstaktik* was just not taken on board:

> Even after studying the Prussian and German armies for decades, the US military showed 'difficulty interpreting' the concept of *Auftragstaktik* and most officers would not come closer to it even when they attended the next higher military education institute. Only very few American commanders such as George C. Marshall, George S. Patton, Matthew B. Ridgeway and Terry de la Mesa Allen understood the concept, even though it had never been taught to them in American military schools. (48:174)

The Hartness/Wedemeyer Reports

The Americans were given ample opportunity to study the concept of *Auftragstaktik* because American officers were welcome for years at the Kriegsakademie (War Academy). The Americans were able to participate in the entire programme, with only mobilization plans remaining closed to them. Those Americans attending provided detailed reports on all topics that had been discussed. Although the similarities between the American Army Staff College at Leavenworth and the Kriegsakademie were constantly emphasized in these reports, the differences could hardly have been greater. While Leavenworth emphasized the principle of dogma, the Kriegsakademie focused on creativity.

Hartness and Wedemeyer were, in a sense, the exception; their reports emphasized the differences and pointed to the advantages of the system maintained by Kriegsakademie. However, such reports had to be tabled in moderation, as the culture within Leavenworth and the Command and General Staff School left little room for people to think differently. Their reports mentioned such advantages as the German system of and requirements for admission such as the entrance examination to the Kriegsakademie, the exchange of officers between the various branches of the armed forces, the excellent quality of teaching and the emphasis on the importance of leadership.

They also praised the practical nature of the teaching material and the way in which various scenarios were discussed and analyzed, in contrast to what was offered in American training, i.e. 'a detached, contemplative solution' that 'may function as a proper product but not as a life and blood proposition'. They also touched the heart of the matter when they wrote: 'Since no two tactical situations are identical, no schematic solutions can be formulated which may be applied now and later to difficult problems . . . In the discussions of the problem no "approved" solution is offered, since every problem will have several satisfactory and workable solutions.' It is thus clear that they preferred the German approach to their own.

Their reports were presented to the Command and General Staff School, although they were 'obviously not read by the staff and the faculty'. Wedemeyer went on to a shining career in the US Army, one of his last postings being as commander of all US forces in China from 1944 to 1947. He then played an important role as Army Chief of Plans and Operations during the Berlin Airlift in 1948 and 1949, where his earlier expertise in the field of airlift operations in Burma, China and India proved invaluable. (48:174–7)

Due to the absence of a clear framework, many institutions such as the United States Military Academy at West Point and the Virginia Military Institute drew up their own curriculum. However, there was no coherence between the institutes, either horizontally or vertically; for example, within the American Command and General Staff School at Fort Leavenworth there was no overarching 'school of thought' or guiding documentation that could lead to a common doctrine and training programmes, such as existed in the German Army. At these American institutions, officers in training were mainly taught to repeat the standard solution that the institute had formulated for a specific combat situation, with little or no room for discussion or personal input. As a result, the American Army entered the Second World War with what might be termed 'thin intellectual baggage' and had to fall back on simple concepts and rely on overwhelming superiority in men and materiel.

2.13 The reality of the battlefield: Monte Cassino 1944

The Battle of Kasserine in 1943 had rid the Americans of any ambition to fight the Germans other than on the basis of a massive superiority in men and materiel and to a strict plan. The Italian campaign shows how the Allies fought their way through the German lines in the following years. The struggle for the Gustav Line, the German defensive position that stretched across Italy, and in particular, the battle for Monte Cassino, are examples of this. Monte Cassino was the key to Rome and the north of Italy, and during the period from 17 January to 17 May 1944 it took four offensives to break through at this point. Significantly, however, this breakthrough was entirely due to the North African troops of the French

Army led by General Alphonso Juin. On one of his first trips to the front he had immediately noticed that the abundant mechanized transport of the Allied forces had a serious downside. Driving from Salerno to Naples he noted the following:

> Along the whole road . . . we ran into the 7th British Armoured Division in close column, incapable of leaving the road and deploying in a terrain completely given over to mountains. I immediately concluded . . . that the widespread mechanization of the British and American forces constituted a serious obstacle to any swift progress up the Italian peninsula. (16:332)

As the Allies did not exactly excel in traffic-handling, this factor, in combination with over-complex planning, frequently led to traffic jams, at times bringing an entire offensive to a standstill.

At Monte Cassino, an American infantry division had initially tried to fight its way through a valley defended by well-positioned German units. It is striking and yet characteristic that serious reconnaissance was not carried out in advance; such an exercise would have been an absolutely basic tactical condition for the Germans. The Allied forces restricted themselves to the use of maps, so that it escaped their notice that they were fighting in an area characterized by steep, boulder-strewn slopes, small canyons and impenetrable thickets. The American division was subsequently replaced by the 4th Indian Division, which became completely stuck on the steep slopes. The Allied planners then identified the Monastery of Monte Cassino as the main problem and bombed it to destruction; this was a completely senseless act, not only given the earlier consultation between Allied commanders and the Pope, but also because no German soldiers had been present in the monastery, and the rubble subsequently provided them with ideal defensive materials. A second offensive therefore also failed. In preparation for the third offensive in March, it was decided that the city of Cassino should be levelled, but the Allies failed to appreciate that 'heavy bombers cannot make buildings simply disappear, and all they succeeded in doing on this occasion was to tumble masonry into the narrow streets and make it virtually impossible for the New Zealand infantry [who had the honour this time] and their supporting armour to get forward at all.' (16:333)

For the fourth offensive, in May 1944, the troops at Monte Cassino were supplemented with units from the Eighth Army and, fortunately for all concerned, French units. The latter, under the aforementioned General Juin, consisted mainly of North Africans who were experienced in mountain warfare. These units were deployed on the western flank, on land that was considered impenetrable by all parties. Their objectives were to infiltrate the German lines and look for weak points that could be exploited. In other words, this was a combination of *Auftragstaktik*, *Hutiertaktik* and *Schwerpunkt*. The French Army command instructed: 'In this period there must be no rigid timetable for anyone; everything will be decided in response to how the attack progresses . . .'

This approach proved successful. The German defenders were thrown out of balance and had to withdraw; so it was this attack and not the brave frontal assault of the Polish Corps that delivered the much-needed breakthrough. The next phase, the pursuit, again showed the awkwardness of the British, who used three infantry and two tank divisions as a 'corps de chasse'. The resultant mass of people and equipment quickly became stuck on the narrow mountain roads and, when another tank division was added, everything came to a standstill ('Traffic became impossible . . . the jam . . . had coagulated and become a fevered stasis'). The Germans, in the meantime, were able to retreat in a north-easterly direction, towards the Arno and the Gothic line, a more northerly defensive position. The fact that they retreated to new positions with their vulnerable flanks exposed to the spearheads of the advancing Allies shows the disdain they had for the quality of the Allied pursuit. As an American staff officer remarked after the war:

> The pursuit between Rome and the Arno is misnamed . . . It was a rapid advance but 'pursuit' implies getting in behind the Germans. The Germans in this action controlled our pursuit, our rate of advance . . . The operations between Rome and the Arno was far from a rout. It was a calculated withdrawal.

The French units under General Juin, operating in the most difficult terrain, were the only ones able to follow the Germans closely, but they were not allowed to undertake any flanking or surrounding manoeuvres. Therefore, although both the Germans and Allies suffered heavy losses, with 20,000 and 55,000 casualties respectively in the fighting around the Gustav Line, the former were able to quickly rebuild their divisions around the core of the remaining officers and staff, as we have seen on previous occasions.

The art treasures of Monte Cassino

As the Allies advanced further to the north and their modus operandi became clearer, everyone realized that the monastery of Monte Cassino could become a victim of aerial bombing. For this reason, Oberstleutnant Julius Schlegel, commander of the Instandsetzungsabteilung of the Fallschirm Panzer Division 1 Hermann Göring, suggested that the monks of the monastery remove their art treasures to safety. After much deliberation, the monks agreed to use the German unit's trucks to transport the treasures, including works by da Vinci, Titian and Rafael. The bodily remains of St Benedict were also taken from Norcia to Rome. As a result, none of these things were destroyed by the Allied bombing.

When Göring, both art lover and plunderer, found out, he ordered a unit of the SS to arrest and execute Schlegel. Only intervention by the monks and the commander of the division, General Paul Conrath, prevented this, and the evacuation continued. Twenty trucks were used, requiring a total of one hundred journeys to transport all the works of art, including 1,200 books and documents. Out of gratitude, the monks held a mass for Schlegel, and he and General Conrath were each presented with a special certificate in Latin by Bishop Gregorius Dimare. The general was referred to therein as *Dux Ferreae Legionis* or 'Leader of the Iron Legion'.

After the war, Schlegel was accused of war crimes and plunder and arrested by the Allies, but was freed following the personal intervention of the British Field Marshal Harold Alexander. Thanks to the rescue of the art treasures and the library, including the original building plans, the later reconstruction of the monastery was made possible. In the early 1950s Schlegel was invited to a special audience by Pope Pius XII. Following the precedent set by Schlegel, many other Italian art treasures were brought to safety to prevent them from being destroyed by Allied bombing.

The way in which the Allies fought their war on Sicily and in mainland Italy cast a shadow over all their future operations. An American journalist described this as follows:

> Always and everywhere procedures and patterns were the same. German guns betrayed their presence. We called our planes to bomb them, and then we concentrated our own artillery, too numerous to be opposed, and they shelled the German guns. Thereupon the infantry flowed slowly ahead. At each strongpoint or villages there were . . . a few snipers to be blasted out . . . [Then] the news would go out to the world that the place was 'liberated'. This is the way it was, day after day, town after town.

This was to become the Allies' trademark: a largely unrefined system of warfare, but one that eventually yielded the desired result.

2.14 The concert of battle

If we list the above elements against the theoretical background of *Auftragstaktik*, they create a formula which may be termed the 'concert of battle', expressed as: Impact = Exploration × Preparation × Focus × Cooperation × Speed × Mass × Continuation.

The formula of the 'concert of battle'

Impact = Exploration × Preparation × Focus × Cooperation × Speed × Mass × Continuation.

Although this formula can determine the success of an operation, in reality the Allies did not properly regulate any of these elements:

- Explorations: rarely executed
- Preparation: never took place thoroughly, other than in the form of extensive plans
- Focus: often lacking, as there was a preference for attacking on a broad front
- Collaboration: this was not part of the doctrine and always required separate tuning

---

- Speed: long lead times were a feature of Allied operations
- Mass: was often used to an excessive extent, but too much literally leads to congestion and logistical obstructions
- Continuation: even if success was achieved, it could not be fully exploited

The German performance stands in stark contrast. They paid attention to all the elements and as a result were able regularly to deliver the 'concert of battle'.

For the Germans the elements of the formula were of paramount importance. They were described in directional documents, translated into training programmes and clearly recognizable in all operations. Things were completely different on the Allied side. Most notably, the Allies did not carry out thorough reconnaissance. As we have seen, the Germans were willing to fight for information and would provoke skirmishes to test the reactions of their opponents. Furthermore, it was important to the Germans terrain be physically inspected by the commanders involved, because maps and reports so often give a wrong impression. By contrast, the Allies did not appear to consider this important, neither did they search for the *Schwerpunkt*, the weakest point in their opponent's front line. The Allies generally attacked head-on, often over a broad front. General Tuker, the commander of the Indian 4th Division, which had distinguished itself in North Africa, noted after the battles at Monte Cassino:

> I could never understand why the US Fifth Army decided to batter its head again and again against this most powerful position, held by the finest troops in the German army in heavily wired and mined and fixed entrenchments. (16:333)

Infiltration tactics, part of the standard package of the Germans, were also unknown to the Allies, who constantly fell back on outdated tactical patterns. We have already seen, and will see again in the next chapter, that the training of American officers was focused on learning standard solutions which offered no room for creativity or personal initiative.

For example, this led to Operation Epsom, the plan to make a circumferential movement around Caen in 1944, grinding to a standstill because 'the advancing infantry adopted extremely old fashioned First World War mass formations that ignored modern thinking about infiltration or fire and movement.' The attack, which started on 25 June 1944, became basically static after three days, with advance units complaining about sniper fire. In reality there were 'no snipers at all, not a thin screen out in front of the German main battle line; those scattered shots, with an occasional burst of machine-gun fire, were the main German positions, it was all that was left of 12 SS Panzer Division on that front.' The offensive thus petered out. When the Canadians, two weeks later, on 4 July during Operation Windsor, made a second attempt with no fewer than ten battalions of infantry, a tank regiment and the support of over four hundred pieces of artillery, the 428 Germans present supported by two or three tanks and a borrowed piece of 88mm artillery had no problem holding them off. (16:382)

Exploration and preparation, the blind spots of the Allies
We have seen before that the British did not exactly excel at reconnaissance and preparation of troop movements. At El Alamein, the existence of German minefields led to large traffic jams of tanks and vehicles which had to squeeze through a limited number of narrow gaps. In Italy similar scenes occurred both before and after Monte Cassino, while Normandy also saw accumulations of vehicles at strategic points.

During the preparations for Operation Epsom in Normandy, the terrain on which the main attack was to take place was not explored. A village turned out to be a bottleneck for tanks due to debris barring the main road. For unknown reasons no attempt was made to bulldoze a path or to clear routes through the minefields on both sides of the village, despite the fact that the British were not under fire. The same happened during Operation Goodwood, the second battle for Caen: over the main axis of the attack, three divisions each with 3,500 vehicles had to squeeze over six narrow bridges, following which they had to advance through minefields on a limited number of narrow paths. The logistical problems that

> this would cause were not taken into account, and no priority was given to clearing the minefields. It should come as no surprise that there were terrible traffic jams, and these prevented the infantry from moving forward to support the tanks which, when at last able to free themselves from the minefields, were subsequently attacked by well-positioned anti-tank guns. (16:383). Later that same year, the slow advance of British units during Operation Market Garden on a relatively narrow road between the Belgian/Dutch border and the city of Nijmegen again showed that the planners had little idea about the terrain and the obstacles their units would meet.

In addition, the idea of focusing an attack on the weakest point in an opponent's line seemed to remain an unknown phenomenon to the Allies. Patton, for example, never understood what this meant, as is clear from his attack on German positions on the Saar in early November 1944. His divisions attacked on the entire width of the front with the instruction: 'Everybody fire and everybody move'. The result was that 'with every division trying to make a breakthrough, the artillery support was dispersed and . . . [the attack] was able to gain only fifteen miles in eight days. The German line sagged, but did not break, for at no point was it subjected to an overpowering onslaught.' The point that seemed to escape Allied commanders was that to break the enemy's line of defence required all force to be concentrated at one point, i.e. the weakest point, so that fast-moving armoured units could penetrate and advance deep into the hinterland to neutralize command centres, artillery and reserve units.

> The outcome was another slugging match in which the breadth of the front dissipated American strength enough to compensate considerably for German weakness.
>> Professor Russell Weighley, *The American Way of War*

Patton fell back on the same type of tactics at Bastogne in December 1944 and January 1945, after a logistical masterstroke by which he (or arguably his staff) repositioned seven of his divisions within three days. Yet despite having overwhelmingly superior numbers of men and materiel both on the ground and in the air against an enemy who was 'outnumbered, outgunned, out-armoured, holding a hopelessly overextended line', it took five days to reach Bastogne with a tank column, a further week to drive the Germans out of the southern part of Bastogne and another two weeks to reach Houffalize, only 22km further on. 'Patton forsook the advantage of concentration . . . in favour of yet another broad frontal effort to go forward everywhere. In the end Patton accepted Eisenhower's adjurations that to attack on a large scale undermined all ideas of "going like hell". He substituted depth for breadth.' 'Going like hell' was a favourite expression of Patton's, yet the front Patton had actually created was so broad that divisions had difficulty keeping in touch with each other's flanks.

2.15 Get the whips out!

In spite of the Allies' obvious inertia, Montgomery gave the constant impression that in him they had another Rommel, Guderian or von Manstein (or virtually any other German general for that matter). Before D-Day Montgomery was talking about his units being 'sent to this party "seeing red" . . . Nothing must stop them . . . We must blast our way ashore and get a good lodgement before the enemy can bring sufficient reserves up to turn us out.' Documents speak of 'successful strong thrusts . . . kept up alternatively by us toward the Seine and Loire . . . We should retain the initiative . . . keep the enemy moving his reserves from one flank to another.' This sounds like *Bewegungskrieg* with shock and disruption to the enemy's decision-making capacity, or even Blitzkrieg, but unfortunately neither Montgomery nor his 21st Army were able to deliver on the promise. The idea was that the British units on D-Day would conquer Caen by storm and 'almost at any risk' by swarming across the plains to the east and to the north of the city. In reality, the British units quickly became embroiled in insignificant skirmishes, so that the attack on Caen failed to materialize. While the capture of the bridge at Bénouville by British airborne units, the bridge providing vital access to Caen, is always highlighted as one of the great heroic actions of this day, the necessary British tank units never showed up. As a result, the Germans had more than sufficient time to let the 21st and 12th SS and the Panzer Lehr Divisions take up defensive positions around Caen. The city was not conquered until 9 July, more than a month later than planned, after several offensives and destructive bombardments by the British, and it was only on 17 August that at Falaise a definitive breakthrough could be forced that allowed the Allies to advance from Normandy to the north and east.

That did not stop Montgomery telling Eisenhower, 'We have now reached a stage where one really powerful and full-blooded thrust towards Berlin is likely to get there and thus end the German war.' In his view, he was the right person to lead such an ambitious mobile operation. In reality, it would take almost nine months to get that far, and the rest of the war was characterized by a long series of slow-moving Allied offensives.

But despite all these setbacks, Montgomery's language remained steeped in a different reality. During the preparations for Operation Market Garden he spoke of goals that would be achieved with 'thunderclap surprise' and to a time schedule that was 'ambitious to the point of recklessness'. The latter became reality, not least because the British Guards Armoured Division were given the impossible task of covering almost 100km between the Belgian /Dutch border and Arnhem in two days. If blame is to be allocated it was not to the Guards, but to Montgomery's planners: it had taken the same unit almost three days to cover a stretch of only 18km between Beeringen and the Groote Barrier, against much lighter German resistance. As in Italy, the route consisted mainly of narrow roads, running here between marshy meadows with bridges over rivers, and as a result the offensive could only proceed as fast as the vehicle or tank in front. It remains unclear how the idea evolved that any unit, even if facing little resistance, could cover such an ambitious distance in such a short time. The 43rd Infantry Division, which was supposed to support the Guards Armoured Division and eliminate local enemy resistance, lost itself during the advance to Nijmegen in battles with insignificant German units and by reacting to a range of rumours. As a result, contact was lost with the Guards, leaving the latter very vulnerable. When the Guards eventually arrived in Nijmegen on 20 September they decided to camp there and not advance to Arnhem until the next day. However, if they had carried out a reconnaissance at that time they would have discovered that there were no German units of any significance between Nijmegen and Arnhem. Half a day later, the situation had changed dramatically, and soon the front was frozen. General Harmel, the divisional commander of the 10th SS Division Frundsberg, was unable to understand why the British had not kept going: 'If they had carried on their advance, it would have been all over for us.' (30:215) An interesting detail is that, according to some sources, the complete plan of attack for Market Garden was found by the Germans in a downed Waco glider as early as 17 September. It took ten hours before it could be transferred to Field Marshal Model's headquarters, where the plans were regarded as too detailed to be genuine, and were largely ignored.

Even in the last days of the war, at the end of March 1945, Montgomery continued to call for his Second and Ninth Army 'to advance with maximum speed and energy to the Elbe', and he stressed the need 'to get the whips out' so that a rapid advance with fast tank columns could capture airfields that could be used for close air support. In reality, the advance was, in the words of the American supreme commander General Bradley, 'at a turtle-like pace', otherwise known, as previously mentioned, as the speed of 'Montgomery Africanus'. When Montgomery claimed that the expected resistance on the eastern side of the Elbe was too great, the Americans moved Ridgeway's XVIII Airborne Corps, consisting of a tank and infantry division, from the Ruhr to the east at high speed. These crossed the Elbe on 30 April, an action that was mainly motivated by the fear that, as a result of Montgomery's slow progress, the Soviets could advance too far to the west towards Lübeck and Denmark. Ridgeway quickly advanced to Wismar, cut off the Soviets and took 360,000 Germans prisoner. In Bradley's words:

> There was much laughter at the 12 Army Group Head Quarters when they heard of this accomplishment . . . Montgomery had been complaining that the opposition was too great for him to cross the Elbe River. When the 82nd Airborne Division crossed, it advanced thirty-six miles the first day and captured 100,000 prisoners.

All in all, the Allies had to regularly fight the shortcomings of their own system, as a result of which their 'concert of battle' was rarely harmonious. On the one hand, there was no strategic or tactical exploration and thus a lack of preparation, while on the other, plans were frequently far too detailed, with a lack of focus in the form of a Schwerpunkt and far too much concentration on broad frontal attacks with minimal tactical infiltration. In addition, the Allied planning necessary to coordinate the activities of the various units removed the element of speed from offensives, with the consequence that large masses of men and materiel had to be deployed to produce any effect. However, such massive deployment, particularly of mechanized units, combined with inadequate traffic handling caused entire divisions to become stuck in endless traffic jams once a breakthrough had been achieved, thereby frustrating any attempt to pursue the retreating

Germans. In this way, the Allies had no choice but to go forward step by step, using 'brute force' to settle engagements in their favour.

Having outlined the various command concepts and their effects on the battlefield in this chapter, the following chapters will now dig deeper into the various elements of military organization. We will look at structures, coordination and communication, the recruitment, selection, training and replacement system of officers and men, the way in which the command concept impacted on the individual officer and soldier, leadership, morale and shared values. And we will again illustrate the analysis with examples from the reality of the battlefield.

CHAPTER THREE

Structure, *Verbundene Waffen* and *Kampfgruppen*

The command concept of the Prussian/German army described in the previous chapter made specific demands on the structure of the organization. In this chapter we examine to what extent this changed, and how the Allied armies related to it. We look at issues such as the degrees of decentralization within, and cooperation between, various army units. We also examine speed of action and response, paying special attention to the question of ambiguity: was there an overall command concept, was this concept clear, was it propagated and translated into a tactical doctrine and was it known to everyone? Furthermore, and importantly, did everyone adhere to it? We also look at the learning capacity of the organizations involved and the way in which knowledge was handled and enriched. We will discuss the cooperation between units under the title of *Verbundene Waffen*, the *Kampfgruppen*, the *General Stab* as a knowledge centre and *Erfahrungsberichte* (feedback reports) as a means of learning. We will also compare these with the operating methods of the British and American Armies.

3.1 Verbundene Waffen: cooperation between units

As we have seen, within the Prussian and German armies responsibility and decision-making powers were exercised at a low level in the hierarchy, and much was left to the initiative of commanders and their troops. Unsurprisingly, this put high demands on the competence of officers, leadership style and communications systems. Trust also played a role, confidence that officers and their teams could and would carry out their assignments efficiently. In other words, commanders had to 'dare to let go'. However, we have seen that, in addition to independent operation, cooperation between the various army branches (*Verbundene Waffen*) was another important characteristic. This emphasis on cooperation appears to run contrary to the independence required by *Auftragstaktik*. How can you cooperate with other units when you are expected to operate independently? *Verbundene Waffen* is the doctrine that combines these two opposing ideas into a powerful whole. Conceptually, orders on paper are 'passive', while the reality of the battlefield is active and unruly. Therefore the Prussian and German armies invested appreciable time and energy in getting this sometimes contradictory doctrine off the ground, and once mastered, it turned out to be an extremely powerful tool on the battlefield.

The German Army, like every other, was structured along functional lines and divided into branches such as infantry, cavalry, artillery, engineers, and so on. This division into specialized units contributes to the professionalism and quality of the individual parts, but can lead to sub-optimal operation by the whole. The Prussians and Germans had a clear understanding of this, hence the doctrine of *Verbundene Waffen*. After all, the primary function of an army, to fight, requires a context-bound optimal mix of these functional units, and the army organization that succeeds in this will have the edge on the battlefield. Cooperation was thus the central theme within the German Army and was encouraged and practised in breadth and depth in the organization, in order to carry out fluid, mobile operations.

> 'Getrennt marschieren, gemeinsam schlagen!' ('March separately, fight together!')
>
> von Moltke

In order to facilitate cooperation and coordination, the various army units had comparable structures, resulting in exchangeable modules and a fluid organization, without the customary barriers between branches. This modular system with its focus on cooperation meant that frontline units could be quickly combined into what were termed *Kampfgruppen* (combat groups), which were able to respond rapidly to the demands of the battlefield in a particular sector. This focus on cooperation also meant that the German Army, in addition to a large adaptive capacity, had considerable self-healing powers or 'resilience'; units were able to regroup both during and after battle into new combinations and structures, a subject we discuss in the next section. Especially in the second half of the Second World War, the doctrine of *Verbundene Waffen* prevented units from simply disintegrating into armed mobs and held them together as coherent armed forces. This is why the phenomenon of the *Kampfgruppe* was one the most important elements of the Germans' command concept; perhaps what might even be termed their 'silver bullet'.

3.2 Kampfgruppen

The high battlefield performance of the German Army can be explained by its focus on both cooperation and independent decision-making. For tactical operations, the German Army frequently and effectively used ad hoc and locally organized units, the *Kampfgruppen*. (14:132) The underlying philosophy was this: although on the one hand the German Army might be formally described in organizational charts and diagrams, on the other hand, and in more practical terms, it could, as a result of a high level of standardization in thought and deed, be regarded as a 'pool' of men and materiel from which, depending on the situation, different resources could be extracted. In fact, the Germans were able to turn a hierarchical organization into a process-driven one within minutes. In other words, they were able to quickly make the switch from one command concept to another, i.e. von Moltke's concept of marching separately but fighting together.

Kampfgruppen were the key, the accelerator in the conversion from a hierarchical to a process-driven organization with multifunctional teams, thus giving the German Army an unprecedented competitive advantage.

If we take an army 'at rest' it is organizationally built from a number of functional disciplines or competencies, such as:

- Infantry
- Cavalry
- Artillery
- Engineers

However, in combat it is quite likely that situations will emerge requiring a mix of competencies. These could be brought together in a *Kampfgruppe*, in which the various functional units described above were combined into a multifunctional unit. After the battle, all units assigned to this entity were able to rejoin their own 'pool'. With this, von Moltke overcame one of the weaknesses of the *Auftragstaktik* concept, namely the potential conflict between:

- Independence (operating separately, each for himself)
- Cooperation (multifunctional units, operating with each other)

The cooperation in *Verbundene Waffen* was the underlying philosophy that reconciled this conflict, while the *Kampfgruppen* became its manifestation. *Verbundene Waffen* are also an illustration of another concept, that of *Einheit* or communality. Prussians and Germans attached great importance to *Einheit*, creating social cohesion. A unit had to socialize into a group: in sociological terms it had to develop from a *Gesellschaft* (society) to a *Gemeinschaft* (community). The closer the communality within the group, the more effective the *Kampfgemeinschaft* (battle community), and thus its fighting power and resilience. We will discuss the concept of *Einheit* further in the next chapter.

Another interesting feature of this philosophy is that it led to the breakdown of formal boundaries between ranks and social classes. A classic model of army organization is shown in the diagram below. In basic terms, a functional organization is structured around a number of specialisms. However, many such specialisms had their origins in positions in society, which makes the cooperation promoted by the Prussians between the different parts of the army such an interesting feature socially. In general terms, the cavalry represented the aristocracy, the infantry the peasants, and the engineers and artillery the townspeople (more specifically, the guilds). Therefore the cooperation promoted within the armed forces led to important organizational and social changes.

In the second part of the figure there are three *Kampfgruppen*, each with a different composition. The units when 'at rest' are part of the various organizational elements, artillery, cavalry, and so on, but for offensive and defensive purposes they were combined into *Kampfgruppen*, each named after its commander, the most senior officer. So there is a *Kampfgruppe* Friebe, a *Kampfgruppe* Glück and a *Kampfgruppe* Hundertwasser. That meant that an infantry officer could preside over a cavalry unit, two arms that were drawn from totally different social groups, especially in the nineteenth century.

While this may seem a simple concept, it can be very difficult to implement, as organizations do not simply change naturally from a classic hierarchical to a process-driven structure. Furthermore, army organizations have even greater problems with this as a result of existing or cultivated differences between various branches. The British Army, for example, had a reputation to uphold in the ranking and different social positions of its regiments. At El Alamein a cavalry general refused to take

Figure 2: March separately; fight together!

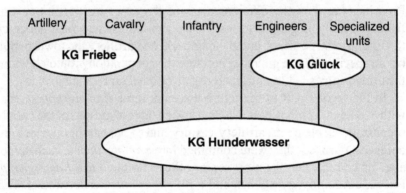

Classical army structure

Artillery	Cavalry	*Infantry*	Engineers	Specialized units

Kampfgruppen as integrating structure

a regiment of the Royal Artillery under his command, stating, 'We only accept the support of the Royal Horse Artillery' (42:111), a unit that had connections with the aristocracy and the royal family.

These *Schnelle Kombinationen* (fast combinations) of *Kampfgruppen* made the Prussian and German armies extremely agile. If you are not used to working and thinking in multifunctional units you have to organize cooperation between functional columns from scratch each time it is required, a process that requires endless planning, tuning, consultation and coordination, and inevitably causes delays. This can create long lag times in responding to developments on the battlefield. No wonder, therefore, that Allied units and armies were described by the Americans themselves as 'slack', 'lacklustre', 'sluggish' and 'timid', as men waited for orders from above, not daring to take the initiative themselves. This meant that the times envisaged in planning and in actual implementation were frequently very different.

Written accounts describe the effects of having to think through everything beforehand, describe it in plans and then discuss it:

> The chief weakness was a ponderous approach to any problem . . . [The British] always tended to organize their movements according to the text-book and official manuals. A whole series of elaborate conferences, often starting at the divisional headquarters and going down through brigade and battalion level, tended to be organized at every opportunity. This consumed valuable time and was much too reminiscent of training schemes at home. (16:380)

The Germans, in contrast, gained valuable time by their approach:

> In contrast to the Eastern theatre of operations, in the West it was possible still to straighten out seemingly impossible situations because the opposing armies there . . . despite their enormous material superiority, were limited by slow and methodical modes of combat. (16:380)

By way of a specific example, the commander of the German 346th Infantry Division reflected that he was never afraid of encirclement, because the Allies created so little real pressure that his units could always fall back easily:

> We were never hurried in these movements because of the tactics of the Allies. When we had been thrown back during the day, we already knew that there would be a pause at night when the enemy would regroup for the next day's operations. It was these hours of darkness that enabled us to retire without suffering many casualties. (16:381)

General Max Simon, commander of the 12th SS Infantry Corps, described the tactics of the Third Army under Patton as 'very cautious and systematic'. About Patton's tank tactics he remarked:

> Had we had the necessary counter-measures – anti-tank guns, airplanes and gasoline – many local penetrations would not have succeeded. The tactics of the Americans were based on the idea of breaking down a wall by taking out one brick at a time. They did this with tanks, against which we had nothing to employ. However, since their tanks were divided amongst several local attacks instead of being concentrated at one point [i.e. the *Schwerpunkt*], we, with adequate equipment, could have repelled these attacks and rejoined our broken line . . . Had you made such attacks [5–20 tanks accompanying infantry] on the Eastern front, where our anti-tank guns were echeloned in depth, all your tanks would have been destroyed. (16:387)

Roncey, July 1944: *Kampfgruppe* Langanke

A superb example of the emergence and later dissolution of a *Kampfgruppe* comes from the Normandy campaign of 1944. Fritz Langanke, the commander of a company of Panther tanks of which only two were operational, was ordered on the evening of 28 July to fight as a *Kampfgruppe* out of a pocket at Roncey towards the south-east to cross the Seine at La Baleine. As he could not get his unit out that night due to chaos on the road, he was forced to wait until the following night, while suffering constant bombing by Allied planes. During the evening of the 29th his *Kampfgruppe* set off, accompanied by Panzer Grenadiers on the left flank and 50–60 parachutists on the right to protect the armour against anti-tank fire. These forces were followed by two StuGs, some trucks, the mechanized artillery of the infantry and several mobile flak guns. At the rear of the column were his second Panther tank and a Panzer 4 medium tank. Just after the departure at 2200 hrs, Langanke's Panther destroyed its first Sherman tank, followed shortly afterwards by an American anti-tank gun. When they later met two other Shermans, Langanke gave the somewhat hesitant StuGs the order to attack, and the two tanks were easily destroyed. Gaining momentum, the *Kampfgruppe* was next faced by a column of American half-tracks. The rear vehicle of the column was set alight by a tank grenade, and several of the remaining half-tracks, by now clearly visible against the light of the flames, were also hit. The remaining Americans fled in panic.

By the time the *Kampfgruppe* reached Lengronne the following dawn it had doubled in size, as 300 German soldiers who had been spread out in small isolated groups had been picked up en route, so that Langanke now commanded 600 men from various units. This now formidable combat group then fought its way to the damaged bridge at La Baleine. It was successfully taken and, on the southern bank of the Seine, the *Kampfgruppe* reached an area that was firmly in German hands. Here, signs indicated where the various 'mother' divisions were located, so men were able to rejoin their own units, following which Langanke's *Kampfgruppe* was dissolved within an hour. On 27 August 1944 Langanke received the Knight's Cross of the Iron Cross in recognition of this successful mission.

Roncey was the first such pocket in Normandy, much like the later one at Falaise that was created by mistakes on the part of the German army command. However, despite the fact that six divisions were originally surrounded, only 5,000 Germans were taken prisoner. Although at Falaise the Allies failed to make large numbers of Germans prisoner, many vehicles were destroyed, which increasingly restricted the mobility of the Germans. (Militaria Hors service 97, Jan/Feb 2016, 76–7)

We have already seen that, following Falaise, the Germans were able to retire relatively undisturbed over the Seine. Reports show that they were not at all afraid of being cut off, since they knew the Allies were incapable of rapid deep penetration or encirclements. In particular, they believed the Allies could not cut the road to the Seine and other rivers, because they were simply not capable of responding quickly enough. In addition, the Allies had become reliant on massive support from artillery or the air, and tended to avoid battle as much as possible.

3.3 Unity in command

The leadership of a *Kampfgruppe* was in the hands of one responsible commander, so there could never be any confusion about who one received orders from. This unity of command was so deeply engrained in the German Army's thinking that each *Kampfgruppe* was named after its commander instead of, for example, receiving a number, as was the usual practice with the Allies. Experience taught that soldiers, as a group, identified readily with the name of their commander, each commander having maximum decentralized responsibilities and powers in accordance with the principle of *Auftragstaktik*. (14:139)

The British Army often disregarded this important principle of unity in command. At the strategic level, for example, where operations involved all three of the armed services, i.e. land, sea and air, command was often conducted by a committee in which the three respective commanders played an equal part, while the Commander-in-Chief had an advisory role and no deciding vote. Furthermore, and particularly during the early years of the war, orders from this strategic level were often seen as advisory at the tactical or lower levels and thus regarded as little more than suggestions, about which anyone could form his own opinion. Not surprisingly, the resulting differences of interpretation led at times to a lack of coordination and concentration within and between units. Combat reports also suggest that during the first years of the war, and certainly in North Africa, the various branches (infantry, artillery and cavalry) operated separately from each other, under their own leadership and without coordination, once fighting started. The more ruthless Montgomery put an end to this free interpretation of orders and forced his commanders to operate within the hierarchy and work to his plan. However, although later in the war the Americans forced the British to adopt the role of the Supreme Commander, which at least guaranteed unity of command within this over-arching structure (27:34), the alignment of the various subordinate units remained a matter of personal initiative. As a result, complete unity in command was sometimes hard to achieve.

The potential diversity of *Kampfgruppen* can be seen in an example from Italy. In May 1944 at Velletri near Rome, a unit of 377 Germans was taken prisoner. To the surprise of the British, the prisoners, who had been fighting like a well-oiled unit for several days, were discovered to originate from fifty different companies of totally different battalions, regiments and divisions. The British Field Marshal Alexander said of this phenomenon: 'In addition, there was the astonishing flexibility in the chain of command which permitted the instantaneous welding together of the most heterogeneous units, from all arms, into effective battlegroups.'

This example shows that units, even those that had suffered severely, could continue to fight as *Kampfgruppen* and could grow over time both in size and strength to form a highly effective force.

On the road to Brussels: *Kampfgruppe* 9. SS Division Hohenstaufen

Lieutenant Colonel Walther Harzer was the divisional commander of the heavily battered 9. SS Division Hohenstaufen, which after its collapse in September 1944 in France, retreated north under Harzer's leadership as *Kampfgruppe* 9. SS Hohenstaufen (the name originated from a noble German family and was retained). The *Kampfgruppe* was commissioned to form an anti-tank screen with its remaining eighteen 88mm flak guns, with the aim of delaying the Allied advance on the route between Paris and Brussels, so that other units could retreat to safety.

Harzer's unit was a shadow of the proud division of only a few months earlier. It had initially been 'loaned' to the Eastern Front and had been in constant combat following a hasty transfer to France on 29 June 1944. On arrival at the front, the division was 18,000-strong, had 179 tanks, 21 StuGs, 287 armoured half-tracks, 16 mechanized guns and 16 armoured cars. It could also field 3,670 other vehicles. Now, as a *Kampfgruppe*, it had shrunk to fewer than 3,500 men with only a limited number of vehicles.

The *Kampfgruppe* had initially excelled itself, but after a fierce battle against a major force of more than 200 Allied tanks, the latter succeeded in forcing a breakthrough in several places. Harzer and his divisional staff remained isolated in the Bois de Bourlon in the Pas de Calais as Allied tanks passed them on either side. They waited until darkness had fallen and then drove their vehicles through the streets of Cambrai, pointed the right way by sympathizers:

Exploiting the night, the SS columns proceeded to drive along the junction between the First US Army to the south

---

and the Second British Army moving to the north. When it became necessary to cross the American line of march, the Feldgendarmerie [Military Police] travelling with the column waved lights and daringly flagged down an enemy convoy. Both sides chose to ignore each other. Dust and exhaustion cloaked the scene with a protective mantle of anonymity. At dawn on 3 September, Harzer decided to lie up and wait again for darkness. Later, the vehicles were festooned with battlefield booty, flags and other souvenir insignia to cover their drive through enemy-occupied villages en route, where victory celebrations were in full swing in lit bars as the half-tracks and vehicles nosed their way through narrow streets. Unattended Allied jeeps were plundered by troopers clambering over bonnets to remove any carelessly left articles of equipment, weapons and supply. They had no idea how long their journey would take, or indeed if they could even reach their own lines; anything picked up on the way was therefore a bonus. On 5 September Harzer's group crossed the main Allied approach route to Brussels and slipped in behind the leading enemy tanks. Maintaining a discreet distance, the column tagged on to the advance. German stragglers picked up en route could hardly believe their eyes when, having been overtaken by the British advance guard, they were then offered lifts by this cheeky German 'rearguard' sweeping up behind it. Eventually, contact was made with the Germans' Brussels garrison which had just evacuated the city, and Harzer's group was directed on to the division. Losses to men and materiel during the march had been nil. Indeed, they had added to their strength, picking up stragglers and a German field hospital with twenty wounded. Even in the face of disaster, the fortunes of war could occasionally smile.

All that remained to this brave *Kampfgruppe* was a single 88mm flak gun and a 20mm gun. (30:11–17, 74)

By using *Kampfgruppen* the Germans were able to execute a very mobile type of warfare. They ensured that these units were equipped with ample radio and communications equipment, an essential means of maintaining cohesion between units operating over a broad and deep front. In order to prevent endless gossip and blockage of the airwaves, men were trained to use the equipment very sparingly and provide extremely concise information.

It is not always apparent what a dominant role was played by the *Kampfgruppen* in the German Army. In reality, they were the organizational form in which the army fought. While the Allies followed plans and had to endlessly align their functional units to guarantee some form of cohesion, the Germans used the *Kampfgruppen* as self-organizing and self-coordinating units. The Allies needed days to arrange all the necessary coordination, while *Kampfgruppen* could be formed within fifteen minutes and be on the road within half an hour. This clearly illustrates the differences in time lag at the tactical level that made *Kampfgruppen* such an elusive phenomenon.

Plans, plans, and again, plans

Where the Germans used *Kampfgruppen*, the Allies used many detailed plans to coordinate their units. These were serious works and sometimes totalled hundreds of pages, in which the choreography of the attack was described. For Operation Torch, the landing of American units in North Africa, the attack plan was the size of the Sears, Roebuck 'General Merchandize' catalogue, the so-called 'Big Book' comprising more than a thousand pages. Subsequent operations such as Husky, the landings on Sicily, also suffered from an excess of paper. It is impossible to reconstruct the extent of the plans for D-Day, but records were undoubtedly broken. D-Day was followed by an impressive number of offensives, each based on extensive staff work; these included Atlantic, Bluecoat, Charnwood, Cobra, Epsom, Goodwood, Jupiter, Martlet, Spring, Totalize and Windsor. Remarkably, these were just the offensives for the period up to 1 August 1944.

Working with extensive plans had two effects:

- It slowed down operations because days, sometimes weeks, were spent on planning
- As soon as a plan was frustrated by enemy action, everything came to a standstill in order to wait for a new plan; also, when opportunities arose, units waited for new orders rather than taking action independently

All in all, this led to situations in which the Germans were regularly given ample time to regroup. As a result, they were not afraid of being encircled or surprised by the Allies, as the latter's plans simply did not permit them to achieve this.

3.4 The reality of the battlefield: Arnhem, September 1944

The reaction of German units to the landings of British parachutists at Arnhem on 17 September 1944 clearly shows the speed of action, initiative, leadership and professionalism the Germans could muster in response to an unexpected attack. At Arnhem a major force of British troops was pinned down within a few hours by a *Kampfgruppe* consisting of units that had not known each other before; some were in training or only partly trained, and others had no combat experience at all.

> We knew from experience that the only way to draw the tooth of an airborne landing, with an inferior force, is to drive right into it.
>
> Captain Sepp Krafft, SS Panzer Grenadier
> Ersatz Battaillon 16 (30:69)

On 17 September at 2.00 pm, 8,000 British paratroopers landed near Arnhem. Opposing them were the remains of the 9. SS Division Hohenstaufen and a varied mix of other combat and training units, including elements from 10. SS Division Frundsberg. As usual, the German units reacted quickly and efficiently. A *Kampfgruppe* led by Lieutenant Colonel

Ludwig Spindler would play a central role in frustrating the attempts of the British to reach the Arnhem bridge:

> In the middle of the afternoon the dispersed quick action company [*Alarm Gruppe*, 'alarm company'] of the 9. SS began to collect together. They arrived on foot, bicycles, horse-drawn carts or in ramshackle cars. Twenty lorries of the Hohenstaufen's transport group operated a shuttle service, moving companies through Arnhem city and out to the western suburbs. They reacted to a simple slogan: 'Follow the sound of the shooting: that is where the front is!'

In the course of the afternoon of the 17th Spindler took command of this motley combination of units, and '*Kampfgruppe* Spindler' became a reality. Spindler has been described as an 'experienced officer, who led by example and was greatly respected by his men'. He had won two Knight's Crosses for his efforts in Poland and the Soviet Union and the German Cross in gold for Normandy, and was therefore exactly the right type of leader for such an assignment. Although his *Kampfgruppe* was made up of men from sixteen different units, it developed rapidly into a smoothly operating unit that successfully frustrated the advance of the British paratroopers. It had originally been made up of just two companies of his own unit, a StuG regiment of 120 men, but without their StuGs. This had quickly moved to the western side of the city from Dieren, a town 8km or 9km north-east of Arnhem, where they joined the 100 men of *Kampfgruppe* Möller, the vestiges of the battalion of the 9. SS Division Hohenstaufen that had already been in combat with the British paratroopers earlier that afternoon and could muster a few half-tracks. Möller had built a line of defence with his *Kampfgruppe* in Oosterbeek together with men from an anti-aircraft unit under Lieutenant Gropp. *Kampfgruppe* Spindler grew in the course of the evening and around midnight it was supplemented by a 300-man battalion led by Major Josef Krafft. This was an *Ersatz* (Training) Battalion, which had no combat experience. However, they had some heavy weapons and had already confronted the British that afternoon, with some distinction. Using these disparate resources, Spindler managed to build up an effective line of defence during the crucial night of 17/18 September and closed the door to the bridge at Arnhem, so that the only British who reached the bridge were 1,200 men led by Major General Frost earlier that day.

In the following days the size of *Kampfgruppe* Spindler grew steadily, sometimes being joined by untrained or even unarmed units such as a group of the *Reichsarbeitsdienst* (auxiliary labour force). Eventually, in addition to the *Kampfgruppe* Spindler, two other *Kampfgruppen* were formed under his leadership, namely *Kampfgruppe* von Allworden, comprising 120 men grouped around the vestiges of Panzerjäger Abteilung (anti-tank troops) of 9. SS Division Hohenstaufen, and *Kampfgruppe* Harder, comprising three companies grouped around the vestiges of the Panzer Regiment of 9. SS Division Hohenstaufen. This unit, despite what its name suggests, did not have tanks, and the tank crews fought as infantry, together with maintenance and logistics units as well as a company of the Kriegsmarine (navy). This latter unit, which was able to field a few StuGs and 75mm guns, had been in action on 17 September north of Arnhem, where it had effectively halted the advance of British units.

It was of course somewhat surprising that a force of 8,000 British soldiers, described in the literature as an elite unit, was not able to break a defence line of a few hundred men, some of them untrained and others with no combat experience at all. This failure, sometimes described by the British as a 'glorious disaster', is often obscured by arguing that two German armoured divisions were present. While there is an element of truth in this assertion, as the Arnhem region was a gathering place for the vestiges of two such divisions, the 9. SS Division Hohenstaufen and the 10. SS Division Frundsberg, these had been in constant combat for three months and their effectiveness was seriously compromised as a result. In all, they probably amounted to 6,000 men, and the major part of the 10. SS Division Frundsberg with 3,500 men and the remnants of its hardware was already on its way back to Germany. Originally it had been the intention that the 9. SS Division Hohenstaufen should transfer its armour and transport to 10. SS Division Frundsberg, as the Germans felt the Arnhem area was safe. The division would subsequently receive new equipment from Germany. However, as 9. SS Division Hohenstaufen was reluctant to lose its vehicles, some thirty to forty half-tracks as well as a number of armoured reconnaissance vehicles had been stripped of essential parts so that they were no longer roadworthy, and they remained behind. When it became clear that British troops had landed, these vehicles were quickly rendered operational again, and by the afternoon of 17 September they had been re-formed as *Kampfgruppe* Gräbner on a reconnaissance mission to check the condition of the bridges at Arnhem and Nijmegen and discover whether any enemy units were nearby. Just after this *Kampfgruppe* had crossed the bridge near Arnhem on the road to Nijmegen, British units under Frost arrived and took up positions. When *Kampfgruppe* Gräbner returned from Nijmegen on the morning of 18 September they were therefore surprised to be confronted by British troops, a scenario familiar from the movie *A Bridge Too Far*, and the subsequent engagements ended in heavy losses. As well as the units of 9. SS Division Hohenstaufen, there was a very diverse array of other units in the region, as can be seen from the composition of *Kampfgruppe* Spindler. They used whatever materiel was on hand; for example, it was unclear where their two StuGs came from or to which unit they belonged.

The diversity and speed of the German reaction soon became even more widespread. Shortly after the landings there was already a unit of forty men of 10. SS Division Frundsberg from Doesburg, 30km to the north, on the way to Arnhem, using confiscated bicycles in search of the fighting; a unit of the coastal battery of the Kriegsmarine from Katwijk, a fishing port on the North Sea in the west of the Netherlands, 120km from Arnhem, was also arriving by bicycle. A request was issued to borrow guns from the Ruhr area anti-aircraft command. This was approved following an agreement that the lender would provide transport, and the guns were already arriving and installed by the morning of 18 September, just in time to catch the second wave of airborne landings. Meanwhile, a railway train containing nine StuGs was loaded and despatched at high speed from Copenhagen, to arrive in Arnhem on 20 September, accompanied by a diverse range of troops including members of the Kriegsmarine and untrained recruits. These units were thrown into battle immediately, albeit with varying degrees of success.

3.5 Composition of a *Kampfgruppe*

Each *Kampfgruppe* had a clearly defined goal and a clear leader who, in turn, was accountable to only one higher commander. The size of a *Kampfgruppe* could vary from that of a division (8,000 to 12,000 men) to a company (100 to 200 men), depending on what it was required for and the availability of men and materiel. The most common size was that of a regiment (1,500 to 2,000 men) or a battalion (300 to 800 men).

Kampfgruppen were operational for only a few weeks. When they had completed their assignment, their men were reintegrated into their 'mother' units. The use of *Kampfgruppen* increased after 1943 and contributed significantly to the resilience of the German Army at this stage of the war, preventing military units from degenerating into armed mobs.

The *Kampfgruppe* concept imposed very high demands on the flexibility and organizational capacity of all involved. In practice, this proved to be no problem, due to the high level of training of both the officers and troops of the German Army, including those on the staff level. (19:78) The combination of *Auftragstaktik* and the deployment of *Kampfgruppen* can be seen as one of the main building blocks for the success of the German Army. If these two elements were in place, the evolution of the concept was complete and the phenomenon of the Blitzkrieg came into being, as illustrated by the Polish campaign of 1939 and the campaigns of May and June 1940.

3.6 The British Army

While the German Army focused on connection, the British Army appeared to concentrate on separation. The reason for this was the influence of the regimental system. Regiments played an important role in the British Army, and it is important to understand the background of this organizational structure.

As a result of the Cardwell reforms of 1873, each regiment was divided in two, one part stationed in Great Britain, while the second served in one or other of the colonies. The influence of the latter commitment was profound. In the period up to 1939 the British Army could rightly be described as principally a colonial army, whose task was the defence of the British Empire. As a result, therefore, any war against European opponents would be fought with insights and experience that had been gained during colonial wars and 'low intensity' or minor conflicts, as described in *Small Wars: Their Principles and Practice* by C. E. Callwell (1896), a work that gained a permanent place in British military culture and military thinking. (46:31) It remains an interesting and readable sketch of British campaigns and opponents from that period, the British way of operating, the terrain, possible counter-actions, tactics, logistics and how to deal with local populations.

The regimental system remained in place after the First World War, by which time it had been further adapted and developed as a result of greater regional recruitment than in the past, this tending to create specific regional identities. For example, the proportion of Scots in the Scots Guards had grown from 42 per cent in 1914 to 63 per cent by 1918. Such a recognizable regional bond strengthened the position of the regiment within the Army, while also increasing cohesion within the regiment itself. (59:208–9) Although recruitment, selection and training were centralized and standardized, the very strong subculture of the regiment prevailed throughout. For example, after a relatively short period at Sandhurst, it was assumed that the subsequent detailed training of an officer would take place within his regiment, this becoming a decisive factor in his further career development. Since each regiment was a society in itself, with its own values and norms, the officer in question was also choosing a life within a certain clearly defined social group. Members of the officer corps therefore identified themselves primarily with their own regiment and its values, norms and traditions, as well as with the microcosm of the officer's mess, and less so with the wider British Army. Infantry regiments had clear ties with certain regions, cavalry regiments with sections of the aristocracy. There might even be a direct connection with the Crown if the regimental commander was of noble birth. As a result, any officer from a middle-class background who wished to advance his career had to adapt to the values and norms of the class that the regimental commander represented. (59:195–8)

The Queen and the regiment
The special relationship of the various regiments with the Crown became clear once again in 1956, when the Queen underlined the importance of the regimental structure during the fiftieth anniversary of the General Staff, thus bringing the position of the regiment back to everyone's attention. This royal intervention took place during a period in which political discussion was taking place, in the context of the Cold War, about the future role of the British Army. The future position of regiments was only of marginal importance, but was seen as a derivative of the future mission of the British Army. (59:215)

The above mechanism of socialization within the regiment still plays a role in the so-called 'fighting' regiments, namely the infantry and cavalry. The technically specialized regiments have a much more open relationship with society. The training of these regiments is also more centralized and their command structure more bureaucratic. (59:195–8)

Over-identification with the regiment

At times, excessive identification with a regiment can become counter-productive. Major General D. N. Wemberley of the 51st Highland Division stressed that its esprit de corps was closely related to the Scottish identity of its regiments. He told his men that 'if wounded and separated from your units, do not allow yourselves to be drafted to other battalions, but see that you can come back to us.' In 1943, 1,200 troops from two divisions, one of which was the 51st Highland Division, were ordered to join the 46th Division inland from Salerno. Three hundred men refused, of whom 191 stood their ground even after their commanders had announced that they no longer had to join their own units at all times. These men were then accused of mutiny. In their defence, it was argued that 'to ask a soldier of the Highland Division to fight with another division is, in my mind [i.e. that of their advocate], akin to asking a Hindu to worship Mohammed'. In 1944, however, the shortage of troops was so great that the barriers between regiments and even army branches fell away. For example, the 2nd battalion of the Scots Guards, regrouping in Hawick, received 400 men from an RAF regiment. The latter arrived dressed in RAF blue while they sang challengingly, 'We are the RAF, RAF, RAF!'

During the course of the war, the Scots Guards became part of the Guards Armoured Division, and the Scots Guards in turn were combined with parts of the Welsh Guards, so that the distinction between the various regiments gradually disappeared in practice. (45:212–13)

In the Second World War, after Dunkirk, larger units such as divisions and corps were needed, as a result of which the regimental system became subordinate to the new organizational structure of the British Army. Alan Brooke, Chief of the Imperial General Staff (CIGS), tried hard during the course of the war to give the British Army a more 'corporate' identity. As a result, although animosity between different regiments was still a reality, the regiment was no longer the dominant structure. (43:214) However, the institution of the regiment meant that it was not possible to create a unified vision of organization and management, and this continued to lead to a fragmentation in thinking and acting within the British Army in all kinds of situations until well into the Second World War. (43:195–8)

Another corollary of the fact that British troops were scattered across large parts of the world was the linking of command structures to geographical areas rather than military units. There were Commanders-in-Chief for the Mediterranean region, India and South-East Asia. In addition to their military function, these officials also played a political and administrative role within the larger whole of the British Empire. These latter tasks often took a great deal of time and led to the creation of regional military substructures to take care of military affairs. This resulted in a cumbersome and undynamic mode of command. In addition, the actual deployment of troops was often dependent on Britain's 'grand strategy' for the region, which had much broader political and strategic implications. For example, at the end of 1940 the successful advance of British troops to Tripoli was suddenly halted by Archibald Wavell, C-in-C Mediterranean Sea, because he needed these units for an intervention in Greece, which was threatened by the Axis powers. (27:38) The resultant vacuum created in North Africa was then quickly exploited by Rommel, with serious consequences.

The lack of an overall vision is also explained by the anti-intellectual reputation of the British Army. This meant that developments were not systematically placed in a broader context with the aim of creating an overall vision or doctrine, a role that the General Staff fulfilled in the German Army. As a result, military solutions had to be sought on a pragmatic 'case-by-case' basis, often because those faced with the task were far from the motherland, and the problems that the British Army faced in their colonies often had little in common. Experiences were limited to the regiments concerned, and it was difficult to learn from each other, develop ideas together and place them in a broader context. (46:32, 34) A central authority, such as a strong general staff, could have combined these experiences and brought the development of a common vision to a higher level. But the British never took this initiative, something which clearly reflects the difference between the British and German general staffs.

The lack of an overall command concept and doctrine, combined with thinking in terms of the regiment and experiences gained from 'small wars' or 'low intensity conflicts', led the British to experiment with a large number of organizational concepts in the early part of the Second World War, particularly in North Africa. A dominant theme here was that British officers, in line with their experiences in the colonies, felt a strongly held desire to command their own 'group' or 'entity'. The belief was that they would then be able to manoeuvre enthusiastically across the battlefield without having to bother about coordination with other units.

In North Africa these small units also fitted the romantic image of many who saw themselves as 'Lawrences of Arabia', ready to attack the enemy unexpectedly and 'kill Jerries'. Sometimes such units were used to good effect, but they often led to fragmentation of scarce resources and to glorious disasters if they fell prey to well-coordinated German units. The units had names such as 'Jock Columns', 'The Long Range Desert Group' and the 'Selby Force', and their activities have formed an attractive subject for films and books. Irrespective of their effectiveness, these actions fitted the British tradition of glorious deeds by small groups of men.

Jock Columns

In September 1940, the British in North Africa came to the conclusion that their armoured units were vulnerable to Italian artillery and aircraft. To counter this, these units were reinforced with artillery and anti-aircraft guns. The artillery was mounted on the body of trucks, while the infantry was also motorized. The spiritual father of this concept was Lieutenant Colonel J. C. (Jock) Campbell of the Royal Horse Artillery. These units appeared unexpectedly in various places to sow death and destruction, to the great alarm of the Italians. Because of their success, later that year more independent units such as the Support Group, consisting of two infantry battalions and an artillery battalion, and the Selby Force, consisting of infantry companies with artillery and tanks, were deployed in the fight against the Italians. (47:119) The success of these units confirmed the experiences gained from earlier 'small wars'. However, they were no match for German troops, the masters in the field of mobile warfare with independent units such as *Kampfgruppen*.

Under certain circumstances, smaller units were sometimes randomly combined into larger ones such as the 'Western Desert Force', 'W Force', 'East Africa Force', 'Creforce' or 'Habforce'.

> None of these formations was particularly effective, and this relatively random way of organizing formations resulted in serious losses of experienced officers and men. (59:38)

After Operation Crusader, one of the large battles in North Africa in early 1942, it was decided, for unclear reasons, that the division as an autonomous combat unit was too large to manage in the desert. (27:24) The solution, in line with the success of the German *Kampfgruppen*, was sought in the formation of what were termed 'Brigade Groups'. The problem was that the concept of the *Kampfgruppe* and its organizational background and doctrine was not understood by the British. The effect was that the newly formed British units had to be pressured to cooperate; moreover, the artillery, the most effective branch of the military, was divided between them. As a result, the Brigade Groups were not a success. Subsequently, a different organizational variant was tested the same year: infantry units were stationed in static reinforcements, or so-called 'boxes', backed by a mobile tank reserve. In practice, these boxes were simply bypassed by the Germans and later on cleared one by one. The frontally attacking British tanks, deployed in small units, were in their turn stopped by a combination of tanks, artillery and anti-tank guns. (10:205–6)

The Lager (or Laager) as a base

In the field, the British Army used a formation termed the 'Lager' or 'Laager', a concept derived from the Boer War, by which support vehicles of a unit were arranged in a circle. They were buried to their axles in the sand and protected by anti-tank guns. From this base, tanks went into battle in the morning, returning during the day to take on fuel and ammunition. The Lager was also used as a base for the night. The range of the tanks was thus determined by the position of their base, which was vulnerable to hostile action because of its stationary character. Lagers were frequently used in North Africa and often overrun by German units, mostly because the British units broke off fighting after sunset to prepare for the night, enabling the Germans to simply follow the British tanks back to their base.

In summary, the institution of the regiment and the later experiments with a number of differing operational units led to a fragmentation within the British Army until well into the Second World War, resulting in an often confused organizational picture. (43:195–8) Although not much is known about these aspects of the British Army in the Second World War, evaluation and observations by the Germans have proved to be a good source of information about them. If evaluation was ever carried out by the British, its results were not evident; and there appeared to have been no interest at the level of the Chief of the General Staff, let alone evidence that evaluation led to any adjustments. It has to be assumed that these were left to the initiative of regimental commanders.

3.7 The American Army: incidental cooperation

There was no explicit focus on the concept of battle groups in the US Army, although this does not mean that different units did not operate jointly on occasion. However, when they did, it tended to be on the basis of an individual plan, as distinct from a joint doctrine. One of the many examples of the drawback of not having such a doctrine was the battle around Aix-la-Chapelle in September 1944. The 5th Armoured Division had successfully managed to drive a wedge 12km deep between the *Heeresgruppe* (Army Group) B in the north and *Heeresgruppe* G in the south. However, because the Americans lacked accompanying infantry to hold their ground, German units regularly and successfully infiltrated the American positions at night and inflicted heavy losses. At the same time, further south, small groups of two to three Germans in seventeen strongholds were able to hold the line against superior numbers of Americans without difficulty. This had nothing to do with lack of courage on the part of the American GIs, but was simply due to bad planning and poor reconnaissance on the American side. The first battalion of the American 110th Infantry Division struggled for three days with this light defensive line until, on the afternoon of 17 September, a unit of combat engineers finally arrived with TNT, some armoured vehicles and Sherman Firefly tanks. Within an hour the obstacles on the road were demolished, and the tanks could open the fire on the reinforcements. Within three quarters of an hour the surviving Germans were captured and the hill was in American hands. Although a good example of cooperation, it also showed how such collaboration on the American side was often dictated by chance. (65:25) Another extremely bizarre example of the deployment by the Americans of a *'Kampfgruppe'* was the raid on the prisoner-of-war camp Oflag XIIIB in Hammelburg, at the end of March 1945, by the 'Task Force Baum', with the aim of securing the release of General Patton's son-in-law. This operation will be described in the next section.

Sometimes personal relationships played a role in collaboration between units. A well-documented example was that of Lieutenant Colonel Creighton Abrams and Major Cohen. The pair were close friends who commanded, respectively, the 37th Tank Battalion and the 10th Armored Infantry Battalion of the 4th Armored Division. Their units worked together closely, and the effect of this collaboration was sufficiently striking that it received a special mention in Wehrmacht bulletins.

Cooperation between tanks and infantry was generally less obvious. US tanks did not have the offensive role assigned to German panzers, but served mainly in support of the infantry. There was a somewhat strained relationship between these services, and many accounts relate the absence of tanks in support of infantry at crucial moments, or their hasty retreat as they came under fire. However, the latter course was not necessarily unwise: the superiority of the German tanks and tank guns, particularly the 75mm and 88mm guns of the Panther and Tiger tanks respectively, made any confrontation dangerous:

> A Tiger could sit all day like a chunk of solid steel, soaking up the punishment, and then blast off one 88 and 'put paid' to the pestering Shermans. [In addition, the infantry complained] that the tanker's insistence on nightly behind the lines 'maintenance' of their machines owed less to mechanical necessity than to the desire for sound sleep. (35:32)

The infantry tried to overcome such behaviour by, for example, adjusting the estimates of the number of enemy tanks downwards. Sometimes tanks were considered to be unwanted intruders:

> Just as SS troops in a French village began to wave white flags to dug-in GIs, two Shermans clanked into the field . . . took no time to ask questions and opened up on the village with their .50-caliber turret guns and .75-caliber turret gun. White flags and Germans – now seeking cover – disappeared in a cloud of dust. (35:32)

However, the infantry greatly appreciated cooperation from the artillery, because the massive use of artillery (and airpower) was often the only way to break German resistance. On the other hand, the US artillery did not have the mobility and the offensive posture that characterized, for example, the German *Sturmartillerie*. In many cases the only thing they could do was overwhelm the Germans with the sheer quantity shells fired from a distance. Another practice was a form of 'hit and run' tactic, by which the artillery positioned itself in the midst of the infantry, fired some shots at the enemy and then pulled back quickly, 'leaving the foot soldiers to absorb the counter-battery fire'. Sometimes, however, a practical solution was found to counter this:

> When each morning in Belgium a British 25-pounder set up, fired ten rounds and scurried away, an infantry-mechanic one day removed the unit's rotor arm, thereby forcing the artillerymen to sample the riposte of the German 88s to which they daily exposed the ground soldiers. They weren't seen again. (35:33)

Probably these were the uncoordinated actions of individual units that wanted 'to teach the Germans a lesson' and show them that the British were there as well. It will undoubtedly have been an exception, but it does clearly show how units sometimes waged their own wars.

3.8 The reality of the battlefield: the liberation of Patton's son-in-law

One of the most bizarre actions of the Second World War on the American side was the attempt to liberate Patton's son-in-law, Lieutenant Colonel J. K. Waters, from German hands. The force involved had many characteristics of a real German *Kampfgruppe*: 'Task Force Baum' was named after its commander, Captain Abraham Baum, and comprised men from various units. Moreover, it was given the kind of challenging mission that would have suited a *Kampfgruppe*. But there the resemblance ends, because this was a case of 'hazardous planning and motives that looked like nepotism'.

So what happened? Oflag XIIIB in Hammelburg held US officers, including John K. Waters. By the end of March, the Americans were only 75km from the camp, and Patton was afraid the prisoners would soon be transferred. He therefore decided a raid was required behind German lines to save Waters and the other prisoners, a total of over one thousand men. Exact details are unclear, but this was clearly a 'hazardous plan'. On 26 March it was decided that a unit of the 4th Armored Division under the leadership of Captain Baum had to set out that same evening, despite the fact that they did not know exactly where the camp was or how many prisoners it housed. Furthermore, the terrain had not been explored, and fuel for the retreat would have to be captured from the Germans (who themselves had insufficient stocks). Another detail was that the Task Force had neither enough vehicles to transport the liberated prisoners of war, nor weapons to arm them. In reality, the Task Force consisted of little more than 300 men with a remarkable mix of weapons, namely ten Sherman tanks with 75mm or 76mm guns, three Sherman tanks with 105mm howitzers, six light Stuart tanks, a Sherman recovery tank, twenty-eight halftracks, a Dodge truck and a Weasel tracked vehicle. Infantry and engineer units were included, plus a medical unit. At 2100 on 26 March the unit tried to break through the German line at Schweinheim with the help of an infantry battalion and three artillery battalions, an attack which eventually succeeded around midnight. The Americans managed to advance smoothly in the following hours, which gives an idea not only of the weakness of the German defence but also of what could have been achieved if the whole Third US Army had followed this breakthrough in classic German fashion with an infiltration behind the front.

If there was any fear of this on the German side, it disappeared early the following morning after reconnaissance by a small Fieseler Storch aircraft; this observed only a ragged group moving in a north-easterly direction, without a clear goal and not followed by any other American units. It was thus immediately clear that this was not an offensive by the full Third Army. An important consequence of this observation was that the strategic reserve of German tanks in the region was not used, because the Germans wanted to save fuel for the expected real offensive. This created a strange situation in which the American Task Force was opposed only by lightly-armoured German units that were part of the reserve or still in training.

As a result, Task Force Baum trundled undisturbed along the River Main, leaving a trail of destruction in its wake: twelve trains at a railway yard carrying anti-aircraft guns and ammunition were shot up, a job that was finished by American fighter-bombers later in the morning, barges on the Main were set on fire and bunkers destroyed. At 0715 the Task Force

91

ran into the first resistance; three tanks were destroyed, and Baum was forced to try to reach Hammelburg by a different route. Further down the road, the column was attacked by an anti-tank unit and two Stukas, but Baum finally reached the camp with twelve halftracks and fifteen tanks at 1800 hrs. Their appearance led to a complete collapse of discipline among the American prisoners of war, who assumed that this was the vanguard of the Third Army. When it became clear that this was not the case, everyone still wanted to make for the security of the American lines; but, as mentioned earlier, the transport of so many prisoners had not been taken into account, since the Task Force was intended to secure only the release of Waters who, incidentally, had been injured by a guard during a skirmish.

After an element of order was restored, the prisoners decided to select a number of their comrades for the return journey. Meanwhile, the local German commander tried to bring troops together to prevent a breakthrough to the north, although the only troops he could field were lightly armed with rifles, machine guns and Panzerfausts (single-shot anti-tank rifles). Eventually, Baum left with two hundred freed prisoners in a south-easterly direction, through an area in which the Germans controlled all the main roads. By the early morning of 28 March it had finally became clear that Baum was in a hopeless situation; he could only muster a little over one hundred men and was already short of fuel, so decided to set eight halftracks on fire, having first drained their fuel for the other vehicles. One hundred and forty-three prisoners returned to the camp on their own, and the injured were left at a location marked with a clear red cross. At 0915 the Americans were surrounded and then attacked, the wounded being caught between the two sides. Before long, Baum ordered that every man should try to find his own way back to the American lines, the Task Force now consisting of nothing more than the smoking remains of the tanks and halftracks. Many of the Americans were eventually arrested, and Oflag XIIIB was evacuated, with the exception of the seriously wounded, one being Waters. When the camp was finally liberated on 4 April, Patton sent two planes with a medical team led by the commander of the medical forces of the Third Army. They repatriated Waters, letting the other badly wounded American officers wait for three days before receiving medical care, thereby reinforcing the idea that the whole exercise had been driven by nepotism.

Reviewing this operation, the raid leaves a number of conflicting impressions. First of all, this was a Task Force that had, in its composition, the characteristics of a *Kampfgruppe*. The Task Force even bore the name of its commander, something which was not customary. In many ways it looked like the *Kampfgruppe* Peiper, which had been sent out to pick up wounded men and guarantee others a safe journey back to their own lines. Taskforce Baum was also able to break through in classic fashion and left behind it a trail of destruction, which, although not the primary goal, was a nice bonus. But Patton had given Baum and his men an impossible assignment with a dubious aim, the rescue of his son-in-law. The fact that news of this disastrous raid never reached the press was due to the death of President Roosevelt on 12 April; this most certainly prevented Patton from having to answer some difficult questions. (23:47, 65–77)

3.9 A 'School of Thought': the German General Staff

Crucial to the organization of the German Army was the General Staff. This, together with the Staff Officer Corps, was of great importance to the maintenance of professionalism; indeed, the Allies had recognized it as the basis of the German Army's effectiveness and promptly banned the institution at the end of the First World War. The Germans took counter-measures, and in secret the General Staff was accommodated in a cover organization, the *Truppenamt*, from 1918, enabling them to start planning and building a new army.

The Allies were particularly apprehensive about the General Staff because it was the brains of the German Army. It played an important role in the development and monitoring of the Army's management concepts and tactical doctrines, because it:

- kept and updated doctrine and tactics, and the methods and techniques derived from them, in the form of Standard Operating Procedures for all kinds of combat situations
- trained the officer corps in the application of the doctrine and tactics, in both theory and practice
- embedded them throughout the command structure in such a way that officers and units actually used the whole system
- selected for key positions officers who met high standards, while rejecting those who did not (42:331–6)

The German General Staff can thus be seen as the 'academy' of the German Army: free exchange of ideas was central to its operation and considered of great importance for the further development of doctrine and tactics. This approach was initiated by von Schlieffen, the Prussian commander of the General Staff before the First World War. He regularly commissioned junior staff officers to work out complex strategic problems, on the premise that in wartime these men would need to have the knowledge and skills to be able to lead large combat units. Von Seeckt, a pupil of von Schlieffen, embedded this culture of openness in the General Staff of the Reichswehr after the First World War. (57:109)

The Staff Officer Corps of the General Staff was an important factor in ensuring cohesion within the German Army. Officers of the Corps, recognizable by the red piping on their trousers, belonged to the elite of the Army, and every intelligent and promising officer was transferred to the Corps for training; here they became, in effect, guardians of the doctrine developed by the General Staff. The training of these officers focused on the consistent application of the doctrine and its associated system of methods and techniques applicable to all kinds of tactical and operational situations. This included the planning of offensives, defensive measures, troop movements and logistics management. There were so many officers in the Corps that all staff positions within divisions, and often within regiments, could be filled by these highly-educated and well-trained individuals. In the absence of an army commander, the staff officer (usually two or three ranks lower than his commander) was generally very capable of managing the regiment, the division, the corps or even the army; and as most commanders originated from the Staff Officer Corps themselves, they knew what they could safely leave to these men. Because the more general and predictable aspects of warfare were therefore often in the trusted hands of staff officers, German commanders in the field could focus fully on the multitude of unexpected situations that occur during every military operation. In addition, they were able to lead from the front. This had not only an enormous motivational effect on combat troops, but also gave the commander a good picture of the front line. (14:136) In practice, the headquarters, manned by staff officers and units of the signal corps, was further behind the front, while the commander himself with his own mobile combat unit (*Gefechtsstaffel*) operated close behind the front line, where he was able to keep himself informed of the progress of the battle and could give prompt and first-hand instructions to the commanders on the spot.

Staff officers rotated between the front and the General Staff, so that optimal use could be made of their experience. In addition, the knowledge of the General Staff was constantly supplemented by evaluation and analysis of important combat actions (*Erfahrungsberichte* – see below). This knowledge was used to adapt the standard methods and techniques and to improve their application in combat situations. (42:127) In this way there was a constant exchange between theory and practice, and concepts and doctrine could constantly be adapted to match the reality of the front. The officers of the Staff Officer Corps functioned almost literally as 'repositories of knowledge' for the German Army.

This way of working led to a high degree of exchangeability of officers and men between the different units and fronts. It was not the personal vision and approach of the individual officer or the army unit that was decisive, but the approach developed by the General Staff and the Staff Officer Corps and tested in practice. By choosing similar approaches and frameworks to evaluate combat actions, structured and unambiguous feedback was guaranteed.

Misconceptions about the German system

The British were aware that the Germans had thought carefully about warfare. A British officer wrote the following in the middle of 1915:

When the war began we were all prepared for the Germans to be successful at first owing to their study of war and scientific preparation, but we argued that very soon we should become better than they, not being hidebound by a system. The exact contrary has been the case. The Germans with their foundation of solid study and experience have been far quicker to adapt themselves to the changed conditions of war and the emergencies of the situation than either we or the Russians have been – possibly even more so than the French. (41:110)

It is clear that the German system was believed to be a rigid framework from which one could not deviate, while in practice it was a way of thinking and working focused on learning and adaptation. Such misconceptions about the presumed limitations of the German system were still common in the Second World War.

As the war progressed, staff officers received further tasks, such as the re-forming of combat units that had been defeated or become fragmented, and the formation of *Kampfgruppen* or *Alarmgruppen*. These latter, stationed behind the front, acted as a safety net and prevented the rapid disintegration of retreating units during the last years of the war. (2:26)

3.10 The British Army: an army without a brain

As we have seen, the General Staff in its role as a brain played a prominent role in the German Army. If any unit showed signs of developing its own doctrines or Standard Operating Procedures, the General Staff and the staff officer corps would ensure that they complied with the general standard.

Such a structure was missing in the British Army, which failed to develop an overall doctrine or philosophy. As a result, its officers remained 'imprisoned' in the regimental system and lacked a common frame of reference in the field of command. It also lacked staff training for officers, and this contributed to the frequently observed low level of training and understanding of doctrine among British officers. (27:31) This was partially addressed during the Second World War, when a structure of staff officers was introduced within larger units, headed by a Chief of Staff (COS), who was responsible for the administrative dimensions of the unit and could represent his commander at a range of meetings. This enabled the commander to focus on the major issues without being bothered by lesser administrative tasks.

However, this was often introduced as a personal initiative and was neither a common feature nor embedded in the organization as a whole. Montgomery, for example, introduced the COS structure in the 21st Army Group, but he saw the COS as having an administrative and supporting role. He continued to make plans and take decisions personally, which the COS was expected to elaborate on in more detail. (27:34)

Montgomery further split his HQ into a Main Headquarters and Tactical Headquarters, the latter being located close to the front from where he led the fighting; this was different to his predecessors, who were often situated 100km to the rear. In addition, he positioned his headquarters alongside that of the RAF in order to optimize cooperation with Air Marshal Tedder.

3.11 Erfahrungsberichte: the learning organization

Many modern students of management will be aware that the origins of what we now know as a 'Quality Cycle' can be traced back to the work in the 1950s of an American professor and management consultant, W. Edwards Deming. However, in practice, the German Army had been operating such a cycle since the beginning of the nineteenth century.

It was this approach that led to the evaluation of the Battle of Jena in 1806 and to evaluations of every significant combat action thereafter. It took the form not of a limited method of feedback with a focus on what went wrong, but of feedback explicitly focused on what could be learned from it. What became known as *Erfahrungsberichte* (evaluation reports) were extremely powerful elements of a quality management system. All combat actions were evaluated, and this could lead to adjustments in the command concept, doctrine and tactics. It made the German Army an unprecedentedly powerful learning organization.

Erfahrungsberichte were concise and quickly shared. For example, when British tank units in North Africa attacked one of Rommel's tank divisions in the morning using a new tactic, a second British tank unit met disaster when it tried the same tactic against another German division hundreds of miles away in the afternoon. The commander of the first division had briefed his colleague on the basis of the *Erfahrungsberichte* so that he could take appropriate counter-measures.

Not learning leads to unnecessary casualties
The British experienced major problems in learning from their experiences. An example of this came in one of the first confrontations between British tanks and German armoured units in North Africa. A British officer 'had seen the Hussars charging into Jerry tanks, sitting on top of their turrets more or less with their whips out.'

As the commentator drily remarked, 'They had incredible dash and enthusiasm, and sheer exciting courage which was only curbed by the rapidly decreasing stock of dashing officers and tanks.' (42:111) This was a poignant example of underestimating your opponent, or of what some might less kindly term 'imperial pride'. The British had apparently learned nothing from the experience of the May battles of 1940.

Yet another example of the failure to evaluate combat experiences and embed them in training and education can be seen in the fighting at Monte Cassino in 1944, when the Royal Scots Fusiliers were particular disconcerted 'to come over the top of hills to discover Germans dug in on the reverse slope, something we had never envisaged'. This is particularly surprising since digging in on the far side of a hill had, since 1917, been one of the standard principles of German defensive tactics. Apparently no one had ever paid any attention to this.

The failure to learn from past battles always leads to more and unnecessary casualties, a lesson that the British should have taken seriously and which was reflected in their low battlefield performance.

The strictness of German evaluation can be demonstrated by the Polish campaign of September 1939, an offensive which was widely seen as being perfectly executed. However, on the basis of the *Erfahrungsberichte*, the *Oberkommando des Heeres* (OKH, or High Command) declared itself very dissatisfied with the Army's performance. Some conclusions from these *Erfahrungsberichte* about the Polish campaign were:

- officers of all levels should be present at the front and not lead from behind
- front commanders tended in their *Erfahrungsberichte* to exaggerate their losses, the strength of the enemy and the difficulty of the terrain, and thus had to learn to report more accurately
- units were not sufficiently trained to perform adequate reconnaissance missions

In addition, the OKH found that:

- cooperation between the various army units was insufficient
- the infantry received too little support from its own heavy weapons and from the artillery
- infantry fire was often uncoordinated
- infantry marching discipline was insufficient
- troops formed too much of a linear defensive position instead of the elastic defence demanded by the doctrine
- the infantry was not always adequately equipped to fight at night or in difficult terrain
- traffic handling was not satisfactory (45:230–2)

A more worrying criticism was the lack of initiative among lower ranking and non-commissioned officers, a subject of great importance to the senior levels of the army, as we have seen. As a result, from that moment on, the senior levels in the Army focused on the importance of taking the initiative within the limits of the given assignment; officers should not wait for orders, but must learn to rely on their own judgment (31:237). The disappointing performance of the officers and non-commissioned officers was largely put down to a large influx of new officers and NCOs after 1935. (34:60)

All of these lessons placed additional demands on leadership in future campaigns and were incorporated in a training programme entitled *Ausbildung des Feldheeres* (Training of the Field Army). Central themes of this programme were:

- conducting reconnaissance missions
- coordination and discipline in shooting by the infantry
- cooperation between infantry, artillery and tanks
- offensive and defensive tactics at dusk and during the night
- the transition from offensive actions to defensive positions

Monthly evaluations of the combat effectiveness of the various divisions and units were linked to this training programme.

The second part of the programme focused on the officers and non-commissioned officers, and emphasized the importance of leadership by reserve officers and NCOs, especially in combat situations. The role of the non-commissioned officer as leader, trainer and teacher was highlighted, a role that we will examine in more detail in the next chapter. Finally, the need for discipline was emphasized. This thorough and comprehensive overhaul was reminiscent of the training programme from the autumn of 1917 in the new offensive doctrine of *Angriff im Stellungskrieg* (Attack in Trench Warfare). It also shows how critical the German Army could be of itself and how swiftly it responded to any weaknesses found, an attitude that was typical of the force throughout the Second World War. This critical approach was basic to the Reichswehr, with its focus on efficiency and effectiveness, combined with a necessary sense of security and trust within and between all levels of the organization. As a result, during the Second World War, the Germans were constantly able to learn and adapt to changing circumstances.

In the next chapter we will discuss the role of officers and non-commissioned officers in the Prussian/German Army; with their teams, they were the key to its success.

CHAPTER FOUR

Leadership

In this chapter we will discuss the views that the various belligerents took of officers, NCOs and leadership. We look at the recruitment and selection of officers and NCOs, as well as subjects such as authority, respect, trust and the attitudes expected of these leaders. In addition to their personal qualities and the knowledge and skills that they were expected to possess, we also look at how they guided the men entrusted to their care in their personal and professional development, and how they promoted unity or 'team-building' in the field.

Perhaps most significantly, we also judge whether this worked as expected in the reality of the battlefield.

4.1 *Auftragstaktik* as a leading principle

In accordance with the concept of *Auftragstaktik*, officers and their units in the German Army were expected to use their own initiative as much as in responding to unexpected situations. This necessarily made considerable demands on the style of leadership and the officer corps. Von Moltke, the founder of *Auftragstaktik*, issued the following guidelines in 1858:

> In general, one should not want to order more than is necessary, nor to regulate more than can be overseen, since circumstances in a war situation change rapidly, and rarely will planned and detailed orders be fully executed . . . The higher in the hierarchy, the more concise and more general the orders should be. The next command position will add the necessary detail to them, and these details must be able to be presented orally or in the form of a brief command. Everyone can move freely within this framework and make decisions in accordance with his responsibilities. (49:106–7)

101

In later writings, von Moltke stressed the importance of taking the initiative and utilizing the independence of soldiers, assuming that they are led by an intelligent officer corps:

> In general, it is better in doubt and in unclear circumstances to take the initiative instead of waiting for the opponent's moves . . . The commanders of the various units must keep these guidelines in mind, instead of marching towards the thunder of the guns. Orders . . . must be critically examined against the light; they might have been given under circumstances that did not take into account the course of the battle . . . The assignment [*Auftrag*] should only relate to that – and no more than that – which the subordinate cannot determine for himself for the achievement of a certain goal. The various units must have a certain degree of freedom. Independently organized, they must be able to carry out the intent of the supreme command under unforeseen circumstances according to their own judgment . . . What is ordered must be carried out, but never should anything be ordered that is not feasible.

In order to prevent this freedom from being interpreted too broadly and leading to anarchy, von Moltke emphasized that if 'the intent of the supreme command is to be implemented everywhere in the same way, discipline is of great importance. Discipline is the pillar of every army and maintaining discipline is a blessing for all.' He also remarked that attention to hierarchical ranks is of great importance, since the creation of bypasses in the organization undermines the authority of the person who is passed over and does not generally contribute to more effective performance.

In this way, von Moltke linked the element of independence in *Auftragstaktik* to the need for discipline in command and execution of combat actions. The preferred style of leadership as another element of *Auftragstaktik* was described in a number of guiding documents in the early 1920s, including Regulations Nos. 5 and 6 of *Führung und Gefecht der Verbundenen Waffen* (Leadership and Fighting with Combined Arms).

In the vision formulated by this style of leadership, great value was placed on being able to think and act quickly, decisively and flexibly, and on being prepared for the unexpected. The need for independent thinking and a sense of responsibility were constantly emphasized in both officers and men. In the spirit of this concept, officer training did not prescribe standard solutions but focused on personal qualities such as responsibility, imagination and initiative, in order to deal with the ever-changing battlefield.

The following characteristics were of great importance and served as a framework for officers:

- logical thinking in combat situations, with particular appreciation of speed
- sound tactical considerations, followed by clear and consistent commands
- conducting well-timed and offensive actions, taking into account a number of basic methods and techniques
- gaining and retaining the initiative

Much attention was paid to transferring the intentions of the officer in question to his units by means of short orders and commands. In addition, a high standard of integrity and behaviour was required of candidates for the General Staff. The trainers served in this respect as role models for their pupils. (46:212)

A further elaboration of von Moltke's ideas can be seen in Regulation 5 of the guidance of 1 September 1921. This describes the role of the officer as follows:

The officer must have the trust and the esteem of his unit. A prerequisite for this is having a strong will and a good character in addition to knowledge and expertise. There are no rules, however, that cover the question of how to act in all kinds of tactical situations. This would lead to too much ambiguity that that does not take into account the vicissitudes of the war . . .

The main characteristic of the officer is his sense of responsibility. All officers must be constantly aware of this . . . For officers of all levels, it is very important to keep in personal touch with the men entrusted to them, so that the officers can assess the needs and capabilities of the men on the basis of their own observations. If the unit knows that the officer is dedicated to his men and shares with them love and sorrow, they will be willing to spend their last forces to achieve the goal, but are also capable of withstanding failures. In the case of failure, the true inner nature of the officer is expressed, from the first to the last man of the unit.

This is a clear statement of the views of the supreme command of the Reichswehr on the preferred style of leadership and the need for team-building (*Einheit*). Officers were held responsible for the development of the units entrusted to them, the creation of social cohesion within the unit and the establishment of mutual respect and trust in the relationship with their NCOs and men. We will discuss this in more detail below.

The elaboration of *Auftragstaktik* in practice is outlined clearly in Regulation 6 of the aforementioned guidance:

The basis for leadership is the assignment [*Auftrag*] and the circumstances. One should always focus on the assignment, even though the circumstances will not always be clear . . . uncertainty remains the rule at war. A watchful and trained commander will be able to draw important clues from small points of reference. Sound judgement and the ability to respond with decisive power, is the basis of success . . .

The [non-commissioned] officer makes a decision weighing the assignment and the circumstances. If the assignment can no longer be carried out because of the circumstances, this must be taken into account when making the decision. The [non-commissioned] officer bears full responsibility if he does not fulfil his assignment or changes it. He always has to take the larger framework into account.

[Emphasis was also placed on a proactive and offensive attitude]. Awaiting further orders is rarely a sign of active leadership and easily leads to major mistakes. (49:171–3)

Because of the mission orientation of the German Army, communication could be relatively informal, and even half a message or order was often enough, due to the force's unity of thought and action. Being able to act on receipt of broadly-based spoken orders rather than detailed and rigid plans added to effectiveness, since the latter were often rendered irrelevant by the reality of the battlefield. Consultation in combat situations often took place ad hoc, leaving much to the further elaboration and initiative of subordinates. (36:48) While officers often received 'global goals', they had to use their own initiative to achieve them.

The importance of leading from the front was also emphasized. This was partly based on the experience of the First World War. Although German officers were always in the front line (and this led to worrying losses), there was criticism of the fact that at the level of divisional commander and higher the presence of officers on the front fell sharply.

The regulations in *Führung und Gefecht der Verbundenen Waffen* laid down a clear foundation for the style of leadership and the modus operandi of the German Army in the Second World War. They combined von Moltke's theory with the experiences of the First World War and led to a command concept that has stood the test of time and is considered by many to be a 'next step' model, an ideal that organizations will aim for but few will achieve.

The result can be best described as follows: 'On closer inspection, the picture of an army evolves that successfully combined opposing characteristics such as obedience and initiative, drill and creativity, authority and independence.' (49:176) Unifying these contradictory aspects in the aforementioned combination of independence and cooperation offers an example of vision and management of an organization which has never been surpassed.

4.2 Non-commissioned officers and officers of the Prussian/German Army

Any discussion of the German officer corps must also include analysis of non-commissioned officers, since the Germans considered this level of management to be extremely important. (31:206) While the Treaty of Versailles limited the size of the Reichswehr, it also had the effect of enabling it to select only the very best officers and non-commissioned officers. The Treaty also extended the service period to twelve years, as a result of which the training of NCOs was intensified. This in turn made it possible to ensure that non-commissioned officers were able to lead units two levels above that of their normal command. Moreover, attention was explicitly paid to the training skills of the candidates, so that numbers of fully qualified NCOs enriched the overall quality of the officer corps; this assisted the rapid expansion of the Reichswehr in the 1930s.

The limitations of the Versailles Treaty

The Versailles Treaty limited the size of the German Army to 100,000 men, including 4,000 officers. While it was allowed to comprise seven infantry and three cavalry divisions, the weapons of these divisions were restricted. The Reichswehr was only allowed rifles and light field guns; heavy field guns, tanks and aircraft were forbidden. However, as a result of the high educational and training level of the troops and officers of the Reichswehr, growth from ten divisions and 100,000 men in 1934 to thirty-one divisions by the end of 1935 was easily achieved. The main goal of this 'new' army was to train recruits. After 1935 the Reichswehr was renamed the Wehrmacht (14:112), and in order to strengthen the cadre, many former officers from the First World War were recalled to active service. Qualified conscripts were promoted to officer, and a substantial training programme for new officers was set up, leading to an almost exponential growth of the Army thereafter.

Recruitment and selection of non-commissioned officers was decentralized, with junior NCOs being selected for officer training after a year of service by the commander of their unit on the basis of central guidelines. In this way, the various units enjoyed a necessary freedom of choice within an overall framework. This method of selection had its origins in the former imperial army and contributed to the strong bond between non-commissioned officers and their units.

In particular, non-commissioned officers were, apart from other leadership tasks, expected to monitor closely the competencies and development of the men in their unit, not just their personal qualities, but also a common feeling of belonging (*Einheit*), leading to the creation of a *Kampfgemeinschaft* (battle community). The NCOs' role was key, since they had the greatest influence this area. (20:167) Their role fitted into the wider importance of *Einheit* within the German Army, with its particular attention on issues such as group cohesion and dynamics, and thinking and acting as an unit.

> Whereas in the United States the officer was one cog amongst others in the huge machine, in Germany the officer was considered the switch to the machine or its whole power source.
>
> Jörg Muth, *Command Culture*

Non-commissioned officers also enjoyed realistic opportunities for promotion. The careers of officers and non-commissioned officers were originally completely separate. This led to tensions towards the end of the First World War, when young, inexperienced officers fresh from school joined up and had to give orders to experienced NCOs. This strict separation of career opportunities was abolished in 1919, and 1,000 non-commissioned officers were commissioned. The division between NCOs and officers became correspondingly less pronounced, and in the Second World War tens of thousands of non-commissioned officers were promoted to officer; by 1945 eleven German generals originated from the ranks of NCOs.

The quality of recruitment, selection and training in the interwar period made it possible, within the framework of *Auftragstaktik*, to delegate many operational responsibilities to non-commissioned officers. As a result, officers were able to concentrate more fully on organizational tasks. This considerably improved efficiency, flexibility and cohesion within the German Army.

Officers

In the period up to the Second World War, officer training took two years and three months. The career of an officer began with registration with the commander of the regiment of his choice. Officer candidates were expected to be educated up to university-entrance level. After an initial six months of service in the *Reichsarbeitsdienst* (state labour force), the candidate received one year's training as a non-commissioned officer. During this period he was coached by a sponsor, usually an older officer who had the task of 'ironing out the wrinkles' and teaching the recruit the behaviour and attitudes expected in his future military role. Until 1926, the regimental commander then determined whether the candidate was admitted to officer training at a *Kadettenschule* (Cadet School). The candidate's personal qualities, of good character and strong will, were particularly important criteria. Remarkably, the *Kadettenschule* had a more liberal character than the then often authoritarian civilian schools. Reward rather than punishment was central to their approach, and this found fertile soil among the young students. The culture was quite different from the American system, for instance, where the four-year officers' training could be horrific, as we will see. The main objective of German training was to make the officer a role model for, and a comrade of, his men. Although *Auftragstaktik* required independent thinking and individual responsibility, weaknesses in academic subjects could be compensated for at the *Fähnrichsexamen* (Ensign Exam) by leadership qualities and perseverance.

After passing the exam, the candidate officer, or *Fähnrich* (Ensign), went on to a *Kriegsschule* (military school) or was placed in a regiment where he would be able to follow the syllabus of the *Kriegsschule*. Ensigns who had been selected or had indicated a preference for the engineers or artillery received separate training. On completion of his training, the regimental commander decided, in consultation with his senior officers, whether the *Fähnrich* could be appointed an officer. The candidate thus finally gained his first substantive rank, that of second lieutenant, after at least two years and three months in the Army. (32:161)

Psychology always played, either implicitly or explicitly, an important role in the training of an officer. Due to a growing interest in the psychological aspects of warfare, a central psychological testing centre was established in 1926. Over two days, officer candidates were given what we would now call an assessment, in which the social functioning of the candidate within a group was examined.

Assessment of officers in the German Army

Officer candidates were subjected to a two-day assessment in groups of four or five. They were observed by a colonel, a medical officer and three psychologists. Each candidate was put in charge of a group of soldiers and asked to instruct them on how to assemble a weapon. Following this, the candidate had to give a presentation about a subject that interested him and carry out a number of additional assignments. The assessors paid particular attention to the reactions of the men who were entrusted to the candidate. If they were interested and reacted positively, the candidate could get high scores. In the period between 1930 and 1932, 2,500 candidates were examined in this way.

LEADERSHIP

Officers and non-commissioned officers alike were expected to:

- motivate their men
- mould the men into a socialized and trusted team (create *Einheit*), through dialogue and connection
- be genuine in their approach and show interest in others
- communicate the 'why' to their men, not just the 'what' and 'how'
- have the ability to quickly analyze complex subjects, assess their importance and act accordingly
- have the discipline to go through subjects from start to finish
- make their team think and act unambiguously

These requirements were constantly emphasized and represented the criteria for an officer's promotion.

The criteria were reformulated in the 1920s to reflect more the personal qualities of the officer: honour, a sense of responsibility, willingness to commit and to sacrifice. The ability to win and retain the confidence of his men was seen as one of the chief features of a good officer. (11:142) Here again, the emphasis lay in psychology, the skills to forge a team into a socialized unity.

The *Kriegsakademie*

A next step in the training of officers was the *Kriegsakademie*, or Higher Staff College. Every officer with five years experience could attempt the *Wehrkreis Prüfung* (military district examination), the entrance exam to the *Kriegsakademie*. In addition, and very importantly, he needed a letter of recommendation from his regimental commander. To pass the entrance exam, the aspiring candidate had to study while still undertaking his normal duties. At the *Kriegsakademie* there was an open and friendly atmosphere, with the *Hörsaalleiter* (teachers) drawn from the cohort of successful veterans, men with extensive experience and good teaching ability. In order to keep the teachers in touch with real life, they were appointed for no more than three years, a rotation system comparable with that of the General Staff. There were no ranks and levels at the *Kriegsakademie*. The students and teachers enjoyed an informal relationship, which extended to social activities such as trips and joint sporting events. In this way, comradely relations were developed which were of great importance for the creation of cohesion within the Army.

The Kriegsakademie did not provide 'academic solutions' as such; anyone could contribute ideas, and thus creativity was stimulated. This reflected the reality of the battlefield, where conformity to a set plan was often impossible due to sudden shifts or events. The students had to learn to deal with these uncertainties and with the 'fog of war'. Playing war games, students were tested for flexibility in thought and leadership, with a free exchange of ideas. They were also taught *not* to follow orders 'when justified by honour and circumstances'. Not obeying orders was part of the German officer's culture and known as *'Führen unter der Hand'* (leading behind your superior's back). As Generaloberst Ludwig Beck, Chief of Staff of the Wehrmacht, said, 'Military obedience has a limit where knowledge, conscience and a sense of responsibility forbid the execution of a command.' To further their flexibility, students were also familiarized with other arms of the service, through a three-month assignment each year to another unit: cavalrymen were taught artillery, artillery officers learnt infantry tactics, and so on. This cross-training broadened the candidate's knowledge of the potential and limitations of other units, and relationships were forged that could come in handy later on.

The transformation of the Reichswehr into the Nazi Wehrmacht in the 1930s made it necessary to bring the training and social requirements of the Army into line with Nazi ideology: the notion of the *Volksgemeinschaft* (people's community) dictated that the officer corps, by the outbreak of the Second World War, should represent all classes of society. (11:133–9. 57:104–5) As the war progressed, it became increasingly difficult to maintain the existing system of training and promotion, with the result that both commissioned and non-commissioned officers were sometimes promoted in the field on the basis of their proven qualities. Increasingly, seniority and the competence of the person involved played a role in promotion, and a new criterion, whether an officer was *Krisenfest* (stress-resistant), made its appearance. The advantage of the system was that proven courage and competence were rewarded; the drawback was that the homogeneity of the officer corps and its esprit de corps were diluted. (4:141)

Wartime training at all levels was practice-oriented. Learning to march or memorize the weapon manual were no longer required. (14:113)

Rommel on leadership

Rommel was a typical member of the German officer corps, a general with specific views on command and leadership style from which contemporary managers can still learn a lot. His daily letters to his wife, Lucie, sometimes read like a management manual, particularly his view that the commander should not limit himself to planning and staff matters at a distance, but should show himself at the front. He gave his reasons for this as follows:

- The correct execution of the commander's plan by his subordinates is of great importance. It is naïve to suppose that every officer will understand the meaning of his specific assignment within the larger whole.
- Most subordinates will try to choose the easiest way: an excuse will quickly be found as to why predetermined goals cannot be achieved. The fact that a subordinate realizes his commander is present at the front helps prevent him dropping out quickly. The commander must be the driving force on the battlefield. The troops must realize that he is the one in control.
- The commander must strive to ensure that his troops are always aware of the latest developments in the field of tactics and their practical application on the battlefield. Junior officers must be taught to respond quickly and adequately to sudden events. A commander must ensure that his troops receive proper training, because that avoids unnecessary casualties.
- It is also important that the commander knows what is happening at the front and what problems his men face. He must keep this knowledge up to date, because otherwise he leads purely from theory and with a limited knowledge of reality, as if war were a game of chess. In other words, a true leader is someone who continually tests his own views and ideas against the circumstances in which his troops find themselves, instead of going into battle with a fixed framework and rigid rules.

> • The commander must remain in contact with his troops. He must know their feelings and think like them. The soldier must have confidence in him. There is an absolute principle here: one must always be sincere to the men and never try to fool them for whatever reason. The soldier has an excellent nose for what is truth or a false representation of reality.

An important requirement for officers was that they should be present on the front line in order to personally evaluate the battlefield and enemy positions. This had a beneficial effect on soldiers' morale, but led to relatively heavy losses of officers in combat. This relationship between officers, NCOs and their men was noted and recorded by the Allies during interviews with German prisoners of war: 'Almost all non-commissioned officers and officers at the level of the company during the campaign in Western Europe were considered brave, efficient and compassionate by the German soldier'. (11:129). A better compliment is scarcely conceivable.

Authority and trust
Establishing authority and winning the trust of their men were central themes in the training, evaluation and promotion of non-commissioned officers. They were expected, on the one hand, to show clear leadership and initiative and to promote an aggressive esprit de corps, and on the other, to have a watchful care for their subordinates and to supervise and coach them. Officers and NCOs needed to create a sense of trust and security within the unit that they led and to stimulate socialization within the unit; good personal relations were all-important. (31:11) The bond between officers and men was reinforced by the use of the term 'soldier' for both. As a result, the troops had to salute not only their officers but also each other. Because officers and men received their training in the same units, contacts between them outside the service were frequent and encouraged from above. (11:129)

We have already seen that that the mission-orientated nature of *Auftragstaktik* demanded trust and a sense of equality: the idea was to work together on every assignment. However, both subordinates and superiors were sufficiently realistic to know that such trust was not a given; as with authority, it had to grow over the course of time as a result of their behaviour shown before, during and after combat. To promote this process, units were kept together as much as possible along the principle of *Einheit*. (49:270)

Rommel as a leader
Military organizations are generally well documented, even when it comes to managing men in a competitive environment. Rommel had a number of interesting views about his role as a leader, the authenticity of which can be judged from the fact that he often gave these informally, or off the cuff. For example:

> There is always a time when the commander should not be with his staff, but with his men up front at the front. It is incorrect to assume that the morale of the troops is solely the responsibility of the battalion commander. The higher the rank, the better the example. The men generally do not care for a commander who is safe in his headquarters far behind the front. They need his physical presence. In times of panic, fatigue, disorganization or when extra efforts are required, the personal example of the commander can do wonders, certainly when there is already myth forming around his person.

The latter was, of course, true of Rommel, and the myth was so great that Churchill in 1942 forbade his name from being used.

Openness in the vertical hierarchy

The German Army placed great importance on good personal relationships and an atmosphere of openness and trust within the vertical hierarchy. An important reason for this was that open communication meant it was possible to keep an eye on the functioning of units and their commanders. By creating a sense of security within the vertical hierarchy, commanders were able to critically examine their own efforts and those of their troops through the system of reviews, the *Erfahrungsberichte* (17:22). The commanders, in turn, expected to hear from their superiors if there were weaknesses in their performance. There was, however, no question of not complying with this system: the Army Supreme Command, the *Oberkommando des Heeres* (OKH) demanded honest and accurate reports on the quality and combat power of the various units. If a unit underperformed, its commander was expected to report this and take measures to attend to the weaknesses identified. If he did not report a weakness, the commander was held responsible. (45:22)

The attitude of a good officer was reflected in a special appreciation by his men, a phenomenon that we will discuss in the next chapter. However, at this point we will look at some instances in which officers displayed exemplary behaviour.

The end on the Eastern Front: Walther Krönke
For Walther Krönke the war ended in March 1945 in Hela, East Prussia. He was a company commander in the 505. Schwere Panzer (Tiger) Abteilung and had served on the Eastern Front from 1941 until 1945. In March 1945 the Abteilung had no more tanks (their impressive *Königstigers*, or King Tigers), so it was a case of just waiting for the war to end. While his men were searching for food, Krönke went to the port of Hela, where he found three *Schnellboote* (fast attack 'E boats'). He asked the guard at the pier if he could speak to the commander of the flotilla, and a friendly conversation ensued with Kapitänleutnant Howaldt, who turned out to be not much older than himself. Krönke asked if he could arrange passage to a safer place, and Howaldt agreed; but when Krönke asked if his troops could join them, the Kapitänleutnant replied that this was not possible because of the many other refugees who wanted to leave. Krönke therefore politely refused the passage offered to him, on the principle that an officer never lets his men down, and he rejoined his troops. On 8 May 1945 the inevitable followed: he was taken prisoner by the Soviets and separated from his men, whom he would never see again. In June 1948 he finally returned home from imprisonment, exactly ten years to the day after he had joined the Wehrmacht. (34:129–31)

On the wrong bank: *Kampfgruppe* **Ölkers**
SS Junker Lindemann took part in the later stages of the Battle of Arnhem as part of *Kampfgruppe* Ölkers, fighting at the bridgehead in front of Doorwerth castle. The *Kampfgruppe* originally consisted of five companies but had suffered heavy losses during the river crossing. The brickworks, the target of the action, was taken on 2 October, but holding

the bridgehead was absolutely meaningless in the opinion of Ölkers, the *Kampfgruppe*'s commander. The group was being hit by fire from artillery and mortars, about thirty shells landing every ten minutes, and was taking constant casualties. The senselessness of the whole thing was clear to everyone, but Ölkers was forbidden to leave the bridgehead by his superiors. He eventually ignored this order and left on his own initiative on 10 October. Of the 120 men who were originally transferred, only 35 were able to make the crossing back. However, the evacuation was a success:

> The battalion commander was, characteristically, the last man to leave the bridgehead, in a dinghy which, Lindemann remembers, was 'shot full of holes'. They had made it. When asked whether he had ever despaired at their situation, Lindemann declared, 'We never felt abandoned, because of Ölkers' leadership.' (30:320)

This represented perhaps the greatest compliment an officer can receive, and it epitomizes the strength of the German Army and its officer corps. The ordinary soldier never had to feel afraid of being physically or emotionally abandoned, since he could trust the High Command and its officer corps always to act professionally and take care of him. There were exceptions, of course, but the overall picture from the literature is clear, confirming the finding of the previously mentioned American research project which described German officers as 'brave, efficient and compassionate'.

Shot down

During the Battle of Britain a Heinkel 111 was shot down and forced to land in the English countryside. The local policeman and farmers armed with pitchforks and rifles rushed to the site, prepared for anything. Once the plane was located, they found the crew standing next to it, guarding the corpse of one of their comrades. While the British watched in amazement, the crew lined up by their deceased comrade and saluted, following which (and to some consternation among the crowd) they got out their guns, but then gave them to their commander, who in turn handed them over to the local policeman. Forty years after the war, one of the farmers who had been there recalled that he had been most impressed by the captain, who was clearly deeply affected by the death of his crewman. When asked about it, the captain had said, 'The deceased is the youngest member of the company, and I am personally responsible for his welfare.'

Operating up front
Officers were expected to operate from the front as much as possible. Their presence in the front line had several effects: it stimulated morale, and by being at the front, an officer was able to:

- Get to know the terrain
- Get to know the men, who got to know him in return
- Gain optimal feedback, sometimes in 'real time'

'For a commander there is no substitute equal to his own eyes.'
General Patton

Being there. Where? There!
Colonel Wolz, the commander of one of the Flak regiments of the Afrika Korps, was consulting with General Nehring during Operation Theseus as all hell broke out around them:

In the middle of the chaos, I discovered a few Flak 88s. We raced to them and to our surprise we found Rommel, completely surrounded by panicking troops. He angrily told me that my Flak regiment was guilty of all this, because we didn't shoot back. I managed to stop three Flak 88 units and formed them into a defence line together with the Flak 88s from the *Kampfstaffel* (mobile protection unit). The armada of twenty or thirty enemy tanks approached quickly and was only 500m away from us. They drove trucks from the supply units in front of them, all extremely vulnerable to tank guns. In the midst of this tangle of vehicles were Rommel, the headquarters of the Afrika Korps and communication units: in short, the core nervous system of a combat division at the front. (17:157)

Thanks to assistance from other batteries, ultimately an anti-tank screen of 3,000m was created, with a total of sixteen 88mm flak

---

guns. This made it possible to halt the attack by the British tanks towards the evening. (19:136)

Rommel also appeared elsewhere that day. Von Värst, commander of the tank regiment of the 15th Panzer Division, had himself been involved with one of his unit in a fierce battle with British tanks which had led to heavy losses on both sides. The British eventually withdrew:

> The company commander of the tank driving up front called von Värst on the radio demanding directions. Even before von Värst could answer, his adjutant called back, 'That way! There is Rommel! Follow him!' And there indeed was Rommel, standing upright in his halftrack, driving over the battlefield that was strewn with smoking wrecks, at the head of his armoured troops. (28:57)

This was what is today referred to in management literature as personal leadership; many examples of it can be found in wartime.

What Rommel did was perfectly normal in the German Army; generals like him were supposed to be 'up front'. They could do this because they were able to leave much of the preparation of an action to their staff officers, and once a battle had erupted, central control was in any case often no longer possible. Allied commanders, on the other hand, remained true 'chateau generals' at their headquarters with large maps in the background, waiting for information from the front so that they could check whether and to what extent their plan had achieved success.

A day in the life on the Eastern Front of General Heinz Guderian

On 24 June 1941, Heinz Guderian left his headquarters at 0825 and headed for Slonim, where the 17. Panzer Division had arrived. Between Rozama and Slonim his staff unit was fired at by Soviet infantry. A battery from the 17. Panzer Division and the accompanying motorcyclists returned fire, together with Guderian himself, who fired at the enemy units with the machine gun on his halftrack. After some time they managed to dislodge the enemy, and Guderian was able to report at 1130 at the headquarters of the 17. Panzer Division in Slonim. During the meeting with General von Arnim, the commander of the division, Guderian suddenly heard rifle and machine gun fire. A burning truck was blocking the view, so it was unclear what exactly was happening, until suddenly two Soviet tanks emerged from the smoke. Firing fiercely, they tried to break through to the village, pursued by German PzKpfw IV tanks. When the Soviet tanks saw the German officers they immediately started shooting from very close range, wounding one officer who reacted too slowly. The tanks managed to reach the centre of the village before they were finally knocked out.

After this brief but frenzied period of action, Guderian visited the front at Slonim and drove on board a tank through no-man's-land to visit the 18. Panzer Division. At 1530 he was back in Slonim after he had given the 18. Panzer Division and the associated infantry division their necessary orders. He then travelled back to headquarters, but not without further incident: at the city boundary of Slonim, Guderian stumbled upon Soviet infantry who were just disembarking from a number of trucks. He ordered his driver to carry on through the Soviet troops at full speed. They were so surprised that they did not have time to fire their weapons, although the General was recognized and his death was announced a few days later in the Soviet press. After his turbulent day, Guderian reached headquarters at 2015 to evaluate the combat situation and plan the following day.

4.3 British officer and NCO training

British officers were generally less well trained than their German counterparts, and this was reflected in their position, responsibilities and powers. German officers were expected to be able to lead units one level up from their usual rank. A major, who usually commanded a battalion, was expected to be able to lead a regiment consisting of three battalions, and a captain was often expected to lead a battalion. This ability became ever more important as losses of officers mounted during the First World War. Whereas the Germans were able to fall back on their well-trained officer corps, the British started at a disadvantage because of their lower level of training and things grew worse as the war went on. (41:108) It was said that British non-commissioned officers took five years of training to achieve the level that their German equivalents reached after two. (57:102) Here too, the regimental rotation system between Great Britain and the colonies undoubtedly played a role. Due to the lack of a solid corps of non-commissioned officers, British officers were forced, for example, to lead platoons and carry out work that was done in the German Army by corporals or sergeants. In other words, they were sucked downwards in the organization. As a result, losses among officers rose, which meant that valuable experience was lost and the officer corps was not able to develop the next stage of professionalism. The final result of all this was that the junior British officer generally functioned at the level of the German NCO, and senior commanders sometimes had to intervene at four levels below them ('four down') to prevent mistakes being made by inadequately qualified subordinates. The rapid growth of the British Army also diluted the knowledge and experience in the higher levels of the organization. Before the war, there were just 447 officers with a degree from the Staff Colleges of Camberley and Quetta, too few to fill all the staff positions. In 1918, the number of staff positions had grown to about 10,000, many now filled by officers without staff training.

The majority of these positions were filled by wounded officers or officers who were no longer deployable at the front. These men did not have the background for complex staff work such as planning logistics, preparation of combat actions, and so on. This combination, of officers who functioned at a low level, non-commissioned officers who were not able to fulfil all tasks, and staff officers who lacked the necessary training, led to a dangerous cocktail of incompetence.

The loss of officers

According to the British Official History, the loss of officers had major consequences for the fighting capacity of units:

> When British troops lost their officers, they were . . . apt to fall back, not because they were beaten but because they did not know what to do and expected to receive fresh orders.

> Perhaps the large numbers of officers commissioned and the fact that a sergeant rarely held command of a platoon for more than a few days lessened the prestige of the commissioned officer. (57:158)
>
> The Germans made comparable observations on the British during the Second World War. Because of the rigid command structure, the high dependency on officers and the lack of training in taking the initiative, British attacks soon petered out if the officers became casualties.

The lack of adequate training meant that the British Army was unable to operate sufficiently flexibly during the First World War and led to a lack of initiative at the operational level. The British were forced to fall back on rigid, linear formations, attacking enemy positions in consecutive waves. Needless to say, these were particularly vulnerable to enemy machine gun fire, resulting in appalling losses and a dramatically poor battlefield performance. (57:160)

The Germans clearly recognized the weak points of their opponent. Their evaluations were enlightening, as for example that of the German IV Corps in the first month of the Somme offensive, July 1916:

> The frontal attacks on open ground against a portion of our unshaken infantry, carried out by several British cavalry regiments, which had to retire with heavy losses, give some indication of the tactical knowledge of the [British] Higher Command.

In June 1917, the 44. Regiment, fresh from the Eastern Front, rated the operations at the tactical level of the British infantry as inferior to that of the Russians, and this view persisted in the Second World War:

> This brigade [the British brigade at Got el Ualab in the Western Desert during Operation Theseus] was the living example of the strengths and weaknesses of the British soldier. Exceptional courage and perseverance were combined with unprecedented rigidity in terms of speed and flexibility.
> Field Marshal Erwin Rommel, in *Rommel in his Own Words*

The Battle of Jena was a massive encounter of more than 200,000 men. The disastrous outcome of the battle forced the Prussians to thoroughly re-examine their doctrine.

Helmuth Bernhard Karl von Moltke, the founder of *Auftragstaktik*.

Landing craft at Anzio. The lack of initiative on the Allied side under the leadership of Lucas provoked Churchill to write, 'I had hoped we were hurling a wildcat into the shore, but all we got was a stranded whale.' (US NARA)

The commander of the Tank Regiment of the German Wiking (Viking) Division consults with his counterpart of the Panzergrenadiere. German panzer and infantry functioned as integrated units as much as possible under the principle of *Verbundene Waffen*.

A Panther tank and an Sd.Kfz. half-track of the Wiking Division working together. Both needed the other to survive on the battlefield; hence the Germans continually emphasized the need for cooperation so that units could support each other at all times.

The most important 'manager of change' on the British side was Montgomery, a very difficult individual but a real leader. 'His great talent for leadership was shown in the way he managed to exploit even the negative sides of his character to positive ends.' (IWM)

German units were able to cross the Strait of Messina between Sicily and the mainland of Italy without much difficulty. Here, one of the many ferries used for this enjoys a calm passage due to the absence of any attempt by the Allies to frustrate the crossing. (Anderson Collection)

Kampfgruppe Peiper on the move: StuG IIIs together with Sd.Kfz. half-tracks form a protective shield for the sixty ambulances and other vehicles that brought wounded men from the trapped units of the 298th and 320th Infantry Divisions to safety.

Unimpressed by the Allies' lack of urgency, the Germans are able to retreat at a leisurely pace to the new, more northerly positions of the Gothic line.

New Zealand units advance through Cassino after it had been heavily bombed by the Allies. However, as 'heavy bombers cannot make buildings simply disappear', the debris of both this city and the many others to follow offered the Germans ample opportunity to build defences. (US NARA)

German troops and their StuG (Sturmgeschütz). The much loved StuGs were an integral part of German infantry units and gave them an extra punch that was often decisive. These units are a good example of the principle of *Verbundene Waffen*. As the StuGs were part of the artillery, their crews did not wear the black uniform of the armoured units.

The officers and men of *Kampfgruppe* Stephan discuss new goals during Operation Crusader in November 1942. While the Allies struggled to follow plans exactly, the Germans needed only short breaks to set new goals and coordinate activities. They were therefore, in popular management language, particularly 'agile'. (Klein Collection)

Men of the Fallschirm-Panzer-Division 1. Hermann Göring in Italy pose without helmets – totally unthinkable in a combat situation – with their MG 43 (Maschinengewehr 43), one of the most feared weapons of the Second World War due to its high rate of fire and effective means of deployment.

Arnhem showed the ease with which German units fused together. Here, an officer probably from the Waffen SS Division Hohenstaufen takes charge of a unit consisting of troops of the Luftwaffe and Kriegsmarine, an exotic combination to say the least. (Bundesarchiv Bildarchiv)

Kampfgruppe Krafft – an Ersatz (training) Battalion consisting of recruits – receives relatively little attention in this book, but it was the first German unit that frustrated the British advance at Arnhem by halting the British 3rd Battalion, as well as the Jeeps of the 1st Air Landing Reconnaissance Squadron. In doing so, they allowed Kampfgruppe Spindler to position itself. (IWM)

A Tiger tank on the steppe in the Soviet Union, the ideal habitat for this vehicle which, thanks to its superior 88mm gun and directional equipment, could destroy enemy tanks at very great distances. While the Soviets were able to field more or less comparable tanks, Americans and British tanks were in no way equal to the Tiger.

Rommel with his men, seen here in North Africa with the Flakregiment 33. Unlike Allied commanders, German officers to the level of the Army Group were always at the front with their troops. (Klein Collection)

The Germans invested a great deal in communications equipment to keep in touch with units which were often spread over large areas, particularly in the May campaigns of 1940 and later in the Soviet Union. Here is an Sd.Kfz. half-track under the command of Guderian, one of the founders of the German armoured arm, in France during the campaign of May 1940.

An American half-track struggles through the mud of the Hürtgen forest, where the Allies were engaged in fierce fighting with German units.

The Allies enjoyed great superiority in artillery, while the Germans could offer only a limited response, albeit with guns of high quality. Seen here in the Hürtgen forest is an sIG (*schweres Infanterie Geschütz*) 33, a 15cm gun that fired grenades of 38kg, each containing 8kg of TNT. It was the standard heavy infantry gun during the war.

A Sherman tank, this one from the British Guards Armoured Division, with its crew in a classic pose. The crews of the venerable Shermans had a healthy respect for German tanks and anti-tank guns. They knew that the Allied supreme command would accept high losses because they had a large stock of tanks in reserve.

After an overwhelming classical artillery bombardment, British Churchill tanks from the Coldstream Guards drive through the streets of a totally destroyed Overloon. Note the spare chains mounted on the tank as extra armour.

'For a commander there is no substitute to his own eyes.' Generalleutnant Walther Hörnlein follows the advance of his units with binoculars while standing on the hood of his Sd.Kfz. 251 during one of the first days of *Fall Blau* (Case Blue), the 1942 German summer offensive in Russia.

In general, the perseverance and courage of British soldiers were praised, but they were not deployed in an intelligent way and did not succeed in exploiting their successes. Tactics from the First World War were repeated in the Second without significant differences. (41:168) The weak points outlined above were not recognized or acknowledged after 1918, and no changes were made in the design of training courses for soldiers, non-commissioned officers and officers. Moreover, as we have seen, in both wars there were misconceptions about the German Army, which was regarded as a rigid fighting machine with little room for personal initiative and no learning ability, an image that is still enthusiastically propagated in the media and the literature. Nothing could be further from the truth: the German Army was a well-oiled learning machine that adapted quickly to changing circumstances.

Due to the lack of a coherent system of doctrine, tactics and training, the emphasis in the Second World War was on the courage and commitment of the ordinary soldier. These were attributes that British soldiers had in abundance, but the real problem, as observed by Air Marshal Tedder, commander-in-chief of the RAF in the Middle East, was that the British Army in 1941 and 1942 suffered from an 'excess of bravery and a shortage of brains'. (42:111) In the years to follow, the British Army did not give the impression at any time that much had changed.

4.4 American officers' training

American officers' training showed the painfully large differences between American and German practice. American training facilities were each linked to a state, and there were a number of central institutions such as the United States Military Academy, West Point, the Virginia Military Institute and the American Command and General Staff School, Fort Leavenworth. Although only a few US officers were trained at West Point, it provided most of those in high positions and thus had a major influence on the doctrine of the US Army. As we have seen before, the Americans did not have a clear doctrine, nor did they have a common view of the role of officers, the way in which they should be trained or what should ultimately be the 'end product' of that training.

There also was no interconnected training ladder by which an officer could reach the higher levels of education. Each institution offered its own curriculum, but West Point was the most prominent, which is why we will look most closely at it.

The Infantry School

A high point in the American training system was represented by the Infantry School during the 1920s, the period when George C. Marshall was its assistant director. Under his leadership, practical cases became part of the curriculum, and the cadets learned how to handle tanks in modern fashion. He did everything he could to teach the officers in training to think independently; he often gave them outdated maps and fragmentary information, or forced them to make their own decisions by breaking the lines of communication with their commanders; he confronted them with surprises to stimulate their creativity and ingenuity. One of his first changes to the school's culture was to ensure that 'any student's solution of a problem that ran counter to the approved school solution and yet showed independent, creative thinking would be published to the class.'

Junior officers also learned to give brief orders, and Marshall showed foresight in stating that 'organization and planning that are based too largely on theoretical grounds result in cumbersome organizations, too large staffs and too lengthy and complicated orders.' (48:194)

Marshall based his vision of training on a thorough study of the German Army. At this date there were often German officers at the school, and their advice and tips were highly appreciated and fell on fertile soil. But Marshall and the Infantry School were an exception in the American system, and as one individual he was unable to make fundamental changes to training.

West Point was founded in 1802 as a training institution for military engineers. During the War of Independence, defensive structures and forts had proved to be of great strategic importance, and knowledge of these was seen as indispensable for the officer corps. Irrespective of real contemporary needs, the focus of the curriculum until after the Second World War remained on mathematics, physics, chemistry and engineering. There was little or no attention to military history or modern infantry tactics, let alone leadership.

Successive administrations at West Point were able to block reform so successfully that the President himself had to step in to enforce it, Theodore Roosevelt declaring that 'mathematical training is a necessary thing for an engineer or an artilleryman, doubtless; but I esteem it to literally no importance for the cavalryman or infantryman'. (48:47) Only after this presidential intervention did some change occur in the curriculum, more attention being paid to leadership and command.

Hazing

To create group cohesion, American academies went in for the 'hazing' of freshmen. This process lasted a year and included some very violent episodes; it was said to be 'so contrary to all leadership principles in an army and yet has always been a part of the American academies.' (48:49). In practice, 'these techniques represented simply a compilation of what young males cornered in an extremely steep hierarchy can do to each other when unobserved and after refinement of techniques over many decades.'(48:50)

Hazing often consisted of enforcing heavy physical exertion and usually stopped only when the first-year students collapsed or fell unconscious on the spot. Ordeals included push-ups over broken glass or being tied up next to an ants' nest after being smeared with syrup. Despite attempts to suppress hazing, every freshman had to undergo it, with the consequence that many promising students dropped out prematurely and sought refuge in university education.

The different boards and the teaching staff knew about the practices (they themselves had often been trained at West Point) but were reluctant to tackle the issue. Most of the students who had been suspended from the academy for hazing simply returned after a short while. Hazing often turned those who had suffered the most into sadistic 'upperclassmen', who showed no remorse and encouraged their fellows to go even further by claiming that hazing was 'manly'. Hazing undoubtedly contributed to the creation of some form of group cohesion, but in general the recruits found it a horrible experience, as many written memoirs have reflected.

In addition, there were important misinterpretations of the Prussian/ German approach within the American training system. The first of these concerned the training for officers introduced by Frederick the Great: according to the Americans, this was a 'hard and merciless system', but in reality the Prussian Army had some of the most advanced regulations of the time and paid specific attention to good relations between officers and cadets – 'When it came to the handling of recruits, physical punishment of officers or officers aspirant was forbidden by the king himself.' (48:59) This *Reglement vor die Königliche Preussische Infanterie* was adopted as standard by the armies of many countries. Equally surprisingly, the Prussian/German system was interpreted by the Americans as creating a caste of officers completely separate from ordinary conscript soldiers. In 1919 a lieutenant observed in a newspaper article that 'it never entered in his head that the enlisted men under him were of the same flesh and blood'. The generally held view of the Prussian/German system was that 'to hold the men down while in idleness, repressive, hard discipline and a caste system is employed'. (48:79)

After completing his training as an officer, thinking in terms of caste was deeply rooted in the American cadet. The ordinary soldier had a good nose for these views, and they caused a good deal of mutual tension. Social and psychological studies after the Second World War described the gap between officers and men as 'a yawning social chasm'.

Cameras on the Battlefield

We have already examined various depictions of German and Allied soldiers during and after the Second World War. However, there is one important distinction: while Allied soldiers were strictly prohibited from taking cameras with them on active service, German soldiers were free to use them. This has resulted in an unprecedented number of photos of German units and soldiers under all kinds of circumstances. On the internet alone, many thousands of photos are on sale every day, and the number taken must have run into millions.

These photos provide a faithful and sometimes intimate image of men in battle and beyond. The strict control of photography on the Allied side, however, has left us with mostly posed images, and it is often difficult to ascertain what actually happened or how people dealt with each other. For example, the only images one sees of the battles in Normandy are of dead German soldiers and Americans clambering over disabled German equipment, or Sherman tanks driving through liberated cities.

On the German side things were completely different: entire photo series were taken by the men themselves of their units en route to, during and after battle. These provide a detailed picture of the life of the soldier, the material with which he fought and the circumstances under which he lived. In addition, the *Propaganda Kompagnie's* war reporters were always 'embedded' in units, and even magazines such as *Signal*, perhaps the best-known German propaganda organ, often showed a realistic representation of the struggle, with photographs taken on the spot. Only in the later years of war did the tone of magazines such as *Signal* become more forced and propagandistic, with less depiction of the real struggle.

Someone who keenly felt the deficiencies of the American system was the American author James Salter, in training as an officer at West Point in 1943. In his autobiography, *Burning the Days*, he sketched his dislike of the training he underwent and, on the other hand, his almost ecstatic relief when he studied German literature on leadership (in German) and saw that there was also 'another world'. His is perhaps the most vivid description by an American author of what the German Army demanded of an officer:

There was one with the title 'Der Kompagniechef', the company commander. This youthful but experienced figure was nothing less than a living example to each of his men. Alone, half obscured by those he commanded, similar to them but without their faults, self-disciplined, modest, cheerful, he was at the same time both master and servant, each of admirable character. His real authority was not based on shoulder straps or rank but on a model life which granted the right to demand anything from others. An officer is like a father with greater responsibilities than an ordinary father. The food his men ate, he ate, and only when the last of them slept, exhausted, did he go to sleep himself. His privilege lay in being given these obligations and a harder duty than the rest . . . It was not his strength that was unbreakable but something deeper, his spirit . . . When he looked over his men he was conscious that a hundred and fifty families had placed a son in his care. Sometimes, unannounced, he went among these sons in the evening to talk or just sit and drink, not in the role of superior but of an older, sympathetic comrade. He went among them as kings once went unknown among their subjects, to hear their real thoughts and to know them. Among his most important traits were decency and compassion. He was not unfeeling, not made of wood. Especially in time of grief, as a death in a soldier's family at home, he brought the news himself – no other one should be expected to – and granted leave, if possible, even before it was asked for, in his own words expressing sympathy. Ties like this would never be broken.

This was not the parade-ground captain, the mannequin promoted for a spotless record. It was not someone behind the lines, some careerist with ambitions. It was another breed, someone whose life was joined with that of his men, who had reached the peak of human condition, admired, feared and loved, someone hardened and uncomplaining upon whom the entire struggle somehow depended, some almost fated to fall.

Salter describes how he identified with this figure and his relief 'when I realized that every quality was one in which I had instinctively faith, I felt an overwhelming happiness, like seeing a card you cannot believe you are lucky enough to have drawn, at this moment, in this game. I did not dare to believe it but I imagined, I thought, I somehow dreamed, the face was my own.'

In the West Point system, the cadets suffered not only from an excess of mathematics, physics and chemistry, but also from prevailing educational theory and the character of their teachers. 'Bi-directional teaching in communication with the cadets was unknown', and discussion was not encouraged; the cadets had to learn the theory and the approved answers by heart. The teachers at these military academies were officers for whom training was just their next placement. Often they were simply officers who could easily be spared from their units; knowledge, background or teaching ability played no part in their selection. They had to teach those subjects that had been allocated to them, and there was no check on their suitability. Some had to teach French, for example, despite having no background in the language; and the vast majority of teachers were West

Pointers themselves, which further contributed to the closed culture of the institute.

> Tactical studies in German books were considered 'too ambitious for the typical American student officer' and as a consequence 'simplified for the American officer students'.
>
> Jörg Muth, *Command Culture* (48:117)

The same pattern was apparent at Fort Leavenworth, where academic solutions were the norm: for every kind of tactical situation, a course of action had been formulated that had to be strictly observed. This was based on the idea that when modern weapons were used, the outcome of a battle would be inevitable as soon as the forces on both sides were known; the rest was just a mathematical exercise. In the 1930s war games were introduced, but they became choreographed exercises in which there was no room for surprise. In this way, Leavenworth turned out officers who had never learned to deal with complex or unexpected situations. They had been taught a staff mentality in which the map was the main source of information, and they were not expected to lead from the front in close contact with their units. The student officers absorbed this mentality and, as at West Point, the motto was 'cooperate and graduate' rather than 'question and challenge' – despite the fact that there were officers there who could have contributed their knowledge and experience and enriched the training. This made Patton sigh that 'no one is thinking, as everyone is thinking alike.' (48:190)

In the First World War, shortcomings among officers were found in the fields of 'resourcefulness, initiative and adaptability to new ideas', all subjects on which of German officers scored highly. There was also a 'lack of leadership capabilities and the humane treatment of men', a defect that was not remedied in the Second World War. When the Inspector General of the US Army addressed these deficiencies in 1924, he was told that more attention to leadership could unfortunately not be fitted into the already crowded programme.

> 'West Point: 120 years of tradition unhampered by progress'.
>
> West Point cadets

Fort Leavenworth also had difficulty in adapting itself to changing tactical challenges. Despite the fact that the First World War had developed into a struggle in the trenches, at Fort Leavenworth no course was dedicated to static warfare and the lessons learned from it; all the attention was given to 'open warfare'. The graduates streamed into staff positions in divisions at the front to plan military operations with their irrelevant knowledge – with, of course, predicable consequences. At the beginning of the Second World War not much had changed: graduate officers had not been taught to develop leadership qualities during their training, and they had had no contact with enlisted men. They had no knowledge of military craftsmanship – unless they were placed with the engineering corps – and no knowledge and experience of up-to-date tactics. They had been taught that the solution to every tactical problem could be found in the training manual, and that the school solution was the norm; not that it could be found in personal leadership, in going to the front line, observing the situation there and perhaps throwing everything they had learned overboard and finding a new creative approach.

'The Academy does not pretend to turn out finished Army officers.'
General Matthew Ridgeway, in *Command Culture*

This led to a proverbial 'educational desert' within the American training system, which changed only after the Second World War. A leadership course was introduced, but even in 1976 a committee, the umpteenth, observed that West Point had to change drastically to be able to train real combat commanders. The fact that the training supplied many officers who later made it to general was, according to an analysis of their biographies, due not so much to West Point but because 'their upbringing in solid families already had formed personalities that gave them the means to survive the harsh military academy regime without it doing them intellectual harm'. (48:187)

The travelling general

A major problem for the American Army was that its officers often lacked leadership and daring. Those who did have these characteristics can be counted on the fingers of one hand. Joe Lawton Collins was one of them, and this general travelled up and down between the fronts in Europe and the Pacific, being deployed for operations that demanded dangerous or demanding leadership, such as opposed landings or forcing breakthroughs. He led operations in the Pacific in the period 1942–3 and was then transferred to Normandy, where he led the 7th Corps.

American officers and their men: an unbridgeable gap
As we have seen, the training of officers contributed little to the formation of good relationships with their subordinates. This was painfully highlighted on troopships to the front, in the Pacific or Europe, when the gap between officers and men became even more obvious:

> Shipping out made manifest the break with home and often signalled the approach of battle. At this juncture of considerable vulnerability, young soldiers would have welcomed officers' expressions of support, indeed of any mutuality. Instead, strict separation seemed designed to seal off enlisted men from any sympathetic contact with their officers. On a transport bound for the central Pacific, the troops were ordered to run through repeated abandon ship drills and while 'hot, sweaty, bruised and ill tempered', commanded by the captain, the officers 'cool, clean, well dressed and smiling' scouted the ship. Private Robert Thobaben recoiled: 'It was at that moment that the glaring gap between officers and enlisted men, between equality and inequality, was driven home to me in a lesson I shall never forget. It was us and them. It was an unbridgeable gulf. It was human estrangement, alienation and isolation, in its most exacerbated form.'

This was something that the Germans tried to avoid at all times in their training and their vision of the role of officers. Indeed, every right-thinking military organization will try to avoid it. The allocation of space on board was one of the first things that made the GIs angry. For example, the ratio of officers to men of the 100th Division was 1:17, but half the accommodation on board was reserved for the officers. The officers had private dining rooms and lounges, but the men could only find room to eat with difficulty: 'En route to North Africa, Robert Welk and his friends ate twice a day, standing up; officers ate three times a day, seated.' (35:191) The GIs felt particularly offended by the reactions of officers if they trespassed on 'officers' territory': 'Don't you know enlisted men are not allowed on the boat deck?' In addition, the differences in food supply caused bad blood:

> While the men ate terrible food twice a day standing up, the officers, in an elegant restaurant several decks above, sat down to white table

linen, nice cutlery, friendly service by stewards and infinitely better food, hardly different from the cuisine rich transatlantic passengers had enjoyed before the war. (20:15)

This did not contribute to a positive atmosphere, whereas German officers and their men ate in the same mess, thereby creating a bond.

'Surveys in social psychology among U.S. personnel showed a catastrophic relation between enlisted men and their officers.'
Gerhard Weinberg, in Command Culture

Feelings about the differences on board could become so heated that, following an incident, Richard Tobin, correspondent of the *New York Herald Tribune*, noted:

The GIs involved are as close to mutiny as they will ever be . . . One young soldier, in tears, keeps telling his mates that he will not be surprised if his own first lieutenant, whom he has not seen below decks since the trip began, becomes an early casualty in the invasion fighting'. (35:189)

These differences remained: officers had access to strong drink, better food – 'The officers get the best; the men get what is left' (35:191) – better housing, their own canteens, own transport, own latrines, a better choice of prostitutes, and so on, and 'such blatant discrimination first surprised and then angered the enlisted men.'

Yet actual instances of conflict between officers and men were rare. At the front, the inevitable relaxation of formal discipline meant that the relations between officers, non-commissioned officers and men became more informal:

A junior officer, Ralph Ingersoll, discerned 'an easy democracy' in the way his company's officers and man ate and slept together in forward areas. Eugene Sledge noted that during the fighting, relations between riflemen and their officers were 'all buddy-buddy'. [The danger of getting hit] placed a premium on cooperation. [Arthur Miller was told that] 'officers wear the

130

same uniforms we do and you call them by their first name. Bars don't mean one little damned thing'. [Now the pendulum swung the other way.] Such modifications owed much to the new, large, lethal significance of bars as an objective for enemy fire. With German and Japanese snipers targeting officers, survival required the elimination of all signs of rank: officers' insignia, uniform variations, salutes, conversational references to titles that might be overheard, differences in weaponry.

This wave of democratization was thus a form of survival strategy on the part of officers. And finally, 'the shocks and costs of battle often scrambled hierarchical roles': in the chaos of the battle, ordinary soldiers assumed a leading role, surviving men replaced officers and NCOs, officers and troops were pushed into each other's arms. (35:203) Men often gained in this way more respect than their officers. For instance, during the campaign in Normandy, an officer ordered his men from the 101st Airborne Division over a 3m-high hedge. They did not climb fast enough to the mind of the officer, who himself had not moved, but then, 'Reaching the top, Donald Burgett looked back and retorted, "Don't worry, joker. I'm ahead of you and so is everyone else. Get your ass up here and go with us."'

What was quite normal in the German Army – officers giving a helping hand in manual tasks – was exceptional for the Americans. When their men were carrying shells weighing 60kg over the entire 200m length of a ship, German officers joined in:

> Even some of the officers helped. It makes you forget the heavy work that you are doing when you see the officers pitch in . . . To see an officer work with the crew is great for morale. The men will respect him and naturally go out of their way to help him. (35:207)

The importance of earning the respect of your men was emphasized in the German Army. Respect would lead to authority and prestige and contribute to the *Innere Führung* (internalized discipline) of men and units. If you have no authority, your only power as an officer derives from your place in the hierarchy and you will have to enforce obedience, a relationship which was normal in the American Army.

4.5 British officers, NCOs and leadership style: rigid guidelines

To gain an insight into the British style of management, we will examine the First World War, during which the British used a strictly hierarchical command structure. Command was centralized, orders were detailed and the various hierarchical levels within the organization served only to pass on orders from above. The reason for this was, as previously discussed, the low level of training and education of officers and men. (27:17) Centralized control by the army and corps command led to a high degree of inflexibility at the level of the combat unit. The general practice was that commanders decided on the deployment of units 'three down', i.e. three levels below their own. In practice, this meant that the location and deployment of units within a division was determined by the divisional commander. In comparison, German officers were pressed to limit their interference to 'one down', and only in a worst case to interfere with a lower level in the organization. The British practice resulted in corps and divisional commanders being swamped with an enormous amount of information, to the extent that units sometimes literally could not move without the approval of the central command. Units were given limited goals in the form of written orders, which they had to achieve at all costs. (57:140–2)

Due to the amount of their administrative work, senior British officers did not have time to evaluate combat actions or develop new tactics. We have seen before that few ideas were developed about the effective role of innovations such as the tank and the fighter plane, or cooperation between these new weapons and the infantry and artillery. As a result, any collaboration between the various arms was organized ad hoc, at a lower level in the hierarchy. (27:17) Centralized control of units also had an effect on the employment of reserves. Here the rule was 'two down', in other words a corps commander had a brigade of each division under his command. This meant that a divisional commander could only dispose of two of his three brigades; so when these brigades were deployed in the front line he could not, in the event of a sudden opportunity or crisis, deploy his 'own' reserve brigade without first obtaining permission from the corps commander. His only available troops would be the reserve battalion that he could use directly on the basis of the 'two-down' principle, one that greatly limited the flexibility of the British Army. As long as operations were running smoothly there were no problems, but at the moment rapid decisions had to be taken, the long lines of communication to the corps headquarters and back to the front prevented a timely and adequate response: that is, if these long lines of communication were still functioning and the corps headquarters could still distinguish between major and minor issues. In the German system, the responsibility for the use of reserve units was decentralized, and commanders were able to respond quickly to unexpected situations. As long lines of communication were avoided, much was left to officers' own initiative and they were expected to respond to situations in real time.

There are many examples from the First World War of the British command and communication system leading to loss of the initiative or to substantial casualties, because all actions that deviated from the agreed plan had to be submitted for approval to the corps command. In one case, the commander of a brigade could not stop an attack by his own battalions which had been based on orders from the Corps headquarters but which circumstances had since rendered redundant. Corps commanders successfully ensured that absolute obedience was one of the central themes of command and that deviation from orders would never enter the mind of a subordinate officer. In other words, 'Obedience is far more important than initiative', a variant of the American principle that you should not think for yourself but follow orders. Considering that during a major part of the First World War the British strategy was limited to attack at any cost, it is easy to imagine the effect this had on the morale of the troops. Apparently, however, it was taken for granted. In addition, it has also been suggested that, in the opinion of the British commanders, only strict obedience to orders could drive the 'culturally degenerate working class' out of the trenches and forward towards the enemy. (57:148)

The class society

From descriptions of officers, men, their mutual relations and the command structure, it becomes clear that the British class system was mirrored in the separation between officers on the one hand and non-commissioned officers and men on the other. This was succinctly reflected in an officer's comment: 'In England the salute is

> intended to mark the fact that the officer is acknowledged to belong to that class whose hereditary function it is to command.' A German who served with the Home Guard in Great Britain complained to Liddell Hart in 1942 about 'the tremendous gulf between officers and men . . . Our C.O., and we have had quite a few already, never says a personal word to us, nor does even a subaltern.' (42:124)

This style of leadership did not change fundamentally in the period between the two world wars. In analyses of combat actions from the Second World War, problems in the chain of command and control can still be observed, and lack of initiative on the part of officers in combat situations is still apparent. The reasons for this are the rapid growth of the British Army after 1939 and its low level of training and education. Of course there is more: German officers were trained to take the initiative in unexpected situations; British officers much less so. The problems described in the command structure indicate that much value was still attached to centralization of command and a hierarchical method of leadership. In Rommel's own words:

> Any delay in one's own actions can lead to an acceleration of the actions of the enemy.
>
> Erwin Rommel (42:52)

Training in the British Army, as we have seen, took place at regimental level, and although at one level this could stimulate esprit de corps and team-building, it could also perpetuate the class distinctions within British society. In addition, it prevented, in contrast to the German system, the promotion of competent non-commissioned officers with combat experience to the rank of officer, so that the precious experience of so many NCOs was not used to enrich the officer corps. This cadre of experienced non-commissioned officers was maintained throughout the Second World War, a quality confirmed by the Germans' own observations. For example, they noticed after Operation Crusader in North Africa in 1942 that 'British troops generally fought well . . . Officers were courageous and sacrificed themselves, but showed little initiative. Non-commissioned officers were good across the board.' It was this lack of initiative that time and again meant that breakthroughs and opportunities were not exploited, in North Africa and later in Europe. It was also unclear whether and to what extent non-commissioned officers were involved in the preparation of combat actions and could offer their opinions.

The position of the (non-commissioned) officer

German evaluation of the fighting in Italy in 1944 clearly revealed a number of weaknesses within the British Army which they linked to formal advice for their own units:

> British attack formations were split into a large number of small units led by officers; non-commissioned officers were rarely properly involved in the attack plan, so that if an officer was wounded or killed, the non-commissioned officers were unable to act in line with the original plan. The result was that, in rapidly changing situations, the junior officers showed too little flexibility and initiative. For example, when a goal was achieved, the enemy failed to exploit it and generally began digging defensive positions. The conclusion is: try to take out the opponents' officers and take the initiative. (42:127)

Such observations fitted seamlessly with the experience of the First World War and showed that the British command concept still had the same fundamental flaws, which even Montgomery was not able to repair. On the contrary, he continued to focus on ever more detailed plans, while maintaining the gulf between officers and men, so that there was rarely a personal note in the conversations between them. (28:124)

Senior British officers also did not really seem to be interested in addressing the fundamental weaknesses in their command concept or its tactical translation. Whether they simply did not realize it, or were unwilling to reflect on their own experiences, is not clear (42:124); but as we have seen, they were not encouraged by the High Command to think or exchange ideas, probably because the Command itself simply did not see the problems.

As we have also seen, Montgomery in North Africa made short work of any individual quirks or interpretations in the implementation of central plans. Although there was room for everyone's ideas in the preparatory discussions, once he had reached a decision he demanded it be strictly adhered to and implemented. The days of informal meetings with everyone on the battlefield, discussion of different command concepts and opinions about the scope of orders, were over. In Montgomery's view, only by a *dirigiste* style of leadership and hard training could the Eighth Army purge itself of its weaknesses and become the fighting force that he envisaged. (46:209)

In the later phases of the Second World War the deployment of personal initiative was completely subordinated to the use of *force majeure*. The Allied material superiority in all areas made initiative and flexibility in thinking, the essential factors in exploiting opportunities after breaking through the enemy line, to a large extent superfluous. The Allied armies lacked officers and NCOs with initiative and perseverance, and the ones they had were insufficiently valued and utilized during the later campaigns. (42:129) This made the entire campaign in the west predictable, something about which even the Germans complained in their *Erfahrungsberichte*.

Having discussed the officers and NCOs and the various dimensions of leadership in this chapter, we will continue in the next chapter with the analysis of men, teams and team performance.

CHAPTER FIVE

Men, Teams and Training

In this chapter we look at the attitudes of the belligerents towards their men, with special attention to teams and team performance. How did these translate into recruitment and selection criteria, how were the men trained and to what extent were the psychological and sociological aspects of individuals and groups taken into account? What was actually expected from teams, and how much attention was paid to team building? Were the relationships between men, officers and non-commissioned officers characterized by power or by authority, and more generally, how did these individuals relate to each other? We also discuss concepts such as trust and discipline, which are of great importance to the cohesion of an army its individual units.

5.1 New round, new chances

As described in Chapter 4, the German Army after the First World War faced major challenges due to the limitations placed on it by the Treaty of Versailles in terms of numbers of men, officers and permitted armaments. In addition, the General Staff, regarded by the Allies as one of its most important elements, had to be dissolved. However as we have also seen, this was secretly kept in operation within the *Truppenamt*.

These demands forced von Seeckt, the new German Commander-in-Chief, to hold a thorough re-evaluation of the functions of the organization. Although all the warring parties had gained experience during the First World War, notably as a result of tackling the problems posed by trench warfare, the Germans were the only ones who subjected their war experience to a thorough analysis with a view to formulating possible solutions. In total, seventy-five committees were set up by von Seeckt to study the war in breadth and depth. These committees were led by staff officers and comprised experts from a large number of relevant fields. More than 400 officers, or 10 per cent of the permitted officer corps, were eventually involved in these exercises. The Germans once again showed a willingness to learn from their mistakes, just as the

Prussians had from their defeat at Jena in 1806. The remarkable thing is that the victors in the First World War, the British, French and Americans, despite their considerably greater losses and their much lower battlefield performance, never analyzed their experiences in depth. In the Second World War they would reap the bitter fruit of this lack of interest.

The Germans' evaluation resulted in the previously mentioned *Führung und Gefecht der Verbundenen Waffen* (leading and fighting with combined armed forces), published by von Seeckt in 1924. Although relatively unknown, it is one of the twentieth century's most important documents in the field of military doctrine and organization. As its title indicates, a central theme is the cooperation between the various branches of the armed forces, in the form of integrated units. The document can be seen as an elaboration of existing ideas and it formed the theoretical framework for the further development of the Reichswehr's command concept in the years between the two world wars.

The concepts and structures described in the previous chapters are of no use if the men and the leadership to implement them cannot be found. In this respect, the Versailles Treaty can be seen as a 'blessing in disguise' for the German Army. Although the Treaty forced the new Reichswehr to limit its size drastically, this in fact created an opportunity to select only the very best officers and NCOs. As a result, the qualities of those involved were explicitly and thoroughly checked, and selection focused on those able to convey ideas effectively and oversee group processes. It created a pool of men of unprecedentedly high quality, particularly in educational and psychological terms, and they provided an excellent basis for the further development and later expansion of the Reichswehr in the 1930s.

Shortly after the ending of the First World War, von Seeckt formulated clear principles for the officers and men of the demoralized Reichswehr in the document *Grundlagen der Erziehung des Heeres* (basics of army education). This prevented the various units from setting up training programmes based on their own experience and insights, but which did not fit within the larger whole. Responsibility for the training of recruits was indeed delegated to the individual divisions, but a very high degree of consistency in approach was maintained. (42:125) The principles of *Grundlagen der Erziehung des Heeres* would be further elaborated and implemented within the Reichswehr in later years.

5.2 Recruitment, selection and the psychological dimensions of warfare

The Germans were aware at an early stage of the importance of psychology: to ensure the right man was assigned to each role; to strengthen morale; and to harden troops against the tension and stresses of modern technological warfare. This is perhaps unsurprising, since Germany and Austria had been the cradles of modern psychology. The First World War had shown that a new type of soldier was needed: no longer someone who merely functioned under the all-seeing eye of his officer, but a man who could operate independently at the front and in no-man's-land. Psychological techniques focused on creating this new soldier, in line with preferred leadership styles in the context of *Auftragstaktik*. In addition, it was realized that the psychological aspects of new weapons such as tanks and aircraft demanded more than just knowledge and skills; they also imposed demands on the personal qualities of the troops.

In contrast to the practice of the British and American armies, German recruits were tested not only for intelligence, but also for social, emotional and character traits: in modern terms, not just IQ but EQ (Emotional Intelligence). Thus the supreme command attached more value to the psychological qualities and the emotional stability of recruits than to formal knowledge or physical strength. A lot of energy was put into developing methods to analyze and strengthen the willpower, endurance and mental resilience of officers and men. The Germans also realized that a subsequent war would be mainly technological in nature and would require nerves of steel in its soldiers, especially men in special units, such as paratroopers, tank crews and the crews of anti-tank guns. It was not long before psychologists concluded that truckers did not necessarily make good tank drivers, or pilots of commercial airlines good fighter pilots. Technical knowledge and skills needed to be supplemented by the mental qualities required of a soldier.

To achieve this, profiles were developed for the different types of role. Tank crews, in particular, were carefully selected. They had to be highly individualistic and able to perform independently, have a good feeling for technology and be prepared to sacrifice themselves for the homeland. Such strict selection and subsequent intensive training contributed to a large extent to the successes of the German tank divisions. Other elite units, such as the crews of anti-tank guns, had to have nerves of steel, strong willpower and perseverance. The latter units were called *Panzerjäger* (tank hunters), a name that suggests the aggressive attitude expected of them. Everything was directed at preparing officers and men as well as possible for the battlefield of the future. Despite initial scepticism and some opposition, the application of psychology found a broad basis of acceptance within the Reichswehr and the Heer. In the period up to the Second World War, more than six hundred publications on the subject of psychology and warfare appeared in Germany. In addition, the Army employed two hundred psychologists, who could base their work on the findings of thousands of academic psychologists in universities and hospitals. (32:154–8)

Socializing: welcome to the Kindergarten!

Socialization into a community (*Einheit*) is a complex process, and the Germans attach great importance to it. The 'kindergarten phenomenon' may reveal how this is done. In Germany, children go to kindergarten at the age of three. Each child is then linked to a child of five. The older child is, within limits of course, responsible for his younger companion. He introduces the child into the group and supports it in games and other activities. During festivities the two children stay together, and at activities outside of school they go hand-in-hand. If the five-year-old is absent, there is a *Stellvertreter* (a four-year-old substitute) who takes over the role. In this way, the five-year-old gains a sense of responsibility for someone who is less mature, and the three-year-old learns to trust an older person. It is a remarkable way to instil a sense of community in groups and teams.

If these children later learn a trade, they will enter a similar system, starting as a *Geselle*, or 'journeyman'. In the course of time, as their knowledge and skills expand, they can reach the position of *Meister*, or 'master'. Here, too, the subtle game of trust and sense of responsibility plays a role, and in organizations this implicit hierarchy, based on authority, will be an important part of relationships. Such mechanisms, laying the foundation for operating independently within a broader framework of trust, were also to be seen in the German Army.

Strict parade-ground drill, seen in other countries as one of the most important aspects of discipline, was abandoned by the Germans long before the First World War. They had decided that this way of training troops did not fit with their view of modern warfare.

Drill

In contrast to popular views of the German Army, drill was used only to a very limited extent. Ludendorff strongly disliked drill and considered it an ineffective way of increasing social cohesion within units. He called it 'mechanical' and 'external' and compared the drilling of large groups of men to the training of dogs, as an approach that deprived young people of their individuality. The method he proposed was aimed at gaining 'internal' or 'self discipline' (*Innere Führung*). He emphasized shared values, norms and a sense of duty. This *Innere Führung* would ensure that the men knew their responsibilities even without direction by their officers, and fulfilled them as independent-thinking individuals. (57:100)

Almost the opposite was the case in the US Army, where breaking down the personality of the individual recruit was always the beginning of his education. The drill sergeant was, and still is, responsible for this.

Partly due to the influence of the psychologists, the harassment of recruits by German officers and NCOs was ended by the 1930s, and strict guidelines on the subject were introduced. Any officer who did not adhere to them was transferred to a punishment unit, where 'the qualities of the officer in question would be better used'. (32:167)

Due to this attention to psychology in the German Army, it experienced very small numbers of psychiatric cases compared to other forces, even after six years of war. The recruitment and selection system, the training, the rotation system and the emphasis on team-building (*Kampfgemeinschaft*) made the German soldier particularly resilient psychologically. (63:93–4)

Training

Superficially, training in the German Army differed little from that in other countries. However, this outward appearance was deceptive. In the first place, *Auftragstaktik* as a command concept offered clear training objectives for all army units, and these were made operational in the aforementioned *Grundlagen der Erziehung des Heeres.*

The training programmes were extremely practical and aimed first at developing the capacities of the individual soldier, then those of larger units. The only restriction was the lack of sufficient military training areas where larger combinations could be rehearsed. It was only after the conquest of Poland and France that really big areas became available to the German Army. (2:82) The overall training programme was detailed, methodical and carefully monitored. (45:237)

In addition to learning to deal with the technical aspects of military life, training also served to establish an aggressive mentality in troops and staff. In order to strengthen psychological resilience and prevent the outbreak of panic in combat situations, German troops were constantly exposed to stressful situations during training. For example, one third of all exercises took place at night, with specially trained units deliberately trying to cause chaos among the troops being trained. Teaching men how to deal with this type of situation was partly based on a large-scale psychological study conducted in the period 1933–9 on the effects of artificially generated panic among soldiers and civilians. The results of this training were clear: there were only a limited number of cases in which German units actually panicked, and as we shall see, these mainly involved what were termed *Ersatz Bataillone* (replacement units), which had not yet been fully integrated. (32:167–8)

These training courses found fertile soil because of the high level of education of recruits. This was is in contrast to the education and training level of recruits in other countries, who often signed up in peacetime. (14:112) The long service and dedication of many German officers and non-commissioned officers further contributed to social cohesion and provided a store of knowledge and experience.

The British and French had their own perceptions of the German training system before the First World War. They believed it encompassed rigid and often inhumane methods of drill and training, when in reality the emphasis was on self-motivation (*Innere Führung*), with the German soldier regarded as a thinking and feeling human being. (57: 56, 99) The German training of recruits was also extremely functional, focused on what a soldier would need in combat.

5.3 Recruitment, selection and training in the British Army

We have seen that the recruitment and selection of British recruits was mainly a matter for individual regiments, which often had a regional focus. However, in the Second World War this system was forced to change due to the shortage of men, resulting in an increased blurring of the boundary between regiments and other units. Much against the wishes of the regiments, the recruitment and selection systems were reorganized by the Adjutant General, Sir Ronald Adam.

The new arrangements required recruits to report first to the General Service Corps, where their knowledge and skills were tested in order to assess where they could best serve. They were then assigned to the different regiments on the basis of functional requirements rather than their regional origins. In this way a general assessment framework gradually emerged which better guaranteed that the right man was matched with the right job and the available manpower was optimally distributed across the various units. (59:213)

Training

One of the recurring themes in descriptions of the British Army in both the First and Second World War is the low level of training and education of both officers and other ranks, resulting in part from the absence of clear central direction and co-ordination. Training programmes were developed by the regiments themselves, and while some were excellent, others were unrealistic. This variety of regimental and personal interpretations resulted in a high degree of inconsistency, not only in the training itself but in its 'end result', i.e. qualifications, because there was no common command concept, doctrine or solid testing framework. (42:112)

The fundamental weakness in the training of officers and men in the First World War was not addressed in the interwar period, as can be seen from complaints by various commanders in this period. Thus General Hobart, commander of the Mobile Force in Egypt from 1938 (which eventually became the 7th Armoured Division), described the officers of the cavalry regiment as socially very nice people, devoted to the regimental tradition of swords and spurs and quickly satisfied when results were achieved, but ready to blame technical factors or the tanks when things went wrong. They spent a lot of time on sport, such as polo at the Gezira Club, or tennis, while at five o'clock all business finished and they dressed formally and reverted to socializing. (42:111)

Sport

British officers had a fascination with sport. Officers in the First World War are recorded as saying things like, 'I should say [riding] is one of the things that matters most for an officer . . . Men will always follow an officer who has got the sporting spirit' . . . [The Army used to be] a paradise for men, in which a subaltern thought very little, but kept fit and hunted for two days a week during the season.'

An officer who also served in the German Army complained that German officers had to work in the mornings and in the afternoon and had no time for 'the sports, so central to a British officer's life'. The same officer believed that relations between officers and men in the German Army had to be bad because 'everybody is being kept so busy that there was no time for sporting activities, which would bring them together.' It should be noted, however, that officers and men engaged in different sports. (57:166)

The Germans attached great value to good qualitative and realistic training. In comparison with the British, this training was so thorough that before the First World War a German professional soldier received more training in two years than his British equivalent in four. (57:162) One reason for this may have been that the battalions of a German regiment all remained in the same place, while the British rotated, one battalion stationed at home for training and the other being sent overseas. However, the overseas units suffered constant attrition, mostly due to tropical diseases, and this led to replacement and movement of men which disrupted training. (57:99) British training was also characterized by an emphasis on keeping uniforms and weapons in good order, marching to the music of the regiment's band, serving officers in the mess, keeping the barracks clean and all kinds of other housekeeping duties; these activities were often 'high-demand' in terms of cleanliness and maintenance, and were a logical consequence of serving in the tropical climates where battalions were often deployed. In addition, marching with the band and outward military display clearly suited the mission of an Imperial army that needed to 'show the flag'. All these activities, however, took up a lot of time and meant that it was seldom possible for troops to practise military tactics together at full strength. (57:163)

British units were continually asked to provide men for administrative and facility duties within the regiment or at the headquarters and bases. The Germans attempted to limit this type of activity as much as possible in order to focus fully on training. British reservists, who would later form the bulk of the British Expeditionary Force in 1914, for instance, also received relatively little training after removal from active service compared to their German counterparts. This lack of training meant that British soldiers had to be told constantly what to do and how to do it: in other words, they had to be led in a highly directed and hierarchical way. When the British Army grew rapidly at the beginning of the First World War, the quality of training became correspondingly poorer, due to the lack of experienced officers and NCOs or sufficient equipment. The emphasis in training was mainly on drill and marching, and much less on learning how to handle combat situations or take the initiative on the battlefield. (27:16)

Confrontation at Landrecies

The Germans attacked Landrecies in northern France on 25 August 1914. In response, the commander of a company of the 3rd Coldstream Guards ordered his men to fire in bursts:

> The fire-commander whistled and then gave the word of command, on which the men emptied their magazines into the darkness ahead. The Germans quickly got used to this. At the sound of the whistle they rushed to cover and as soon as the burst of fire was over they began to work forward again. (59:165)

This sort of mechanical and repetitive technique was characteristic of the British Army and would lead to large losses. The classic whistle followed by 'going over the top' was a well-known example, as were massive introductory artillery bombardments in advance of an attack, which gave away any element of surprise.

Montgomery, who was considered to be an excellent trainer of men, confirmed these shortcomings in describing the state of the Eighth Army when he took over: 'The condition of the Eighth Army . . . was almost unbelievable . . . Gross mismanagement, faulty command and bad staff work.' Divisions were split up into small units over the desert, tanks were spread out and there was little or no understanding of how to concentrate artillery. Another divisional commander told the author Liddell Hart after the Second World War that he was shocked at the poor results of two years of training of the 44th, 51st and 56th divisions in England. According to him, another division, the 50th, had learned nothing at all during two years in North Africa and kept making the same mistakes: 'If I told you what I had seen myself among these divisions, you would not believe it. It was nothing to leave the tanks to hold a position at night and retire the infantry – for a rest! This would let the enemy infiltrate back and take the position.' (42:126) It is clear that its low level of training and education, and inability to learn, were the most fundamental and persistent weaknesses of the British Army.

5.4 Training in the American Army

The Americans' view of training mainly focused on breaking the psyche of the recruit, so that his individualism was subsumed in the identity of the group:

> The military's awareness that the American individualistic ethos did not lend itself to easy subordination led it to design basic training as 'intensive shock treatment', rendering the trainee 'helplessly insecure in the bewildering newness and complexity of his environment'. A regime in turn intimidating, exhausting and overpowering would shear from soldiers their idiosyncrasies and contrariness. Individuals had to be broken to powerlessness in order that, collectively, their units might become powerful. As a US marine particularly noted, 'The erasure of individuality would create a malleability to discipline; repetitive actions would instil that automatic response for which the service strove.' (35:186)

This was in every respect contrary to the German view and explains many of the deficiencies noted in the American military:

> Training then was to be the process in which the soldier would learn, through forced subordination, that the individual was unimportant relative to the organization and would be persuaded, through daily chastening, that indiscipline would bring down on him penalties that ranged from annoying to life-altering . . . It took no more than a day of basic training to comprehend that military life accorded no premium to intelligence. [As one commentator noted] 'The first the Army teaches you is if you got any brains it's best to keep them to yourselves.' (35:193)

> 'The purpose . . . is to break you down, and then rebuild you into the person the Marine Corps wants.'

In addition, men were threatened with draconian punishments. Recruits were menaced with what were often grossly exaggerated penalties, such as a 25-year term of imprisonment for absence without leave, a burial of a carelessly-tossed cigarette butt beneath a heap of soil or cleaning the latrines with a toothbrush for a week. These exaggerated threats, the endless drill, brushing of shoes and cleaning of weapons were all designed to enforce submission on the part of recruits.

All this clearly shows that the American Army strove for *Aussere Führung* (outwardly enforced discipline) instead of *Innere Führung* (self-discipline). The threat of punishment was used to instil discipline, something totally alien to the German view of individual and group dynamics. The result was reflected in the rapid collapse of the discipline among Americans when this external pressure was removed. It also laid the foundation for thoroughly disturbed relationships between officers and men.

5.5 Team-building (*Kampfgemeinschaft*)
The core philosophy of the German Army was the socialization of a group of people into a team, or *Einheit*, combined with a constant focus on strengthening the agility and resilience of the unit thus created. However, because personal initiative was also encouraged, the combination of independence and cooperation (*Auftragstaktik* and *Verbundene Waffen*) was

extensively rehearsed, in order to teach units how to deal with any animosity that might naturally still remain, for example, between cavalry and infantry. Leaders were expected to look beyond the boundaries of their units and actively promote cooperation, a policy that had considerable benefits:

- Units frequently sought mutual contact instead of avoiding each other
- Units alone or together had an unprecedentedly high resilience, because they had learned to trust each other as teams
- Units had a particularly high regenerative capacity: units that had suffered losses or were beaten back formed new combinations (*Kampfgruppen*) that made them into effective armed forces as distinct from disorganized mobs
- The focus on cooperation between teams led to a much higher relative battlefield performance compared to other armies, a feature that endured throughout the war

The result was that, during times of crisis, Allied units often had a tendency to disintegrate, while German units tended to integrate to a higher level.

The Germans expected three things from teams and their responsible officers and NCOs:

- To perform, i.e. to achieve their goals in accordance with *Auftragstaktik*
- To be able to reflect and learn on behalf of their own team as well as for the Army as a whole
- To socialize, to become a unit

Within teams, large or small, much emphasis was placed not only on the craftsmanship and professionalism of the men, but also on the creation of mutual trust and connections; and formal links were considered less important than informal ones. This was all part of the strongly democratic nature of decision-making in the context of *Auftragstaktik*. More generally, teams and their responsible officers and NCOs had to pay regular attention to the social and psychological dimensions of the group. This was reflected in the assessment framework for promotion of officers and NCOs, as we have seen.

Everything in the German training and personnel planning system, from the recruitment and selection of troops within a well-defined geographical area (*Wehrkreis*) and the divisional rotation system, to the reception of rehabilitated troops within their own units, was aimed at achieving and maintaining a high degree of social cohesion. In a military context this meant everyone in a unit knowing each other well and sharing the experience of combat. It was assumed that this would ensure units functioned more smoothly, remained cohesive in combat and disintegrated less rapidly. (2:80) Creating *Kampfgemeinschaft* was central to the resilience, toughness and survival strength of a unit. There is a good example of this in scenes from the TV series *Band of Brothers* in which Germans who have surrendered are shown marching into captivity. The troops may have been beaten, but they are still marching as unbroken units, giving an impressive demonstration of *Gemeinschaft*. Another good example comes from the last episode of the same series, when a German commander thanks his men for their dedication in the past years and wishes them a peaceful future. His men are lined up and, although clad in a mixture of different uniforms, still clearly show unity and unbroken cohesion. Whether this was an effect that the directors of the series intended is a moot point, but both are very strong scenes that might leave some viewers puzzled or even uneasy, particularly if they had served in the Allied forces, with their rather more casual approach.

The mute army

What stood out in the behaviour of American soldiers in the Second World War was their lack of communication in battle, to the dismay of many observers such as Colonel Lyman Marshall, a journalist who would later become the Army's Chief Historian of European Theatre Operations. While Japanese and German soldiers and officers talked to each other, discussed things and gave and received instructions during the fighting, as a result of which their forces remained cohesive, it was often uncomfortably quiet on the American side. This lack of close communication was, in Marshall's view, a direct threat to the cohesion of American units. He attributed it to 'a definite blind spot in our training – the inability to impact awareness that "when you talk to others and they join with you that your action becomes more important".' He concluded that America went to war against the Axis with 'about the mutest army we ever went to war with'. (35:28)

In addition, units in the German Army were remarkably democratic. In the context of *Auftragstaktik*, the emphasis was on jointly reaching goals as a team and thus on horizontal communication. This was in contrast to other armies, where communication between officers and men was conducted in a vertical, hierarchical way – order-orientation rather than the Germans' mission-orientation. If men were involved in the definition of goals and how to reach them, they were better able to grasp the whole mission and see it in a larger context. Having done so, they were then able to carry through the mission independently, even if their officers were killed.

Respect and authority

By the end of the First World War the Germans had learnt from the differences that had arisen between officers, NCOs and their men. They wanted to avoid this happening again at all costs, which is why they attached great importance to creating a new type of relationship between all ranks, while at the same time preserving the outward appearance of discipline. They wished relationships to be based not on power, but on authority and mutual respect. As a result of this, from the beginning of his training, an officer was urged to win the confidence of the men entrusted to him, without jeopardizing his authority. (56:215)

Trust

In the Second World War a young British lieutenant who had earned his spurs in the African and Italian campaigns gave this view of the all-important element of trust: 'Trust depends on a man's knowledge that his commander thinks of him as a person and therefore treats him fairly, and looks after him . . . as well as conditions permit.' (35:227)

On the German side, men's confidence in their superiors was always high, even though, for example, Luftwaffe squadron commander Johannes Steinhoff received strong criticism from Reichsmarschall Hermann Göring of the Luftwaffe's commitment during the Sicilian campaign. Reflecting on this after the war, he said:

In my answer lay that trust in one's superior – a whole attitude to life – had been instilled into us, into our fathers and into their fathers before them. For we soldiers this had hitherto

---

been the only right attitude, indeed the only conceivable one. The obedience practised for centuries by the German soldier had always presupposed an unshakeable trust that the orders he received would be sensible orders and the high command would search their hearts very carefully before sacrificing whole formations. And the many who were sacrificed died in the certainty that this was so. (35:234)

The Germans therefore did not have separate messes for officers and men, or other privileges for officers that could negatively affect mutual relations. By contrast, this was one of the chief criticisms of the American and British armies.

> The obedience practised for centuries by the German soldier had always presupposed an unshakable trust that the orders he received would be sensible orders and the high command would search their hearts very carefully before sacrificing whole formations.
>
> Johannes Steinhoff, commander of
> Jagdgeschwader 77 and later Chairman of
> NATO Military Committee

5.6 *Wehrkreis* and the rotation system

Each German division recruited its men from a well-defined geographic area, the *Wehrkreis*. As a result, many recruits had known each other for years before they were called up, which provided a healthy basis for the socialization process. Divisions trained their own recruits within the framework of the overall training programme, so that all recruits, including those called up to replace losses, could immediately be fully integrated into their division.

The Army itself was made up of the Field Army (*Feldheer*) and the Reserve Army (*Ersatzheer*). The former was under the authority of the commander-in-chief; all other units came under the control of the *Ersatzheer*. (11:43) Once a division was on active service in the field, a training battalion remained stationed at the home base as part of the *Ersatzheer*. This *Ersatz Battaillon* was responsible for training troops and delivering them to the division at the front. There was a rotation system in which officers and NCOs with combat experience, often including men who were recuperating from wounds, were deployed to the 'mother' units of the *Ersatzheer* at the home base. The importance of this system should not be underestimated, since it ensured that recruits quickly got a feeling for the *esprit de corps* of the division and were trained in state-of-the-art combat tactics. (2:81–2)

This method also avoided the risk of recruits being trained by officers who had remained on the home front and had lost contact with active service.

The officers of the active division at the front and their counterparts in barracks were expected to maintain close personal relationships with each other, in order to achieve an optimal alignment of training with practice.

After training, troops travelled with their officers as a group to the front. This meant that they supported each other during this period and could form an immediate integrated and effective fighting force if, as could happen, for example, in the Soviet Union, their train was attacked by partisans.

To ensure a smooth transition from theory to practice, each division of the *Feldheer* had what was termed a *Feldersatz Battaillon*. This provided additional training and acclimatization to newly arrived men and officers from the *Ersatzheer* during breaks in battle. (4:72) The three companies of the *Feldersatz Bataillon* each had a close relationship with the three regiments of the division. The officers and non-commissioned officers of these regiments, the future commanders of the men, were attached to the companies as instructors, with the aim of stimulating good relationships between officers and their men at an early stage. In addition, junior officers taught the newly arrived troops about the peculiarities of their specific part of the front, to reduce the risk of 'greenhorns' being killed during their first days in battle.

This training and rotation system also ensured that even divisions that had been almost annihilated could quickly be rebuilt around the core of officers and NCOs in training. It also gave rise to a team spirit that encouraged units to continue fighting in circumstances which might have caused men in other armies to give up. In other words, like the concept of the *Kampfgruppe*, it prevented an organized force from disintegrating. (2:81–2)

Untrained in battle: Arnhem 1944

The Battle of Arnhem was largely settled by German soldiers who were either untrained (from the *Reichsarbeitsdienst*), from other branches of the armed forces such as the Luftwaffe or Kriegsmarine, support staff such as maintenance and airport personnel or still in training. Sending such men into battle was completely contrary to the German philosophy, but the High Command simply had no choice. They were taken care of by the experienced troops of 9. SS Division Hohenstaufen and absorbed into the division to create units of a very mixed character. Their combat experience and strength grew day by day, but the men were approaching the limits of their ability during the fierce house-to-house battles that heralded the beginning of the end for the British. By 25 September:

> Inexperienced reinforcements that had been used to supplement the depleted German attacking battalions were now causing some concern. Casualty rates were becoming excessive...the concentrated British forces fought desperately and ferociously for every house and every position. The attack had little success because our troops had little experience in house and woodland clearing.

Because these inexperienced units did not take time to reconnoitre the area thoroughly, they began to take heavy losses against the well-camouflaged British units. When a German company advanced without realizing that they were within range of British machine guns, 'they were totally oblivious of the potential impact fully-automated fire could have upon their densely packed ranks. The inevitable consequence was "very satisfying" for the British troops.'

In another incident, a German unit came under heavy fire when they had to cross a street:

> But before they could cross the street, the enemy opened up such a volume of fire from the occupied houses that the operation collapsed. The assault force leader, a sergeant, was

killed instantly, and other casualties both killed and wounded compelled the assault force to withdraw. [According to Rudolf Lindemann, an officer in training, these units had] 'no idea of fighting, as was also the case of the Kriegsmarine, the *Reichsarbeitsdienst* and the Luftwaffe'.

Because of this, Harzer, the commander of the 9. SS Division Hohenstaufen, regrouped his units on 25 September: 'It was no longer a case of forming large *Kampfgruppen*, but forming units of veterans for the decisive attacks.' (30:292) But the fact is that all these inexperienced units were ultimately supreme at the critical moment and contributed to the defeat of Operation Market Garden.

The Allies had essentially been fought to a standstill by untrained or partly-trained troops that had been quickly formed into ad hoc combat groups, or *Kampfgruppen*, consisting of 16- to 17-year-old teenagers or old and infirm men taken from NCO schools and logistic organizations from all three services: army, navy and air force. Soldiers had been summoned from headquarter staffs, defunct airfields and coastal defence batteries and were required to fight as infantry in units where only an average of 10 per cent had any previous service experience.

Divisional commander Harzer wrote twenty years after the battle:

It is with personal pride that I regard this German victory, because it was achieved not by regular units, but by railway workers, *Reichsarbeitsdienst* and Luftwaffe personnel as well, who had never been trained for infantry work and were actually unsuited to house-to-house fighting. (30:310)

5.7 The American replacement system

The descriptions in this chapter of the German system are in stark contrast to the American Army. American officers and men travelled separately and, as replacements, often arrived singly. There was no *Ersatz* system aimed at introducing and socializing new units or men at the front or teaching them the tricks of the trade for that part of the battlefield.

The Americans simply did not recognize the need for this kind of integrated approach. For example, as the losses in the months after the Normandy landings were much higher than expected on the Allied side, streams of newly trained men appeared; but very quickly the quality of combat units deteriorated, due to defects in training and the lack of a proper introduction to the front. The Americans did little to address the most obvious issues, with the exception that these new units were called 'reinforcements' instead of 'replacements' in what was termed 'The Communications Zone' (the area concerned with administration of the landings and the campaign). Reinforcements arriving from America stayed in the Communications Zone until they were transferred to their designated division. However, whilst in the Communications Zone no attempt was made to prepare the newcomers for life at the front, neither were tips and advice provided: the men were only there for administrative purposes. They were also confronted by soldiers who had recovered from wounds and were returning to battle, from whom they inevitably heard frightening stories about life at the front.

As a result, the new units were inadequately prepared. An officer from the 28th Infantry Division put it thus: 'The replacements, both officers and men, are green. They don't know how to take care of themselves. They become casualties very fast sometimes. They don't know their leaders and their buddies well, and it is hard to get them worked in as members of a team.' For example, at a very basic level, none of the newcomers was familiar with the rules of personal hygiene in the field, the most important of which was the regular changing of socks to avoid trench foot. Furthermore, many did not meet the qualifications that were listed on their forms; for example, some could not swim, and consequently drowned in action.

Troops frequently travelled singly to their assigned units, and this could cause psychological problems, as men arrived on their own and often at night. They were then largely ignored by those who had often lost comrades whom the newcomers were replacing, 'and because replacements were seen as clumsy and doomed, the veterans kept their distance.' This created a vicious circle:

Those who had seen combat talked to new arrivals in their own ranks diffidently and differently. Many campaigners clung to silence on the ground that replacements would 'find out soon enough for themselves'. Many replacements resented the veterans' reserve and, no less, some of what was said: it sometimes seemed the veterans had given them false information.

Being ignored had a demoralizing effect on newcomers, anxious as they were about what was to come, and it also ensured that they did not socialize, so that group cohesion was diminished and the combat effectiveness of the unit was accordingly reduced. As a result, the newcomers' chances of survival were also reduced, and this higher casualty rate only added to the continuous coming and going of new men. (35:28) Furthermore, poorly led units preferred to give dangerous assignments to new recruits, thus avoiding the risk of losing experienced men but adding further to the high casualty rate among newcomers:

> One day at Anzio we got eight new replacements into my platoon. We were supposed to make a little feeling attack that same day. Well, by the next day, all eight of them replacements were dead . . . But none of our old guys were. We weren't going to send our own guys out in a damn fool situation like that. We had been together since Africa, and Sicily, and Salerno. We sent the replacements out ahead. (20:98)

This practice meant that newcomers were often killed or wounded before anyone in the platoon or company knew their name. Paul Fussell in *The Boys' Crusade* rightly posed the question asked by many others:

> How did this idea arise of inserting infantrymen singly as strangers into experienced units? It could make sense only to someone trained in business methods. While drawing up tables of organization and elementary guides to tactics the higher echelons appear to have neglected a sufficient study of actual human behaviour. (20:99)

An American company commander described the problems that arose from this dangerous mix of weary veterans and untrained soldiers during the battle for Fort Driant, in the Lorraine campaign of autumn 1944:

> We could not get the untrained and inexperienced troops to move. We had to drag them up to the fort . . . The three days we spent in the breach of the fort consisted of keeping the men in the lines. All our leaders were lost exposing themselves at the wrong time in order to get this accomplished. The new men seemed to lose all

sense of reasoning. They left their rifles, flamethrowers, satchel charges and whatnot laying right where it was . . . Why? They would not fight. Why would they not fight? They had not been trained or disciplined to war.

Some newcomers were more fortunate, such as Arthur Couch, who was ordered to report to the 1st Infantry Division and recalled, 'I was lucky to be with old soldiers who wanted to help a replacement survive.' He learned from them that he had to roll aside after firing his machine gun, because the Germans immediately targeted any place where fire had come from. Couch was lucky, but he was in a minority.

These circumstances led to the disappearance of a large number of deserters, men who furtively withdrew to the rear, alone or in small groups, under the guise of carrying messages, seeking medical help or escorting wounded men. In American official history, the term 'retired' is used to describe them, although 'fled' or 'ran away' would be more appropriate. There were also a good many self-inflicted wounds, usually in the left hand or foot, and these multiplied so greatly in the course of the war that field hospitals set up special departments for this category of patient. The number of these injuries was often in direct correlation with the morale of the units to which the men belonged: 'In actual practice it [the Army Research Branch] found that units with high rates of non-battle casualties were usually reluctant to get into battle and lacked confidence.' (20:110) The fear of being wounded or killed was all the more compelling to men who felt they were on their own, in an army that took no interest in the psychological or sociological dimensions of warfare or the wellbeing of individuals and groups.

> Although the replacement system made good bureaucratic sense and promoted efficient management, it is hard to imagine a system that is more detrimental to the individual soldier's discipline, morale and training.
>
> Michael Doubler, in *The Boys' Crusade*

Joseph Stilwell was the only general, once again in China, who sought a solution to these problems, by training and replacing units in groups of four 'buddies of long standing'. This system was not, however, followed by the rest of the Army, and the result was that the battlefield performance of the US Army decreased over the course of the war. The system whereby new troops were added singly to units, without any effective additional training on site or attempt to include them in the group (insofar as a genuine group existed), and were led by officers who had no eye for psychological and sociological factors, created units without inner cohesion that entered battle as temporary and often accidental combinations. Yet it is cohesion and mutual attunement that create the conditions necessary to play the 'concert of battle' well and survive to its end.

'One irony of this highly modern war was that the Allied ground army grew worse as the war proceeded.'

The odd one out: the American 88th Infantry Division

Amidst the generally poor battlefield performance on the Allied side in the Second World War, there was one unit that positively distinguished itself: the American 88th Infantry Division. This division achieved a battlefield performance of 1.14 and came ninth in a top ten otherwise made up of German divisions. This was in Operation Diadem, the offensive aimed at Rome in May/June 1944, and the table is led by the Fallschirm-Panzer Division 1. Hermann Göring, with a battlefield performance of 1.49. The quality of the 88th Division was acknowledged by both the Allies and the Germans, but at first glance its composition appeared no different to any other's. Closer examination, however, reveals differences in leadership and training, and the man responsible was Major General John Emmit Sloan, the division's commander. He was educated at the US Naval (!) Academy in Annapolis and at fifty-five was technically too old for active service. However, he was appointed divisional commander after distinguishing himself as an instructor at the Command and General Staff School at Fort Leavenworth, and by consistently implementing his vision of leadership, demonstrating exemplary behaviour and dedicating himself to the training of his officers and men, he managed to lift his division to a higher level. According to Dupuy, the characteristic features of his approach were:

- Aggressiveness
- Attention to detail
- Strict discipline

- Inspirational talks and messages
- Personal presence in the front line
- Being sure subordinates had what they needed to do the job
- Making sure every assignment was carried out properly, including those not immediately related to military procedures
- Requiring strict adherence to established standards for military courtesy and proper uniform
- Prompt relief of any subordinate who could not or would not do his job
- Making friendly gestures to establish rapport with subordinate commanders
- Grasping and communicating the 'big picture' and role of each unit in overall objectives (15:116–20)

In short, the vision of Sloan corresponded with that of the German officer corps. After the war, the veterans of this division saw the main reasons for their success as: 'Personal presence in the front line, discipline, courage and aggressiveness . . . They were proud to be in a division that they now knew to be an excellent, outstanding unit, and they realized that the man primarily responsible was Sloan.'

Sloan did more than the above: during quiet times, he trained his division and set up a special training programme behind the front with elements that corresponded to that of the Germans. He showed interest in his men, made sure that they were taken care of and demanded the same professionalism from his officers as the Germans did. Replacements were absorbed quickly and 'imbued with the spirit of the division. When the division was out of line Sloan still insisted upon smart salutes and buttoned buttons, and got them from proud soldiers.' This is reminiscent of the German Army and its officer corps, and it shows that high battlefield performance can be achieved by any combat unit, provided its commander takes a number of principles into account. The same conclusion was drawn by Rommel, when he stated, based on his experiences in North Africa, that the Italians could form excellent combat units if they were well trained and led. The proof of this was the German-trained Folgore parachute division, which distinguished itself particularly at El Alamein.

5.8 The reality of the battlefield: the fight for the Hürtgen forest, November 1944

The Battle of the Hürtgen Forest, south-east of Aachen, in November 1944 witnessed a total meltdown by the American Army. The battle had no effect on the course of the war, but it led to a large number of American casualties. Together with the fighting in the Ardennes, it offers one of the defining images that the Americans had of the war in Europe: a struggle against an invisible enemy in a dark, cold, wet and impenetrable forest cut through by ravines and steep slopes. A total of 120,000 American soldiers were involved, of whom 33,000 were eventually killed or wounded. This battle revealed all the weak points of the American Army:

> This hideous battleground illustrated all at one time the deficiencies in the American system of troop replacements, the insufficiencies of American troop training, the failure of American divisional leadership, the innocence or ignorance of large-unit tactics by corps and army commanders, supply and imagination failure resulting in the absence of appropriate cold weather uniforms, and unjustified staff optimism, the result of basing decision-making on rear echelon map study and rumours instead of actual visits to division, not to mention battalion, fronts. (20:84)

What was the reason for this 'protracted mess' to which so many GIs fell victim? After the capture of Aachen the Americans set their sights on the Ruhr dams, but they believed the Hürtgen Forest to contain a serious threat on their right flank, although in fact it was only occupied by a weakened German infantry division of 6,500 men. The American plan to fight through the forest towards the dams actually rendered the small German force more effective, while the woodland terrain meant the Americans were unable to deploy their tanks, artillery or aircraft. As a German general remarked, it was clear that the forest was 'hard to take and easy to defend', and it would actually have been easier for the Americans to bypass it. As always, the Germans had prepared properly by building reinforcements and planting minefields, and targeting all firebreaks and paths with artillery and mortars, which were able to fire as soon as any movement was observed. But their main weapon was the forest itself. The tall trees standing close to each other made it permanently dark, and thick layers of pine needles, in which it was easy to hide anti-personnel mines, muffled the sound of manoeuvring units.

General Hodges was the responsible commander on the American side, and his uncreative approach led to the forest devouring six American divisions in a month and a half. The 28th Division made a first attempt, followed by the 8th and then the 1st. These were followed by the 4th, the 83rd and finally the 5th Armored. Almost a quarter of the troops deployed were injured by splinters, bullets, grenades or mines. Some units were so demoralized that they gave way en masse to 'unordered flight and even rout, flagrant disobedience, bursting into tears, faking illness and self-inflicted wounds'. (20:86) This report gives a good picture of the drama of the fighting in the forest:

> Squads and platoons got lost; mortar shells landing among assault teams carrying explosive charges set off the explosives and blew up the men; an unfailing chatter of machine guns ripped through the trees when anyone moved. One man, a replacement, sobbing hysterically, tried to dig himself a hole in the ground with his fingers. In late afternoon this battalion . . . staggered back to the line of departure. (20:87)

During this entire period, General Hodges never visited the front, moving no further than divisional headquarters. He thus broke one of Patton's commandments that 'plans should be made by those who are going to execute them'. When winter hit the front at the end of November, the misery gained an extra dimension because the Americans did not have any winter or camouflage clothing. This was because Eisenhower had given priority to the transportation of fuel and ammunition for a rapid advance through Germany, something which did not happen. While the GIs were shivering in their flooded and frozen foxholes they were served cold Thanksgiving Day turkey, a gesture from Eisenhower who, with a view to maintaining morale, had issued an order that all frontline troops, whatever the logistical effort involved, should be able to celebrate the day with this classic meal. But while the American soldiers were forced to stay in their foxholes, the Germans had retreated into comfortable wooden bunkers: this was a poignant reminder of the First World War, when the Allies were stuck in flooded trenches while the Germans were able to rest in their extensive and comfortable dugouts.

It is completely unclear why the Americans were incapable of offering their troops any form of acceptable shelter. Was this lack of knowledge, time or tools, or simply a failure to recognize the men's needs? The Germans were experiencing the same conditions, but without suffering the misery found on the American side. While a very high percentage of Americans suffered from trench foot, due to a combination of cold, damp and the inability to change their socks or dry their feet, the condition was unknown on the German side. Nor did the Germans suffer from psychological problems: while 8,000 American soldiers had to leave the battlefield early for that reason, no similar cases were recorded among the Germans. Of course, the Germans did suffer losses, and their ranks were strengthened over time by the 12. Volksgrenadiere Division and untrained Luftwaffe and police units, often with disastrous results. Eventually, the Americans – after a less than effective bombardment by 1,000 planes – managed to break through the German defences and reach the Ruhr Valley. The battle for the Hürtgen forest made a lasting impression on many American veterans, affecting their view of the war in Europe and of their supreme command:

> There are still survivors whose anger at the whole business will never cool – anger not, as the innocent reader might like to believe, at those formally designated their enemies, but at their own commanders who insisted on and presided over this conscienceless mess.' (20:90, 16:320–5)

As an incidental result of the battle, because of all the American attention to this part of the front, the Germans were able to build up their attacking forces for the Ardennes offensive undisturbed, 100 miles to the south. And the Ruhr dams, the original target of the operation? They were only captured in February 1945.

Do your homework and do it well!

One of the reasons for the excellent battlefield performance of the German Army was that they did their homework well, using a wide range of proven tactics that they adapted to specific situations. Due to their poor evaluation and learning systems, the Allies were

---

never really able to match them, and they persisted in stereotyped behaviour that played into the Germans' hands. In Chapter 7 we will look more closely at a number of clashes, but these introductory examples are taken from *Ardennes 1944. The Battle of the Bulge* by Antony Beevor. The cases are mainly from the Hürtgen forest:

- The Germans aimed their mortars just behind the American line of fire, making it seem like the American shells were falling short. This often led to panic and confusion in American ranks and accusations aimed at their own artillery, and had the desired effect of disrupting the attack.
- In the Hürtgen forest, Arthur Couch, a member of a machine gun team, noticed that 'The German artillery was pre-aimed on forest roads and also had been set to explode when hitting a tree top so the fragments sprayed down on us. This caused many dangerous wounds and deaths.' (70)
- The Germans fired their artillery during American attacks at the edges of the positions of their own troops. Because the shells exploded in the treetops and came from behind, a shower of wood splinters engulfed the American attackers. According to an American colonel, 'It took guts, but it worked.' (64)
- The Germans noticed that the Americans only bothered to carry out reconnaissance when about to attack a particular sector, which thus revealed their objective for the next day. (71)
- Junior American officers were often tempted to pull back at night after taking ground, but the Germans would move in and it would become impossible to dislodge them the next day.
- 'The Germans kept their tanks well dug in and camouflaged, and used them mostly as a psychological weapon.' During the daytime they kept quiet but at sunrise and sunset and during the night they manoeuvred and fired their guns 'just enough to keep our troops in an almost frantic state of mind'. The Americans were forced to position their tanks up front as well, but when they returned in the evening behind the lines to replenish with fuel and ammunition 'infantry tended to panic and retreat'. In contrast, the Germans always brought petrol and ammunition to their tanks up front.

- This could only be prevented by working in rotating shifts, but this was very laborious since the tanks had to be protected by more infantry and engineers needed to clear mines. Moreover, 'Tank crews seem to have been even more frightened than the infantry in the woods.' (71)
- The tanks thus deployed were confronted by the Germans, who had perfected the tactic of destroying tanks at short distances with the Panzerfaust or the Panzerschreck (a reusable anti-tank rifle), which had a longer range. Moreover, many German soldiers had overcome their fear of American tanks by this time because of the cautious and predictable character of the latter's behaviour.
- The American tactic of assaulting a hill via gullies on the flanks was well known to the Germans, and these gullies were always mined and covered by machine guns. (62)
- The Americans still did not realize that the Germans took every opportunity to unbalance their opponents or reconquer territory. When an American unit took possession of the village of Schmidt in the Hürtgen forest, they forgot this: 'Rather than digging foxholes, they went to sleep in houses. Their officers never imagined that the Germans would react immediately, so they did not send out patrols or position outposts. As a result, the battalion was totally surprised when German infantry and tanks appeared at dawn, following a sudden artillery bombardment.' The Americans panicked and retreated head over heels to their previous positions, leaving behind many dead and wounded. (67)

5.9 Self-discipline (*Innere Führung*)

Von Moltke emphasized the importance of discipline as an instrument to connect people: the stronger the discipline, the less need for instructions. Discipline in the German Army ensured group cohesion and prevented units from disintegrating. It was not the *Kadavergehorsamkeit* (zombie obedience) that some like to characterize as German behaviour, but the aforementioned *Innere Führung*. Men were taught, within the larger framework of *Auftragstak*, to think independently and responsibly. All the Army's efforts in the field of psychology and sociology were aimed at creating this, at the level of the individual and the group. This idea that discipline contributes to group cohesion and *Kampfgemeinschaft* was a common thread in the training of officers, NCOs and men. Within the concept of *Innere Führung* all these themes came together, creating the complex image of 'an army that could combine seemingly opposing characteristics of obedience and initiative, drill and creativity, authority and independence, with success as a whole'.

Discipline the American way
Discipline, of course, was also important to the other belligerents, and it was a subject that particularly engaged the Americans. The supposed individualism of the American citizen meant that basic training was mainly aimed at erasing the personality of the recruit, then rebuilding it as part of the unit: in other words, a forced policy, not one built on socialization as in the German Army. There were differences between the US Marines and the Army: 'The effort to neutralize personality, to suppress individual assertion, and create receptivity to command was more resolute at Parris Island [Marines] than at Fort Knox.' (35:225) This approach produced the image we are all familiar with from films: the drill sergeant who breaks his recruits by showing them who is in charge and humiliating them if necessary – this despite the fact that as early as 1906 Ludendorff had correctly observed that such drill deprived young men of their personality and failed to produce the desired *Innere Führung*. It would not take long, once they entered the war, for the Americans to discover the downside of their methods.

The psychology of drill
American officers had a distinctive way of driving out individualism and training recruits in dependence:

> While cleaning a latrine, a group of recruits obeyed an order to wash their hands in the toilets. The instructor next demanded to know whether they would drink that water and received the reply, 'Yes, sir!' Then came the usual reversal of direction designed to sharpen receptivity by sowing confusion and intensifying vulnerability: 'Do you run around drinking

---

165

out of toilets?' First came the dictum: 'You obey orders . . . It doesn't matter if you like it or not. It ain't yours to think.' Then came the link to combat: 'One of them damned Japs or Germans might make you drink out of a toilet. You would be insulted and do something foolish, and get shot . . . you get to be able to take cussin' and insults.'

The conclusion was therefore: 'Do what you are told, don't think and you will survive', or to put it another way, if you think for yourself, your initiative will not be appreciated.

The way in which the American Army used and still uses drill is in line with the concept of *Befehlstaktik*: you do as you are told and do not think for yourself.

The Marine Corps was to a certain extent an exception, in the sense that they showed some interest in creating group cohesion: 'Marine instructors simultaneously strove more strenuously than their Army counterparts to connect.' (35:225) But the end result, especially in the Army, was that in general discipline was fragile and quickly fell away when there were no longer clear power relations, as in the case of prisoners of war. Officers immediately came under pressure in such situations, now that they could no longer use their position in the hierarchy but had to rely on personal authority.

Evans Fordyce Carlson and Carlson's Raiders. A style of leadership the German way

There were of course exceptions in the American Army, men who shared the German vision of leadership. General Carlson, was one of them. He had served in China for several years and had gained respect for the Chinese Eighth Army, especially 'its relationships between officers and men stressing mutual respect under the rubric "gung ho" (working in harmony). Around this concept Carlson was determined to construct a Raider battalion, which he won authorization to organize in February 1942.' Carlson introduced the same ideas as those which formed the basis for the relationship of officers and men in the German Army.

Carlson decreed the abolition of such officer privileges as separate messes and clubs. Saluting became a rarity. Distinction between officers and men, in uniform, equipment, living conditions, diminished dramatically . . . At the heart of Carlson's vision lay the rejection of imposed discipline and its replacement by collective, cooperative problem solving – in other words, American teamwork. In his view, officers were to earn their status by demonstrating superior ability, knowledge and character. All orders were to meet tests of essentiality and justice, officers were 'never to order a man to do anything they are not willing and able to do themselves'. (35:229–31)

This seems like a direct quotation from a German handbook and may indeed have been so: the Americans used German publications in their officer training, as we have seen from the autobiography of James Salter.

Assertive American individualism could cut both ways: on the one hand, spontaneous individual deeds sometimes had a major effect on the course of a battle; on the other hand, they could undermine group cohesion and battlefield performance. Examples of the former can frequently be found in books and movies: indifference to danger, bravado, self-indulgence, all things that in fact undermine the group. But were these individual actions generally effective? What we read about or see depicted are mostly the successes, while the many failures are not mentioned, the times when this behaviour caused multiple casualties or ended in disaster.

This sort of individualism and breakdown of discipline could sometimes lead to complete anarchy:

The war, however, also bared other manifestations of individualism whose consequences were grievous. Especially costly was the propensity of Americans, in struggling to survive drastic pressure, to rely mainly on themselves; in ignoring or clashing with their own organization, they evaded its dictates, but denied themselves its protection. (35:219)

Captivity undermined to a considerable extent men's willingness to adhere to the principles of military organization. The first victim of this was discipline.

Discipline also collapsed in the Hürtgen forest. The cause was not the individual GI, who was brave enough, but all the negative aspects of the American system:

In one attack in early November the 2nd Battalion of the 112th Regiment of the 28th Division, assaulted a difficult ridge in the Hürtgen. After a particularly severe German barrage 'the men suddenly could stand it no more.' Panic-ridden, the men of one company grabbed wildly at their equipment and broke for the rear . . . The impulse to run was a disease, a virulent, highly contagious disease that spread like the plague. Once started the men would not stop, even when confronted with the pistols and carbines of officers ordering them to halt. (20:87)

On the run

German units also sometimes found themselves on the edge of ill-discipline. An officer of Panzer Gruppe III was shocked by events he witnessed on the road east of Klin in December 1941, when the Soviets launched their first real counter-offensive:

Discipline is disappearing. More and more soldiers hurry west on foot without weapons. Some have a calf on a rope, others push a sled with potatoes. The road is constantly attacked from the air. Those killed by bombs are no longer buried. Men of support units (units of the corps, Luftwaffe, supply units) flee in large masses. Without rations, freezing, irrational, they seek safety. Trucks that do not want to wait in the event of traffic jams turn off the road and find their way across the open field and through settlements. Traffic control works day and night and is hardly able to keep the traffic going. The Panzer Gruppe cannot sink much lower than this. (52:314)

The challenge was to get such a mass of people back in line and form them into a fighting unit again. The Germans succeeded time and time again in this, and as the war progressed such scenes seldom occurred, and retreats rarely turned into flight. An example was the Battle of Cherkassy in Ukraine in February 1944, when the Germans did everything in their power to relieve their troops trapped there. The heaviness of the fighting is evidenced by the report of Leon Degrelle, the commander of the brigade Wallonia, who were fighting their way to safety:

> We had hardly started climbing the hill when we saw cavalry rushing down a hill from the south-west. We first thought that they were German Uhlans. When I looked through my binoculars, I could clearly see their uniforms. They were Cossacks. I recognized their little nervous brown horses. They came after us, fanning out in all directions. We were stunned; the Soviet infantry fired at us with machine guns, Soviet tanks chased us and now the Cossacks rushed in after us to finish the attack.

Only one obstacle now separated the Germans from the safety of their own lines, the river Gniloy Tikich, which was between 7.5 and 12.5 metres wide and 2.5 metres deep. To bridge this, the last tanks were driven into the river at 1300 hrs, forming a bridge for the remaining units. They made contact with the units who had come to relieve them and who escorted them safely to their own lines. This disciplined retreat was one of many, and a relative success: of the 50,000 men involved, between 30,000 and 35,000 managed to reach their own lines. Most importantly, many of the wounded and the doctors and the nurses could be saved; it was crucial that the latter in particular did not fall into the hands of the Soviets.

At the end of the war there was a complete collapse of discipline in the US Army.

> The close of the fighting against the Germans on May 8 and against the Japanese on August 15, 1945, exposed for a final time how little the American military drew on internalized discipline that their training had been expected to inculcate. VE celebrations commonly moved beyond control, first in the rear areas where support personnel, unlike the line-soldiers, had no difficulty in grasping that the war could actually end – and without taking their lives.

Many rear echelon troops broke out and began firing weapons, including anti-aircraft guns, threw hand grenades and started fires. Drunken GIs used their weapons to create a Fourth of July sky, and thereafter few semblances of discipline survived . . . Officers continued to post guard-duty rosters, but soldiers seldom appeared . . . The only American diligence was that of a few sentinels whom the men set out to warn of any officer's approach. (35:231)

Out of a group of 250 American soldiers on their way to Mannheim, a third simply disappeared as their train passed Paris, 'for the delight of the city'; the rest enjoyed themselves throwing stones at American trucks on another train nearby. Every time a window was hit, they cheered. Only a third of the group eventually arrived at their destination. 'Their war was over and they don't give a shit for their officers, commands, or any of the trappings of the military', said Lieutenant John Toole. (35:232)

But for many Americans the war would not have been over if the atomic bombs on Hiroshima and Nagasaki had not given history a nudge. For some was this was a blessing: Chaplain Morris Kertzer had watched an Army transport draw away from a Marseilles wharf bound for the Pacific:

The men were not happy. They had been separated from their family for months, some for years . . . If ever I saw misery it was there on Pier E. Theirs was the misery not of sullenness but of rebellion. Americans were fortunate that the Pacific conflict ended only ninety-nine days after the European war. Had peace not brought an end to the transfer of forces between theatres, the government's effort would have provoked indiscipline of unprecedented scale.

Discipline and the British
In comparison, British discipline remained intact even under the most miserable conditions, such as Japanese captivity:

Granted that at the time of their surrender British units retained a higher order of cohesion and British soldiers a higher state of health than their American allies on Bataan and Corregidor, the subsequent resilience of British discipline was nonetheless impressive. The chain of command carried on, intact, even amid such demonic inflictions as the Burma-Siam Railroad construction and hell-ship voyages.

The hardships during these latter voyages can hardly be imagined. For example, during a crossing of sixty-seven days, 325 of 630 prisoners of war died, but discipline was still preserved: 'In the holds, spacing schemes permitted some sleep because others stood, confident of their turn to lie down'. And it held even when things got worse: 'When one ship was sunk by American torpedoes – the Japanese did not mark prisoner transports – the British formed into queues and climbed out in perfect order.' Under these conditions, American soldiers had the greatest difficulty in behaving with discipline:

> The Yanks spurned all notions of social distances separating officers and men, dismissed suggestions of higher capabilities inherent in superiors, derided the Tommies' obedience to orders, and detested the officers' *noblesse oblige*, indistinguishable in GI eyes from arrogance. But the British contract – the willingness of many officers to accept service to the men as an indissoluble component of leadership, the willingness of the men to defer to rank, its orders and its prerogatives – served soldiers well when, in one of the war's sternest ordeals, survival often hinged on the preservation of military cohesiveness. And it was here, for GI prisoners of war, that the cost of American convictions came. (35:224–5)

However cruel the behaviour of the Japanese camp guards, the British did everything they could to preserve group cohesion. In Changi prison camp, Singapore, British officers remained firmly in control, to the astonishment of a GI held there: 'Their enlisted men ... took orders as if there had been no surrender ... We Americans could hardly believe our eyes ... British soldiers stand at attention and salute their own officers, the officers actually pranking around, expecting it.' Sikhs took over some of the surveillance tasks from the Japanese, camp regulations were drawn up, all escape plans were assessed by a special committee and there were all kinds of recreational and educational programmes. In other words, an organizational structure, group cohesion and camaraderie were retained, which considerably increased the chances of survival of those participating. (35:222)

5.10 Regeneration of units, the German way

The German training system ensured that divisions that had been almost completely destroyed in battle could be rebuilt around the core of officers and NCOs that remained at the home base as part of the divisional rotation system. This also explains how divisions that seemed to have been wiped out could reappear at the front soon afterwards, as in the rapid recovery after Falaise and the retreat to Germany via Belgium and the Netherlands, or in the resilience of German units at Arnhem. If a division fell to a certain minimum number of men, the Germans would not allow it to continue to fight, but withdrew it from the front in its entirety to be rebuilt.

Their team spirit developed over time encouraged divisions to continue fighting in situations where units from other armies would long have fallen apart. In other words, German units showed very substantial resilience, meaning that they would not become armed mobs, or even collapse completely. (2:81–2) In fact, German units under fire tended to integrate, while Allied units were more likely to disintegrate.

Operational personal planning

Even when not on active service, a German division in barracks 'lost' 1 per cent of its strength every day due to illness and accidents. At the front, but not in contact with the enemy, an average infantry division lost 3 per cent of its strength each day. In this way, an infantry division in the Soviet Union could melt away to half its original strength in one month. This explains why divisions might gradually 'disappear' during a campaign. Of the aforementioned sick and injured, 50 per cent returned to the division within two months. They had rarely been further away than the medical units at the level of the Corps. The recovered men mingled with 'new' recruits in the Feldersatz Battalion, to be transferred to their own units as quickly as possible. To keep the division up to strength, this Feldersatz Battalion had to transfer 100 to 150 men per day to the regular units of the division. (14:120)

Team performance also played a major role in the principles of *Einheit* and *Verbundene Waffen* that required units of the various army branches to be able to cooperate at all times. For this reason, every effort was made to encourage teamwork. Different methods and models of cooperation were developed for mobile warfare, and new forms of communication between the various units were introduced. Through joint training and exercises, a focus on teamwork was developed which made units automatically seek contact with other units as quickly as possible. (56:217) This all added to the high regenerative capacity of the German Army.

CHAPTER SIX

Shared Values, Morale

Values and norms are, of course, ultimately crucial in whether and to what extent men feel connected to the cause they are fighting for. In Germany, propaganda since 1933 had made most believe that they were fighting for a higher purpose, the future of the German people. Among the Allies, such beliefs were less dominant, not because they had no higher goal in mind, but because their governments had manipulated them far less.

It is questionable to what extent political beliefs actually played any role on the battlefield. In reality, men probably concentrated more on survival, and for this your comrades and your group are more important than any higher cause. This raises the question of that internal cohesion that makes men want to survive as a group, help each other and even make individual sacrifices for their comrades. If this is not present, then the group falls apart under pressure into a bunch of individuals, each man fighting his own war. This chapter examines the belligerents in this context.

6.1 The German Army

The post-1918 Reichswehr attached great value to morale; indeed, in many respects it became even more significant than prior to 1918. Each regiment restored the traditions of its old imperial predecessor, and these were expected to be observed, along with the general honour of serving in the German Army. The Germans also made extensive use of new psychological and sociological insights to train soldiers for this new army. Time and again it was emphasized that young officers should keep an eye on the individual soldier and treat him as a member of a larger community. (42:162)

The senior echelons of the Reichswehr put great emphasis on the social dimensions of the new army, and the barriers that existed between officers and men almost disappeared during the 1930s. This was partly due to the Nazi concept of *Volksgemeinschaft*, and partly caused by the rapid expansion of the Reichswehr, from fifty to three hundred divisions. There was thus a major influx of officers and men from all sorts of backgrounds in civilian life who had to be unified by training and given the feeling of camaraderie which the Army's leadership desired. As a result, a soldier's career was less and less determined by his social background, and increasingly by his own competence. This spilled over into off-duty life, and troops were able to socialize on an equal footing in their free time and discuss all sorts of matters without restriction. (56:233) In this way, civilian and military society merged into one another.

Morale is an important element in combat performance. The Germans recognized that in combat situations soldiers do not primarily fight for lofty ideals such as the homeland or political convictions. These may be decisive in whether or not to join up in the first place, but under fire quite different priorities are likely to take over. The most important of these is the preservation of one's own life and, as a consequence, commitment to your comrades and your team: hence the emphasis on group cohesion. In studying social structures it became clear that a battalion has a lot in common with a tribe, its companies with clans and their platoons with families. The Germans were therefore sensitive to the need of soldiers to belong to something akin to a primitive sort of family focused on the preservation of life. As long as the members had faith in each other and the leaders of the family, clan or tribe, as well as in the tribe's overall effectiveness, they could be asked to do anything. (14:113) That they were successful in this is shown time and again by the willingness of German troops to keep fighting until the last days of the Third Reich.

This raises the question of what role National Socialism played in the culture and morale of the Wehrmacht. It is likely that, in reality, ideological considerations played only a minor role in motivating the German soldier on the battlefield. Enthusiasm for the regime reached a peak in 1937 and then slowly declined, partly because of fear that Hitler's policy would lead to war. During the war, enthusiasm fluctuated in line with the pattern of victory or defeat. All in all, it is assumed that the effect of National Socialism on combat effectiveness was about the same as that of democratic ideals on, for example, soldiers of the American Army. (13:63)

After Hitler's seizure of power, the Nazis developed a keen interest in the military. Until 1939 the Army resisted pressure to conduct propaganda for the regime, though it permitted the wearing of Nazi symbols and indoctrination of its troops with Nazi principles. Just before the Second World War broke out, the Wehrmacht set up its own propaganda department formed of individual units. It was agreed between the Ministry of Propaganda and the Wehrmacht that, at the request of the Wehrmacht, the Ministry would provide propaganda material, and that each commander should be responsible for the morale (*Geistige Betreuung*) of his troops. His responsibilities in this context were:

- Preparing the troops for the outbreak of the war
- The distribution of military and political news in the first days of the war
- Providing daily newspapers and later also military newspapers for the troops
- Monitoring radio listening
- Monitoring movies, field libraries and field theatre

In practice, despite honest efforts, commanders were often unable to manage all of these, and most did not wish to get involved in politics.

In spite of increasing pressure from the Ministry of Propaganda in the autumn of 1940, the Army's Chief of Staff, General Franz Halder, insisted that individual commanders should remain responsible for morale. However, there was an official list of subjects that they had to cover. This included the German people, the German Reich, living space for the German people, National Socialism and aspects of life under National Socialism. With this concession to the regime the Wehrmacht retained control over propaganda and the indoctrination of troops. An attempt in 1941 by Nazi ideologue Alfred Rosenberg to provide the Wehrmacht with literature, lectures and courses on National Socialism for officers was unsuccessful; but following the first major defeats suffered by the Wehrmacht, from the beginning of 1942, what were termed *Betreuungsoffiziere* (care officers) were appointed to battalions and larger formations. The resistance to these was great, and often the least competent officer was given the task; occasionally senior officers had to intervene to prevent Army chaplains from spreading Nazi ideology. (11:85–8)

A second attempt by Martin Bormann was more successful. In December 1943 Hitler signed a decree establishing the function of the *Nazionalsozialistische Führungsoffiziere* (NSFO), or instructors in national socialism. These were staff officers who assisted the commander in the area of *Geistige Betreuung* and who were, without exception, men who had distinguished themselves in battle. They were required to work through the hierarchy; rarely, and then only in the presence of the commander, were they allowed to address the troops themselves. It was not until the last stages of the war that these officers occupied their own place within the organizational chart and were allowed to approach the troops directly. In special training courses for the NSFOs, party officials emphasized patriotism, something that generally made for bad blood with soldiers who had already proven their patriotism many times over. This and other issues meant that the courses needed to be constantly adjusted.

Research after the war showed, without exception, that the majority of German troops were indifferent to these propaganda efforts. Only 5 per cent of prisoners of war indicated that they were more concerned about these matters than their personal problems; another study indicated that the proportion of 'fanatical' Nazis, 'apoliticals' and 'anti-Nazis' was distributed in accordance with the traditional model of Gaussian theory (the 'bell curve'). Approximately 11 per cent could be considered 'fanatic' Nazis, a percentage that tended to be higher among non-commissioned officers and considerably higher among junior officers. Another 11 per cent were fanatical opponents of the regime. The majority of the respondents, however, had no definite views. (11:88)

6.2 The British Army

What applied to the German Army will also have applied to the British, but preliminary analysis suggests that in their personal courage morale must often have been of decisive importance, as only this could have compensated for the weaknesses of the British Army, certainly in the first half of the Second World War. No matter how hopeless the situation, time and again the British avoided disaster through courage and dogged commitment. In addition, they had, and still have, a strong tendency to regard defeats (such as Dunkirk) as 'glorious failures', an attitude that still blurs their image of the Second World War. The phlegmatic way in which they handled setbacks and hardships was extremely significant, and the limited space given to the subject here is no reflection of its importance to the course of the struggle.

Poorly trained and poorly led, with often inferior equipment, troops chose for themselves and tried to run as little risk as possible, because they did not want to pay the price of all the failures on the Allied side. This explains why many Allied units were described by themselves as 'lacklustre'.

For example, during the first weeks after the Normandy landings, British and Canadian units often lacked the aggression to force a breakthrough and were satisfied with simply defending conquered territory. The veterans of the 7th Armoured Division knew their German opponents all too well, and its performance 'gave rise to the suspicion ... which hardened in the following weeks that ... [it] seriously lacked ... spirit and determination ... Many of its veterans ... had become wary and cunning in the reduction of risk, and lacked the tight discipline which was even more critical on the battlefield than off it.' We have already seen that during the Epsom operation to seize Caen the British infantry lapsed into 'old fashioned mass formations', and also that later offensives such as Goodwood and Totalise 'revealed a similar lack of aggressiveness'. Another important reason for this attitude may have been that their overwhelming superiority in weaponry gave the men the idea that no great efforts were required from them. (16:382) Halder, Chief of Staff of the Wehrmacht, stated after the war that the 'historical material superiority' provided by America made the Allies 'display a marked tendency to underestimate the importance of surprise, manoeuvre and improvisation'. (16:385) It simply meant that they were often insufficiently focused, even behind the front, whether in staff work or the role of the supporting units, and all of this contributed to the relatively low battlefield performance of the British Army.

6.3 The American Army

American soldiers often saw the war as a personal, individual fight: 'Soldiers also anticipated that the war they would control would be the war they desired, one of personalized, individualized combat. They spoke as if battles would be decided by hand-to-hand fighting.' (35:9) The bayonet was seen as the ultimate individual weapon. As army correspondent Ralph Ingersoll observed, 'Bayonet fighting was highly personal, the most intimate fighting in the war.' In reality, as in the First World War, when only 2.8 per cent of the injured had stab wounds from bayonets, there was very little bayonet fighting. This was partly because, once at the front, men realized how vulnerable they were and became totally unwilling 'to close in on the enemy at all costs' and settle things hand-to-hand. In Normandy, for example, Lieutenant George Wilson was threatened with being sent on a reconnaissance patrol with his company 'to engage the Germans in a fight, using trench knives, bayonets and grenades', a prospect that appealed to few of them. Wilson stated that only two bayonets and a single knife could be found in his entire company. His commander demanded an explanation and declared that he would undertake an inspection, but this proved unproductive. 'Wilson had been aware from the outset that hand-to-hand combat was about the last thing the men wanted to do.' (35:23) This was a widely held view among all the belligerents, despite the fact that such fighting still features prominently in war films.

We have already seen in previous chapters that the Americans displayed a confusing range of behaviours, caused by their typical view of training and leadership. The nonchalant attitudes of enlisted men, hanging out of cars and slouching on chairs and at tables, demonstrated both a physical and emotional distancing of themselves from the Army. Casual clothing and the 'forgotten' or sloppy salute are depicted as 'cool' trademarks of the Army, at least up to and including Vietnam, but in fact show a lack of discipline or interest and an attitude that 'this is not my organization'. The dialogue in war films tends to underline this, but is probably not totally realistic and does not reflect the situation as recorded at the time. Yet we have also seen that this behaviour was indicative of fragile morale and discipline.

Furthermore, and importantly, the war in Europe was not principally an American war, but a war between European states. This made the GI look down on Europeans, especially the French, who apparently had not been able, yet again in American eyes, to defend themselves. Their feelings cannot be more aptly expressed than in the words of an American soldier written on the wall of a fortress near Verdun:

Austin White, Chicago, Ill. 1918
Austin White, Chicago, Ill. 1945
This is the last time I want to write my name here (20:41)

The French, in turn, kept their distance, particularly because of the trail of devastation that accompanied the Allied 'liberation' of many parts of their country. Yet despite all the above, there was steadfastness and perseverance: the GI held his ground, and fought on.

CHAPTER SEVEN

The Reality of the Battlefield:
Overloon 1944[3]

This chapter was written by Major Ruud Veen (Chief Section Logistics, NLD, Groundbase Airdefence Command) and edited by Jaap Jan Brouwer

7.1 Introduction

In this chapter we will discuss a number of engagements that further illustrate the battlefield practice of both sides. They centre round the small southern Dutch town of Overloon, where in the aftermath of Operation Market Garden, between 30 September and 18 October 1944, heavy fighting took place between the German and Allied forces. Weather conditions

---

[3] This chapter is based on research in the following sources:
- *Actual Hoogtebestand Nederland* (2017), map of Overloon
- Boomer, *Terrein der opgravingen Overloon* (map of German war graves)
- Comité Shermantank Overloon (website) (2017), *De Slag om Overloon*
- Didden, J. et al (2016), *Kampfgruppe Walther and Panzerbrigade 107*, De Zwaardvisch
- Hagenaars, P.J.T.M., 'Geen einde zware wapens', in *Militaire Spectator*, July 2013
- Joint Doctrine Publicatie 5 Commandovoering, Ministry of Defence
- Korthals Altes, A., (2004), *Slag in de Schaduw*, Amsterdam, De Bataafse Leeuw
- Lind, William S. (1985), *Maneuver Warfare Handbook*, Westview Press
- Ministry of Defence, *Joint Doctrine Publicatie 5 Commandovoering*
- Official Military History of the Royal Ulster Rifles (2010), *12 to 13 October – Overloon*
- US Army, *After Action Reports of the Headquarters 7th Armored Division Period 1–31* October 1944 (607-CCA-0.1 to 607-CCA-0.7)
- Zucchino, D. (2004), *Thunder Run: The Armored Strike to Capture Baghdad*, New York, Grove/Atlantic Corporation
- Go2War2 (website) (2017), *Slag om Overloon en Venray, 30 September – 7 Oktober 1944*

were far from ideal during this period: cold, rain and wind made combat difficult. In the area between Boxmeer and Venlo west of the Meuse, called 'Brückenkopf Venlo' by the Germans, were a number of German units, whose purpose was to carry out attacks on Allied forces and to protect the Meuse crossings. Because Overloon and its surroundings were easily defensible, the Germans chose this as their northernmost defensive line. For their part, the Allies had every intention of clearing German resistance west of the Meuse, because forces there threatened the flanks of a future Allied offensive into Germany. The British 8th Army Corps, with the 11th Armoured Division and the 3rd Infantry Division, had made the closest approach to this bridgehead, but needed to rest. In addition, Montgomery wanted to spare them for the invasion of Germany itself. For this reason, the American 7th Armored Division was transferred from Northern France to the Sint Anthonis/ Boxmeer region at high speed to get the job done.

The core of the German force was the *Kampfgruppe* Walther, named after their commander, Paratroop Colonel Erich Walther. This *Kampfgruppe* comprised, among other units, a few Fallschirmjäger (paratroop) battalions operating as infantry. Additionally, the Panzerbrigade (PzBrig) 107 was stationed in the area with its Panther tanks and Panzerjäger IVs, as was a Panzergrenadiere battalion with armoured halftracks. There were also SS units active in the area, with a Panzerjäger (tank hunter) Battalion and a Panzergrenadiere Battalion. This list of units is misleading, however, as they were all far below their nominal complement, just as at Arnhem, and made up of a mix of experienced men and raw recruits; also, the armoured units had little more than ten tanks, which would only be sparingly used. However, as at Arnhem, despite the size and composition of these units, their superior leadership and training made them formidable opponents. In the coming weeks they would face an enemy many times stronger, yet they succeeded in delaying and partially halting the Allied offensive in this area for six months: Venlo, the gateway to Germany, would not be conquered until March 1 1945.

Immediately apparent in the cases we are going to deal with are the inaccurate assessments, poor tactics and slow reactions of the Allies. The Americans had been fighting the Germans for more than two years, and the British for almost five years now. Yet the Allies still appeared to be ignorant of many basic German tactics. On the German side, by contrast, we can observe a range of defensive tactics performed in flawless coordination by the various units involved. The Allies must have been acquainted with

German defensive tactics from their experiences in Tunisia, Italy and Normandy, and during their advance into the Low Countries, but they appear to have failed to learn any lessons as a result.

The Allies' story is always the same: 'fierce' resistance and German units fighting 'fanatically', with the Allies only pushing through 'against all the odds'. The reality, however, was that the German Army was the superior organization, with a well-trained officer corps and tried and tested tactics that were continuously updated and adapted to changing circumstances. In fact, the poor performance of the Allies themselves represented the 'odds' against which they fought. In the cases we examine, the Germans always enjoyed higher relative battlefield performance. The following actions will be described:

- 30 September: from 'Thunder Run' to 'Blood Run'
- 4 October: Flak against Sherman tanks
- 12 October: the rolling barrage
- 14 October: the choreography of the fight
- 16 October: the crossing of the Loobeek

We should always keep in mind the formula, Impact = Exploration × Preparation × Focus × Cooperation × Speed × Mass × Continuation. The organization that controls this best will always have the advantage.

7.2 30 September 1944: from 'Thunder Run' to 'Blood Run'

The leading actor on this day was the US 7th Armored Division. This, like all US tank divisions, consisted of three Combat Commands, namely A, B and R (Reserve). On 30 September 1944, Combat Commands A and B advanced towards Overloon. Their goal was to take the town and then to advance to Venray and Venlo. The plan was for a surprise attack executed with great speed in the form of a 'thunder run', a left-and-right-firing armoured column aimed at penetrating deep into enemy territory. This was exactly the type of action at which German armoured units excelled, but which the Americans had only attempted in situations without serious opposition. The attack of Combat Command A (CCA) on Overloon would be carried out from Oploo by two battle groups, Task Force Chappuis and Task Force Brown. Task Force Johansen of Combat Command B would support this thrust by attacking the forest complex north of Overloon from Sint Anthonis via Stevensbeek.

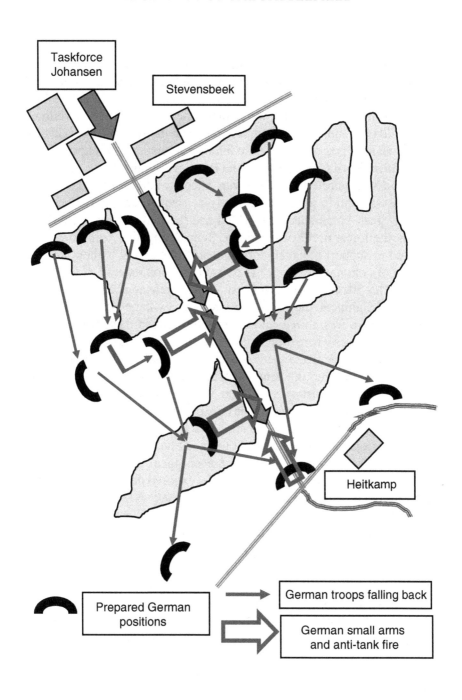

Taskforce
Johansen

Stevensbeek

Heitkamp

Prepared German
positions

German troops falling back

German small arms
and anti-tank fire

The order of battle of Combat Command A on the one hand and Task Force Johansen of Combat Command B on the other was remarkable. CCA would advance over open terrain which presented an ample field of fire and, in principle, required more tanks and fewer infantry; Task Force Johansen, meanwhile, would attack the woods north of Overloon, but would need more infantry, in order to clear the forest. However, Task Force Johansen possessed only two infantry companies, perhaps because the commander of Combat Command B believed opposition in the forest would be weak, since the 'thunder run' attack would be a 'walkover'.

This assumption would have costly consequences, particular if we consider Task Force Johansen, which had the more ambitious task, to occupy the forest north of Overloon. Remarkably, this Task Force was required to support the attack of Combat Command A without making the line of command explicit. As a result, the commander of CCB had to divide his attention between a task immediately adjacent to CCA and his other assignment, the conquest of Vortem, a village 5km further east. However, there was no logical relationship between these two tasks, so that, as in all cases where the attention of a commander is divided between two unrelated objectives, there was a diminution of combat power. In addition, not only did the Americans underestimate the strength of the expected German resistance, but there were other factors preventing the Americans from taking Venlo in one or two days as planned. For example, there were few good roads in the area, a factor whose consequences had not been recognized, with the result that the Sherman tanks were forced to drive on the road in a column to prevent them from getting bogged down in the swampy ground on either side; exposed in this way, they were particularly vulnerable to German anti-tank units.

The bad weather that autumn not only caused problems on the ground, but also made air support less effective; indeed, it was sometimes absent completely. Moreover, there were large areas of woodland to the north and south of Overloon that made it easy for the Germans to manoeuvre, unseen from the air, and set up their positions. The estimates of German forces were also based on regular reports from British reconnaissance units that emphasized the enemy's numerical weakness, but without taking into account his professionalism. Reconnaissance, if carried out at all, was often superficial and overlooked much that was camouflaged. The American 7th US Armored Division, in turn, had little experience of 'heavy' fighting and was therefore probably unaware of the importance of reconnaissance; part of its own reconnaissance had been detached for the follow-up task of the division in the Deurne area.

Stuck in the mud

The weather was bad during the Battle of Overloon. Persistent rain had soaked ground that was saturated with water and had lost its structure. The terrain had turned into a series of swampy fields, where off-road movement was difficult. Many roads around Overloon were still unpaved, and the movement of many vehicles, especially tracked ones, left deep furrows and turned them into channels of mud. Driving over this swampy terrain in tanks caused many problems. The front tank of a column usually still had a reasonable road or undisturbed ground in front of it, but the following tanks often got stuck, and their attempts to extricate themselves then completely destroyed the going. Tanks became immobile, sometimes with their bottom plate stuck to the ground. On narrow roads, in a passage (parade) or at river crossings, the mud posed particular problems, because it was precisely in those places that concentrated movements of vehicles were necessary.

While the Allies' major advantages (mass mechanized operations and mobility) were often decisive, these were lost in the battles around Overloon, because the weather restricted movement on the ground so severely. The Germans seized the advantage, since tanks were forced to stick to the road, where they were vulnerable, or leave it and get stuck. As so often, the Americans and British did not really have an answer to this, addicted as they were to mass mechanization.

On 30 September, following its agreed plan, Task Force Johansen advanced in a column on the road from Stevensbeek to Overloon, supported by the infantry in halftracks in front and behind. However, this formation complicated the way in which tanks were supposed to support infantry, and vice versa. If the German defenders opened fire, it would only be possible to cooperate effectively after the infantry had sought cover and the tanks had been brought in, a cumbersome procedure that wasted a lot of time. This was exactly what the defenders wanted. Unknown to the Americans, the Germans had prepared good defensive positions along the access road, on the road through the forest and in the depths of the forest itself. They also kept a close watch on the movements of American troops, thus removing any element of surprise from the attack. The German defenders even carried out a short but fierce preventative attack of their own with artillery and a tank immediately prior to the American advance. Still the Americans failed to investigate the location and character of these units. The Germans planned to delay the Americans by opening fire at a great distance the moment they started their advance from Stevensbeek, thus forcing the attackers to spread out and slow down. The swampy ground would force any advancing American halftrack and tanks to use the road, where they could be fired on at short range from strong positions on both sides of the road. Additional guns covered full length of the road, with the aim of making it impossible to mount an attack on the German positions. In the depths of the forest, defensive positions had been set up and paths were mined, keeping the American infantry busy for a long time.

As a result, events unfolded entirely in accordance with the German plan from the very start of the American advance. The German defenders immediately opened fire with a PzJgr IV Jagdpanther (tank destroyer) at a great distance, and the attack ran into the ground even before the advance units had left Stevensbeek. The American infantry then climbed out of their halftracks and spread out to confront the German infantry. After offering initial opposition, the defenders left their lines on the northern edge of the forest in an orderly way: the weapons with the longest range were the last to leave. These guns had kept the attackers at bay for so long that the infantry, while still controlling the fighting, managed to detach themselves and fall back to positions further south in the forest. The defenders had prepared many positions, and by repeatedly falling back to these they were able not only to give depth to the defence, but to secure their flanks by allowing units to switch from left to right, and vice versa.

After penetrating the edge of the forest, the Americans then tried to break through the German lines with tanks and halftracks via the north-south roads. They only just made it to the southern edge of the edge of the forest, fired at from all sides and leaving behind burning wrecks and dead and wounded men, then finally managed to reach the area of the hamlet of Heikant, north-east of Overloon, where the remnants of Task Force Johansen were decisively halted by German anti-tank guns, thus ending the attack. They were still 2km from Overloon and 10km from Venray, and it was only two days later that the forest was finally taken by the American infantry, thanks to the massive deployment of tanks and artillery.

The reality of battle in the east

The Second World War was decided in the east, where the biggest and bloodiest confrontations took place. There the Germans also learned much more than in the west, where their Allied opponents displayed considerably less determination than the Soviets, who were fighting to defend their homeland.

In theory, both German and Soviet attacks were carefully planned actions, with infantry, tanks, artillery and engineers working closely together. In reality, only the Germans were able to carry out attacks with the necessary coordination; Soviet attacks were generally poorly executed. One reason was that the best qualified personnel in the Red Army were with the tanks, artillery and engineers. The infantry, which bore the brunt of attacks, was of poorer quality. The Soviet artillery could be effective but was inefficiently managed; their engineers were good, especially at clearing minefields; and the Soviet tank forces were excellent, partly due to the superior quality of Soviet tanks.

While the Germans had a balanced and proven offensive doctrine, the Soviets had to build theirs from scratch after 1941. The Germans, however, lacked as good a defensive approach. The main purpose of Soviet offensives, particularly towards the end of the war, was to punch a hole in German defensive positions at all costs through which their motorized units could advance. It was the Soviet artillery that had to create this hole, since the infantry was not able to break through on its own. German defence was too flexible, and the coordination of German artillery and infantry was too good. A typical Soviet offensive was announced by increased patrolling in the weeks prior to the attack. About three days before the offensive, the artillery moved into position and started test firing.

The attack itself often began with the well-known 'artillery offensive' that lasted two to three hours. Then the artillery shifted its fire to positions further behind the front line to support its own infantry. The Germans, who had entrenched themselves in fortified positions, generally survived such a bombardment, thus forcing the Soviets to use tanks in addition to infantry to force a breakthrough. After breaking the first line, however, the battle was not yet over: the Germans often built defensive lines with a depth of 6–8km. This meant tanks had to be used, because by the time the Soviets broke through they were out of the range of their own artillery. In addition, the Germans constructed extensive anti-tank and anti-personnel minefields throughout their defences and around their artillery positions, and the Russians therefore had to deploy engineers.

This all put severe demands on the coordination capabilities of the Soviets, which were not that well developed. One particular phenomenon that the Soviets had to take into account was the German machine gun nests. One well-placed machine gun, provided it was well protected, with a good field of fire (a special point of attention) and sufficient ammunition, could halt the Soviet infantry over a 1km front for a long period. The Germans could dispose of thirty-two to sixty-five machine guns per kilometre of front, so machine guns that survived the artillery bombardment could stop a Soviet offensive over a wide front for hours. Tanks or mechanized guns from the rear had to destroy these areas of resistance as quickly as possible.

On the other hand, the anti-tank guns were relatively vulnerable to artillery fire. The Germans had three to six anti-tank guns per kilometre of front, in addition to ten to twenty Panzerfausts. One anti-tank gun was able to take out three tanks on average before it was destroyed; a Panzerfaust could account for one tank. The anti-tank guns, however, were difficult to protect against the destructive power of the artillery bombardment and many of them could be eliminated before the battle actually began.

In comparison to these battles on the Eastern Front, the fighting at Overloon was little more than a skirmish. If instead of the 7th Armored Division a Soviet tank division with T-34s had been the opponent, the outcome could have been very different.

7.3 4 October 1944: Flak[4] against Sherman tanks

After these encounters, the battle for Overloon continued on 4 October. The central factors in this episode of the battle were a 'defile' (a narrow passage), a column of Sherman tanks and a unit of German Flak 88 guns, the last being a deadly weapon when used against Shermans.

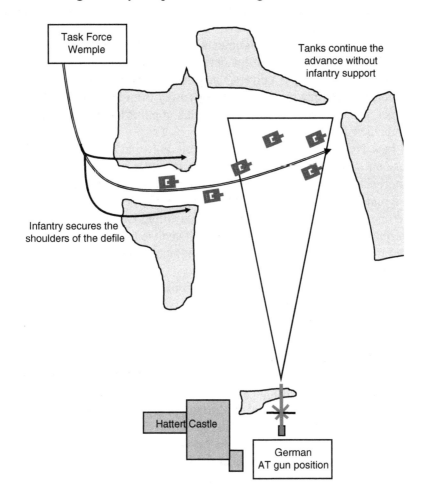

---

[4] There is no hard evidence that the guns fired at Wemple's tanks were Flak. Naturally, there was anti-tank fire, but the German unit near the Hattert was Luftwaffe-Festungs-Bataillon X, which makes one inclined to assume that these were the dreaded 88mm guns.

On 4 October, the wooded area north of Overloon and the forest complex west of Vierlingsbeek were the prime targets of the Combat Command Reserve (CCR) of the 7th US Armored Division, comprising Task Force Wemple and Task Force Fuller. The assignment of Task Force Wemple was to take the forest complex near Vierlingsbeek with tanks, while the infantry of Taskforce Fuller was assigned to support the attack on Overloon by Task Force Brown of Combat Command A; the two Task Forces thus had different assignments and were operating 3km apart. As a result, the CCR had to coordinate two totally different attacks: the main assault on Overloon and a diversionary thrust towards Vierlingsbeek with the objective of drawing German troops away from Overloon to the east. In fact, the Germans totally ignored this attempt by the Americans to divide their forces.

Task Force Wemple was a formidable unit that could even call for close air support (CAS) – a very powerful but rare asset, even for the Americans, its availability underscoring the importance of Wemple's assignment. Wemple comprised three companies, two of Sherman tanks and one of infantry. According to the prevailing American doctrine, the Sherman was used generally as a support vehicle for infantry, in this case in a ratio of two tank companies to one infantry company, with the tanks up front.

Task Force Wemple planned to exploit the element of surprise in their attack on the forest by focusing on the German flanks. However, the Task Force had to negotiate a narrow defile before they could reach their ultimate goal, and this forced them to advance more or less in columns. In such a formation, a force is unable to fully develop its combat power; and in order to avoid an enemy ambush, it is necessary to hold the shoulders of the defile. Passing through a defile without having checked whether its mouth is vulnerable to enemy gunfire is a perilous undertaking.

In this particular case, the defile passed through the forest to the north of Kasteel (Castle) De Hattert, with the shoulders of the defile both north and south in the shape of an open field at the edge of the forest which the attacking force had to cross to attain their ultimate goal, the wooded area west of Vierlingbeek. If the Americans had bothered to reconnoitre, they could have seen that on the southern shoulder of the defile, near the Castle, the Luftwaffe-Festungs-Battaillon X had set up a position with two Flak 88 guns. Although the Battalion was an anti-aircraft unit without combat experience in the field, it had been stiffened by the addition of troops with front-line experience. The Flak 88 was, as its full name *Fliegerabwehrkanone* (anti-aircraft cannon) indicates, developed for use against planes, but proved during the Second World War to be a flexible and very much feared anti-tank weapon. It was, for example, the main armament of the Tiger tank.

The position chosen by the Luftwaffe battalion provided good cover and camouflage. In addition, it offered an open field of fire towards the north-east over flat terrain to the railway line and the Kiekuutweg (road) that runs alongside it, and to the area west of De Hattert. With a rise of just 3m over a slope of 1.5km from east to west, the set-up was chosen perfectly, since targets would stand out in silhouette against the horizon: in short, it was an ideal position for anti-tank guns, particularly since the Flak 88 gun had no problem in piercing the armour of a Sherman tank 2km away.

A number of issues on the American side are immediately apparent. The terrain had not been explored at all, while the ratio of two tank companies to one infantry company seems unbalanced. Moreover, the infantry was given the task of clearing the forest on both sides of the defile, an intensive and time-consuming task for just one company. This curious mix of units had already been apparent on 30 September, even though the same infantry company had then to be deployed for the attack on the ultimate goal. The Americans still did not seem to realize how essential it is to gain control over the areas surrounding open ground.

In good spirits, Task Force Wemple, with its two companies of Shermans (thirty-six tanks) and its infantry company, moved forward in one column towards their goal. Suspecting nothing, the first tank company negotiated the narrow passage through the forest and reached the beginning of the open ground. The Germans let the first group of tanks roll out of the forest, allowing the Americans to occupy all the space, because they did not yet know the exact object of the American attack or where the Flak guns would be most effective. Once the Americans reached that position, however, the tanks were fired on one by one. The Americans were completely overwhelmed; the crews had no idea who had fired at them or where the shots came from. Also they could expect no support from the infantry, who were still busy clearing the forest. Soon five of the first company's eighteen tanks were destroyed and three damaged; two hours later, thirteen more had been destroyed by the anti-tank guns on the southern shoulder. Task Force Wemple had no choice but to retreat, in order to avoid even worse losses.

As an encore, the American Air Force bombed Kasteel De Hattert less than half an hour later, causing a few German casualties; but air support could only be deployed after a reconnaissance plane had marked the target with red smoke for the Allied artillery, a cumbersome American procedure and something that could be achieved more easily, faster and more effectively by tactical air controllers, as used by the British since the Normandy landings.

After this debacle, the morale of the American 'Lucky' 7th Armored Division was broken, and the unit was taken out of the front in the days that followed, leaving no fewer than thirty-five tanks and forty-three other vehicles on the battlefield, as well as losing well over 400 men. The British took over but were given no useful intelligence, so they in turn would go into battle unprepared.

On reflection and by way of summary, this operation revealed poor planning and execution on the American side: the strange ratio of tanks to infantry, the lack of reconnaissance, the failure to capture the shoulders at the end of the defile, and the tanks losing contact with the infantry. Conversely, on the German side, there was a skilful arrangement of gun emplacements, deployed at the right time in the right way, which halted the American attack. Moreover, the inexperienced crew of both Flak guns achieved an unprecedented feat in their first deployment under fire, thanks undoubtedly to the experienced troops supporting them. This was a good example of the flexibility in thought and action of German units, and a remarkable display of sangfroid by the Luftwaffe-Festungs-Bataillon X in particular.

7.4 12 October 1944: rolling fire or 'creeping barrage'

On 7 October the 7th Armored Division was replaced by the British Guards Armoured Division and the 3rd Infantry Division, supported by two battalions of Churchill tanks of the Coldstream Guards. On paper this was a formidable fighting force of almost 25,000 troops, facing German units that could field just 4,000 men, including elements of the PzBrig 107.[5] On 12 October the first attack took place, heralded by a classic artillery bombardment of Overloon and the surrounding area at 1100 hrs. Three

---

[5] PzBrig 107 could field seventeen Panther tanks and four Panzerjäger IV tank destroyers.

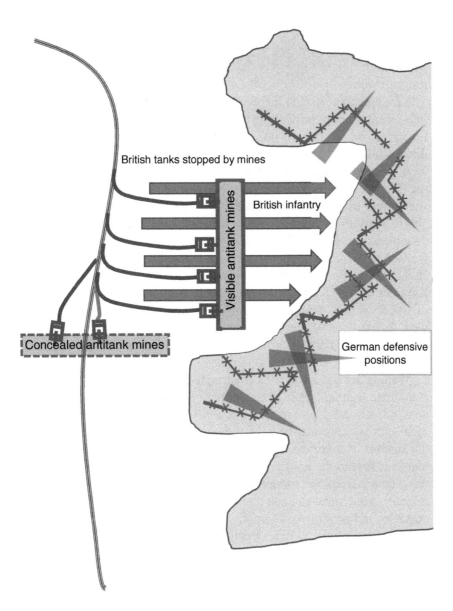

British tanks stopped by mines

British infantry

Visible antitank mines

Concealed antitank mines

German defensive positions

battalions of the 8th Brigade of the 3rd Infantry Division were involved in the attack, one west of Overloon, one to the east and one aimed directly at the town. Ninety-two pieces of heavy and medium-heavy artillery opened fire, and at 1130 hrs this barrage was joined by 216 pieces of 25-pound

193

field artillery, effectively razing Overloon to the ground. At noon a rolling fire, or 'creeping barrage', an important aspect of the Brigade's attack plan and designed to protect the advancing British infantry, started to move forward.

This creeping barrage involved the artillery firing at the German front line and gradually advancing the range according to a predetermined timetable, in this case 100m every five minutes. This rolling fire was directly followed by two of the three infantry battalions: the Suffolks to the west of Overloon and the East Yorks to the east, supported by tanks from the Coldstream Guards. During the bombardment no fewer than 100,000 shells were fired, a good example of the brute force that the Allies were able to apply and leading to great destruction and large numbers of civilian casualties. The East Yorks had to attack the forest complex defended by the Germans, their first goal being the woodland between Hazenbroek and Heikant, directly north of Overloon. After taking this area, the infantry had to cross the Overloon–Vierlingsbeek road to take their assigned part of Overloon and, having eliminated or expelled the German defenders, were then to consolidate in the forest south of that road.

With these goals in mind, C and D companies of the East Yorks advanced.

Waiting for them was a Fallschirmjäger (paratroop) Battalion led by Hauptman (Captain) Paul, who had been preparing for the defence of the area over several days. His unit was a mix of veterans and inexperienced men with predominantly light weapons, although he could count on the support of a number of Panther tanks from Panzerbrigade 107. His plan was first to disrupt the cohesion of the British attack by separating the infantry from the supporting tanks; then to wear down the British infantry in the forest and halt their advance with a combination of various obstacles and gunfire. An additional advantage was that rain had saturated the ground, forcing the British tanks to stay on the small number of dirt roads in the area. Moreover, the British artillery was of little use in the forest, so the infantry had to fight it out themselves.

Initially, the attack went well, as the rolling fire suppressed much of the German resistance. But what the British did not know, having failed to reconnoitre the area, was that the Germans had mined the roads; consequently, the first tanks drove unsuspectingly over anti-tank mines, and this forced those following to forsake the road for the fields; all this was in line with the Paul's plan. To add to the confusion, the tanks were then engaged by German artillery fire, and some which had left the road triggered anti-tank mines laid a few metres to the side which were invisible to tank crews inside their vehicles. Some tanks were damaged by exploding mines; others which slowed down and avoided the mines then stopped and were promptly targeted by Panzerfausts. The infantry, however, kept moving forward under the pressure of the German artillery, because stopping in the open was not an option in the middle of battle. To make matters worse, the British were also fired at by flat-track artillery just before they reached the edge of the forest. In other words, the obstacles that Hauptman Paul had planned were completely effective. Neither tanks nor artillery could support the infantry in the forest, so they had to fight a well-prepared opponent on their own. Paul's tactics had made the forest easier to defend by ensuring the attackers could not operate as an integrated unit. The obstacles were like fangs, wide at the base and sharp at the end, while machine guns covered their entire length, with the ends under fire and mined. The defences ran deep into the forest. The British attack quickly lost its momentum, and the German defenders gained full control of the battle. If the attackers did achieve success in any sector, the defenders simply fell back on positions deeper in the forest, and the advance had to start all over again.

The battalion headquarters of the East Yorks soon lost an overview of the action, which had broken down into a series of small attacks by individual groups. As the battle stagnated, the British commander was forced to deploy his reserve, the A and B companies. While D company of the East Yorks became stuck in the west of the forest, A and C companies eventually reached the Overloon–Vierlingsbeek road, and B company even managed to reach Overloon. But at dusk the attack finally bled to death over the full width of the Brigade's front, still 1km short of its intended target.

On reflection, this British attack was more effective than the American one of the week before. The British, of course, deployed an extra infantry company to clear the forest, but only half the number of tanks. The main difference was in the width of the front: the British front was 2km wide, the Americans' over 8km, so the British could deploy a more concentrated force. The rolling barrage certainly contributed to the initial success of the attack and forced the Germans to leave their positions. However, the defenders successfully targeted the attackers before they could reach the edges of the forest and also managed to separate tanks and infantry so that the latter had to fight it out on their own in the forest. The Germans' approach in the forest was a showcase of defensive tactics. The enormous superiority of Allied firepower ultimately did not produce the result the British had hoped for, and the Germans were able to achieve a great deal with the limited means available to them. But more importantly, although the defenders suffered serious losses, particularly from the rolling barrage, they still managed to retreat in an orderly fashion to positions in the forest to the south of Overloon and fight another day; it was thus by no means a total defeat.

7.5 14 October: the choreography of the battle

The British goal on 14 October was to eliminate the German units on the north bank of the Loobeek river south of Overloon, then to cross the Loobeek and advance towards Venray in the south. This task was given to a battalion of the Royal Norfolk Regiment and one of the Warwickshire Regiment. We shall focus on the Norfolks. The plan of the battalion commander, Lieutenant Colonel Bellamy, was to move south along the Overloon–Venray road with two companies, supported by tanks in the lead and followed by his two other companies, to force a crossing over the Loobeek. His units had to cover a distance of 1,500m across open ground between the forest, which was their starting point, and the river. Bellamy's opponent, once again Hauptman Paul, decided he would open fire on the attackers the moment they left the forest and thus force them to spread out. His plan was then to disrupt the attack by separating the tanks and the infantry with the deployment of anti-personnel mines, a similar tactic to that of 5 October. This would present his opponents with a number of dilemmas, which were intended to paralyze their decision-making. It would slow down their advance, and that was important because Paul wanted to stop them before his men became tied down in close combat, whereupon the British would make it difficult for them to fall back on new positions further south. His intention was to detach his unit from the British after the attack was brought to a standstill, then to cross the Loobeek and hand over the fight to the unit behind him, Panzerbrigade 107. The British did exactly what Hauptman Paul had expected; indeed, the action became a textbook example of how to deal with such a scenario.

The Norfolks and the tanks of 1st Squadron Coldstream Guards left the forest edge at noon and advanced across the open ground. As soon as the German machine guns opened up, the units spread out, the infantry lining up between the tanks and all advancing together to attack. After

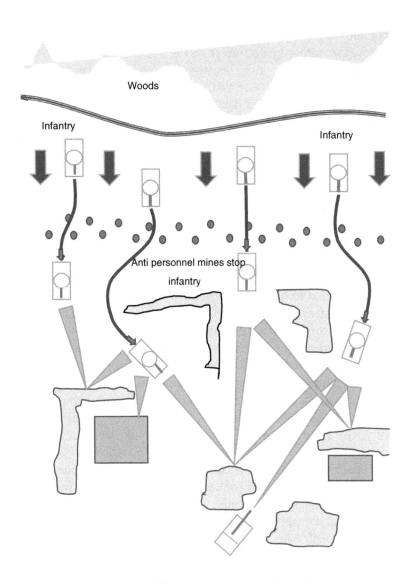

they passed a road and a line of trees, explosions began to erupt and it quickly became clear that they had entered an unexpected – because unexplored – anti-personnel minefield. The infantry stopped immediately and tried to find cover in the flat and open terrain, before beginning cautiously to work their way forward. Their dilemma was that if they wanted to reach the enemy positions they had to penetrate deeper and deeper into the minefield, but the presence of mines left them insufficient space to set up a coordinated attack on the enemy machine guns. Staying in the open was not an option, because the area was covered by machine guns and offered no cover. Behind the infantry, more explosions suddenly sounded: German mortar fire! The fire came closer and forced the infantry further into the minefield; shells were dropping between the front and the rear companies. Combining the front and the rear companies to gain fire superiority and move forward jointly – necessary if the attack was to continue successfully – was impossible, because the rear companies had to get through both the mortar fire and the minefield. Withdrawing was not an option for the front companies either, because they would have to traverse the same mortar fire, and then the attack would surely fail. In other words, the British infantry was in a hopeless position.

The tanks had not noticed this and had rumbled on, consequently becoming separated from the infantry. They attacked the first German line and managed to break through. Then, without the protection of the infantry, they drove further south into enemy territory. They had little choice but to carry on, because now they were fired on by Panther tanks and mechanized guns from Panzerbrigade 107, who had taken up positions at some distance. Hedges and farms seemed to offer some cover, and the British tanks, under fire, sped towards them. Only when they arrived did their commander realize that the infantry had been left behind and they were alone! The tanks were promptly attacked at short range by German infantry with Panzerfausts. One after another, tanks went up in flames or drove over mines.

The attack was therefore halted before the Loobeek, and the defenders detached themselves and fell back to the south bank of the river, handing over to Panzerbrigade 107. In order to cover the retreat of Fallschirmjäger Battaillon Paul, Panzerbrigade 107 had positioned tanks and mechanized guns on the north bank; it was these that had just fired at the British tanks. They took over the defence and, as soon as Bataillon Paul had left, gradually retreated across the river. In this way, Bataillon Paul could safely disengage from the British attackers – albeit not without losses – fall back behind the Loobeek and recuperate. The British sustained eighty casualties that day, including five company commanders, on what turned out to be the fiercest day of fighting in the battle for Overloon; they had advanced just 1km on a front 500m wide, and had not yet succeeded in crossing the Loobeek.

On reflection, this was a remarkable achievement by the Germans: a complicated choreography of *Verbundene Waffen* inflicting heavy losses on the enemy. In the two days since the previous engagement, the Germans had managed to regroup, prepare defensive positions and coordinate activities. The cooperation between the Fallschirmjäger and Panzerbrigade 107 worked smoothly. The British fell into all Paul's traps, infantry and tanks were again separated from each other and both suffered heavy losses. That is the price you pay for predictable behaviour when facing an opponent who has the imagination to turn it against you.

7.6 16 October: crossing the Loobeek

The Loobeek had still not been crossed, and the plan of attack for 16 October had to address this. The task was assigned to the British 8th and the 185th Infantry Brigades. On 16 October at 0400 hrs, units of the Norfolks and the Warwicks of the 185th Brigade were to quietly cross the Loobeek with kapok pontoons to create two bridgeheads on the south bank in preparation for the transition of the rest of the Brigade. Two bridge-laying tanks of the Coldstream Guards would then cross to these bridgeheads, followed by the infantry and then the other tanks. At the break of dawn, a full attack would be launched from the south bank. This was a remarkable choice when one considers that the starting point had not yet been taken from the enemy – an absolute precondition for a successful attack! The infantry of the 8th Brigade led the attack at dawn, advancing from the forest to the river with a battalion of Suffolks in front. As soon as that battalion had crossed the Loobeek, the plan was for the East Yorks battalion to follow. The supporting tanks then would cross the Loobeek on fascines (bundles of rods or branches). The ultimate goal of the attack, however, was not just to cross the river but to advance on and take Venray.

On the German side, Alarm Bataillon Krüger was responsible for defence. They had positioned themselves along the Loobeek, behind flooded areas and anti-personnel mines, virtually on the starting line of the British attack! Their task was to prevent the British crossing the Loobeek, by carrying out counter-attacks if necessary. If the pressure became too great, they would hand over to the unit in the second line of defence, Fallschirmjäger Bataillon Löytved-Hardegg, and then act as a reserve. It says everything about the place where the Germans expected the attack to come that they had chosen this sort of defence in depth. Their position

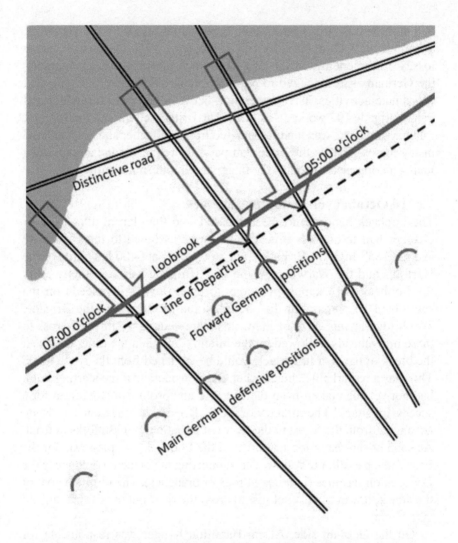

was divided into two: on the left was Fallschirmjäger Bataillon Kerutt, on the right, Fallschirmjäger Batailllon Löytved-Hardegg. In support were mechanized guns and tanks from Panzerbrigade 107.

The Germans had organized their defence along classic lines. They had flooded the area so that the Loobeek was now rather more than 6m wide. This forced the attackers to keep to the drier parts, such as dikes and paved roads. It will come as no surprise that these were covered by German guns. As experienced defenders, they had of course blown the bridges and laid anti-tank mines on the roads. An alternative for the British was to advance over the terrain between the existing roads, but because of the poor condition of the ground, such an attack would soon lose momentum: tanks would get stuck in the mud and the infantry would have to advance on foot across ground saturated with anti-personnel mines – some had even been laid in the bed of the Loobeek itself. Moreover, forcing the attackers to advance on foot was exactly what the defenders wanted, because the former were limited in mobility by the lack of (mechanized) transport. By slowing the attack down, the defenders were able to determine the pace of the action and leave the Loobeek in an orderly and controlled fashion if under excessive pressure, handing over to the units of the second line. Then they could be deployed as a reserve whenever or wherever required. In this way, the defenders would retain the initiative.

On Monday morning, 16 October, the attack began with the crossing of the Loobeek, now widened due to heavy rainfall as well as flooding by the Germans. The Norfolks moved up the main road from Overloon to Venray, the Warwicks battalion followed the secondary road west of it. Between 0400 and 0500 hrs, the Norfolk and the Warwicks were the first to cross the Loobeek using the kapok pontoons. Although one company of the Norfolks had come through a minefield, it had not suffered any losses. The tanks of the Coldstream Guards would have to follow the infantry as soon as the latter had crossed, but the tanks got stuck in the mud, as was to be expected. After a smokescreen was laid over the road and the river, a Churchill bridge-laying tank moved forward and spanned the stream. The moment the tank started crossing its newly laid bridge it became unstable, and the whole thing tilted. Consequently, crossing at this location became impossible, and the Norfolk battalion on the other bank could no longer count on support by tanks.

Half a kilometre to the west, near the Warwicks battalion, that bridge also threatened to slide away, but logs were inserted to prevent this happening. Because of the commotion, the Warwicks had given away any element of surprise and came under fire from Germans machine guns and anti-tank weapons. The Germans were even cheeky enough to mount a counter-attack, despite their numerical inferiority! At around 0900 hrs (more than three hours late) the first British tank rolled over the bridge. This crossing was also very difficult, because the tanks became stuck in the mud on the far bank and came under constant German fire. In pouring rain the Norfolk and the Warwicks pushed on towards Venray, advancing thanks to artillery support, in spite of heavy counter-fire. Gradually more Churchill tanks crossed the stream, and eventually the British battalions managed to force Alarm Bataillon Krüger to retreat.

Further west, the British also faced difficulties. According to their plan, the Suffolks were not to cross the Loobeek until 0700 hrs, but because Fallschirmjäger Bataillon Kerutt had been alerted by the fighting to the east, the Suffolks had to cross under murderous machine gun fire. To seek cover, the British troops jumped into the ice-cold water of the Loobeek, a disastrous move because of the mines laid there. It was not until 1000 hrs that the British succeeded in getting the rest of the battalion across. Here, too, the Churchills of the Grenadier Guards had got stuck in the mud before they even reached the Loobeek. Filling the stream with fascines failed, so a bridge-laying tank was called up and arrived that afternoon. As the Suffolks stumbled on, the East Yorks arrived behind them at the river. Waiting for the bridge-laying tank, they took cover. At 1500 hrs the bridge was finally laid. The problems for the Grenadier Guards, however, were not over yet. The first three Churchills crossed the bridge but got stuck in the mud on the other bank. The tanks, however, could still give supporting fire to the advancing infantry, and by evening the Suffolks had taken the hamlet of Hiept, 1km west of Venray. In the dark the East Yorks crossed the Loobeek and dug in to the left of the Suffolks. There were now four British battalions in a semicircle around Venray. The next day, the battle for Venray began. On 17 October, the first asault failed, and only after the arrival of fresh troops could Venray could be taken, on 18 October.

There are a number of observations to make about this attack. In the first place, it is remarkable that it began when the starting line was not in British hands; secondly, the brigades started their attacks at different times, thereby giving away the element of surprise and losing cohesion. The location of the British attack was exactly where the Germans had expected it. It looks as if the British had underestimated both the difficulty of crossing the Loobeek and the Germans' defensive qualities. Crossing the stream only served to get the British units to their starting line; they seem not to have expected to have to fight their way across. Crossing any river is quite a complex operation, let alone under enemy fire. In addition, the British let themselves be forced to use the roads, thus heading straight at the German defensive positions and losing any opportunity to attack from the flank – a potentially successful tactic given the relative weakness of the German force. The position of the Warwicks was so vulnerable that the defenders even dared to launch a counter-attack. Generally speaking, the British troops were deployed piecemeal, making it possible for the weaker German defensive force to slow down the attack, retreat in an orderly and controlled way and transfer the fight to the second line of defence. In the end, British artillery was needed – again – to force a breakthrough.

Once again, the German defenders showed great professionalism. They stuck closely to the Loobeek as a first line of defence and created defence in depth by using two lines: Alarm Batailllon Krüger up front and Fallschirmjäger Batailllon Löytved-Hardegg as a second line. German fighting strength remained intact, and they even forced the British to deploy fresh troops two days later in the battle for Venray. It shows that the Germans had used the days before the attack to explore the terrain, use all its possibilities and prepare a defence in depth.

7.7 Evaluation

The course of the fighting around Overloon clearly shows the Allies making many mistakes and neglecting the formula Impact = Exploration x Preparation x Focus x Cooperation x Speed x Mass x Continuation. Any coherence between the elements of the formula was pretty much missing in every situation. Astonishingly, time and time again the Allies did not stop to evaluate why they had suffered severe losses, but continued to operate in the same clumsy fashion. The only justifications they offered for their failure was that the Germans were 'fanatics', fought 'fiercely' and were 'hardened' troops, excuses which were supposed to explain the consistent shortcomings of the Allies. A completely different picture emerges, however, from the cases we have examined: the Germans were professionally led troops and were willing to take that extra step in preparation for battle.

There is one other thing that catches the eye. Historians seldom pay attention to the true combat power of the forces deployed. Units are introduced without mentioning the actual number of deployable tanks or men. Panzerbrigade 107 sounds impressive but could in reality never field more than twenty-five tanks and tank destroyers; the Allied divisions, on the other hand, could muster more than 200 tanks and had an overwhelming number of tanks, halftracks and so on in reserve. The same applies to the battalions: nominally, German battalions consisted of 800 men, but in reality they often contained fewer than 200. The struggle for

Overloon appeared to be one of matched forces, since the Allies, despite their superiority in numbers, were unable to push the Germans aside. In reality, this was a battle between two numerically completely unequal sides, and it is clear that Montgomery's principle held good: only with a superiority of 3:1 did the Allies stand a chance of winning.

Calculating relative battlefield performance during the battle for Overloon is revealing. The Americans and British lost 1,878 men and about 60 tanks, the Germans 600 men and a few tanks. Assuming that on average 25,000 Allied soldiers confronted 5,000 Germans, even the Germans' advantage as defenders had little impact on their battlefield performance. With even losses, this performance – assuming that a fighting force of 5,000 in a defensive position has a relative strength of 15,000 – would represent a factor of 25/15 or 166 per cent. The British lost three times as many men, leading to a relative battlefield performance against them of around 500 per cent! And this is not to calculate the performance of the tanks: the Allies had hundreds of them, the Germans a few dozen. In general, this would lead to an absolute battlefield performance of around 900 per cent, the 'going rate' for a Panther or Tiger versus a Sherman or Churchill. The relative battlefield performance is a multiple of the absolute battlefield performance, given the great superiority in tanks on the Allied side.

What was true at Overloon applies to the entire Second World War: the Germans were almost always in the minority, but through superior training, leadership, tactics and their mastery of the concert of battle, time and again they gained the upper hand in confrontations with the Allies, at least when expressed in relative battlefield performance. The Second World War in the west was an accumulation of Overloons, a series of relatively small battles in which the Allies always incurred heavy losses but eventually managed to force a breakthrough due to their superiority in men and materiel; a *Vernichtungskrieg* (war of attrition) so to speak, characterized by a *Materialslacht* (battle of materiel), the type of war that the Germans wanted to avoid with their *Bewegungskrieg*. It is one way of winning, but at the expense of many lives, both among your own troops and in the civilian population.

CHAPTER EIGHT

Reflections and Conclusions

In this chapter we will try to outline some of the main insights we have gained, based on the themes of the different chapters.

The first conclusion is some organizations find it hard to reflect and learn. The Americans and British systematically refused to recognize or acknowledge their weaknesses and the strengths of their German opponents; this remains true today, as debate on the roles of the different belligerents continue. Understanding one's opponent is difficult if one fails to grasp his command concepts and the ways these are implemented. It is clear that this was a weak point of both the Americans and the British. The British seem to have learned little or nothing during the war, other than that in order to achieve success they had to fight the Germans in a planned and controlled way, employing superiority in men and materiel. Relying on overwhelming force and weight of numbers, they showed no interest in a fundamental analysis of the successes of the German Army or the doctrine it used; instead, they treated it as just 'the German way of war'. To some extent they can be forgiven for taking such a line, since ultimately they emerged the victors from two world wars, although the extent of their losses should have given them pause for thought. Analysis of First World War engagements would have demonstrated the differences in battlefield performance if they had cared to look, but they did not.

The Americans had been impressed by the Prussian Army and its command concept, but central elements such as the role and position of the officer corps and the concept of *Auftragstaktik* completely passed them by:

Even after studying the Prussian and German armies for decades, the US military showed 'difficulty interpreting' the concept of *Auftragstaktik* and most officers would not come close to it even when they attended the next higher military education institute. (48:174)

Misinterpretation of the Prussian system also meant that the Americans regarded officers as a privileged caste. In addition, just like the British, the Americans failed to understand all the variables and their connections in the formula Impact = Exploration × Preparation × Focus × Cooperation × Speed × Mass × Continuation. That is why their 'battle concert' seldom sounded 'melodic' and generally ended up relying on the use of massive bombardments. The only factor in the equation which the Allies understood was 'Mass'; all the other elements were ignored by them, and their rigid command and control structures obstructed fast decision making. The Germans consistently took advantage of this, and it allowed them time to withdraw and regroup. The Allies themselves acknowledged their shortcomings in this area, sometimes describing their own actions, as we have seen, as 'sluggish' and 'lacklustre' and their leadership as an 'almost timid operational and tactical command'. Field Marshal Alexander aired his frustration as follows:

> The enemy is quicker than we are at regrouping his forces, quicker at thinning out on a defensive front to provide troops to close gaps at decisive points, quicker in effecting reliefs, quicker at mounting attacks and counter-attacks, and above all quicker at reaching decisions at the battlefield. By comparison, our methods are often slow and cumbersome, and this applies to all troops, both British and American.

The Allies also failed to use the *Schwerpunkt*, the weakest point in the opposing lines, as the focus of an attack, but tended to advance on a broad front. In the words of Patton, 'Everybody fire and everybody move.' This tactic was rarely successful, the Germans ultimately succumbing only when faced with overwhelming Allied superiority in men and materiel. Cooperation between the various army units, perhaps the 'magic bullet' of German *Auftragstaktik*, was usually absent or at best undeveloped on the Allied side. When it did occur at the operational level it was often solely by chance. Reconnaissance by the Allies was generally limited to the study of maps, and only rarely did senior officers come to the front to personally inspect the terrain over which their units had to fight. 'For a commander there is no substitute equal to his own eyes', said Patton wisely, but this precept was rarely followed and was not an integral part of the Allied officers' training. Preparation consisted of drafting detailed plans which considerably limited the personal freedom and initiative of the troops, while institutes such as Fort Leavenworth only taught standard solutions to tactical problems which often had nothing to do with the reality of the battlefield. In short, the importance of the above elements as part of a broader concept was simply not recognized by the Allies, let alone studied or discussed.

If we examine the other building blocks in the success of the German Army, in comparison to the Allies, a number of things catch the eye. Something we have frequently discussed is cooperation, in the form of *Kampfgruppen* as well as a more general tendency to support each other at all times. When under combat pressure, German troops tended to integrate to a higher level, while Allied troops tended to disintegrate. In the words of Field Marshal Alexander:

> In addition there was the astonishing flexibility in the [German] chain of command which permitted the instantaneous welding together of the most heterogeneous units, from all arms, into effective battlegroups.

Kampfgruppen are actually very advanced forms of organization, and even today successful examples are rarely encountered in civilian life. Not surprisingly, the German Army only achieved this level of cooperation and integration through constant training. It is also interesting to note that this form of cooperation was not affected by social barriers: the cavalry, historically staffed by the aristocracy, were quite prepared to work with the infantry, traditionally farmers and workers, and both in turn worked with engineering specialists often recruited from among city dwellers. This may seem perfectly logical to modern ears, but in the middle of the nineteenth century it represented a social revolution. Such collaboration resulted in the great resilience and high regenerative capacity of the German Army, at least in organizational terms. A *Kampfgruppe* could emerge out of nowhere, as exemplified by *Kampfgruppe* Spindler at Arnhem. As a result, it became difficult to predict when and in what form such a phenomenon would occur or how best to respond to it, a problem never resolved by the Allies. The only exception might have been Patton who, copying the Germans, named his combat teams after their commander rather than allocating them a number: but that did not turn them into *Kampfgruppen*.

The German General Staff remained a real enigma in the eyes of all its opponents. It was known to play an important role in the command concept, but not what this role was, or how it was structured. Whereas in the Prussian and German Army the General Staff was actually a centre of knowledge and innovation which ensured that complacency did not set, its American equivalent became a regular staff department, which slowed development rather than stimulating it. Its British counterpart in the Second World War, the Imperial General Staff, could not do more than attempt to reconcile the competing views of the various regiments; independent thought or development of a command doctrine were out of the question.

Something which contributed greatly to the effectiveness of the Germans' command concept were the *Erfahrungsberichte*, reviews which provided feedback on all combat actions and formed the basis of education and innovation. The Germans' opponents also evaluated combat actions, but there is no indication that this led to any improvement: the Allies continued to fall back on methods from the First World War, such as the signature tactic of a massive artillery and air bombardment followed by an equally massive infantry attack. Even though overwhelming firepower would eventually pave the way for victory, it was not a very subtle way of waging war, and caused excessive casualties, both military and civilian.

In the training of officers, German efforts were focused on socializing all those involved into a cohesive group. The Germans were very aware of the sociological, psychological and educational dimensions of groups, group dynamics and the effect of leadership on groups. Their entire training and education programme was permeated with these ideas, which meant that men were not only extremely professionally led, but also directed by officers and NCOs who looked after the human needs of their subordinates. It is therefore no wonder that a survey of tens of thousands of German prisoners of war showed that 'almost all non-commissioned officers and officers at the level of the company by the German soldier during the campaign in Western Europe were considered brave, efficient and compassionate.' Many examples of this can be found in previous chapters.

On the Allied side, the divisions between officers, non-commissioned officers and men were very apparent. In the British Army this was a reflection of a hierarchical, class-based society; among the Americans it was a result of the belief that officers should form a separate caste. While British troops recognized their own society in the system and mostly went along with it, this 'yawning social chasm' stirred up much bad blood among American GIs: 'Surveys in social psychology among US personnel showed a catastrophic relationship between enlisted men and their officers.' This was combined with the typical American view of training, in which the breaking of the will of the individual held a central place: 'The erasure of individuality would create a malleability to discipline; repetitive actions would instil that automatic response for which the service strove.' Men would join the larger whole and thus become subject to its discipline, actions would become automatic, independent thought was discouraged: 'Do what you are told, don't think and you will survive.' This led to men becoming selfish, their sole purpose being survival. This is evident in the way in which newcomers were treated: 'old timers' immediately deployed them at the front, to avoid being wounded or killed themselves.

If one compares this with the German system, whereby newly arrived recruits, who always travelled to the front as a group together with their officers and non-commissioned officers and were first trained away from the battle by front-line units for acclimatization before deployment, the differences between the armies become clear. The Americans overlooked an important dimension, that of human nature: 'While drawing up tables of organization and elementary guides to tactics, the higher echelons appear to have neglected a sufficient study of actual human behaviour.'

This brings us to the subject of morale and discipline. As regards the British, it was a remarkable feat that they were able at all times to maintain discipline, especially under difficult circumstances, for example in prisoner of war camps, where von Moltke's words truly come into their own: 'Discipline is the pillar of every army and maintaining discipline is a blessing for all.' The British showed in captivity that:

> The willingness of many officers to accept service to the men as an indissoluble component of leadership and the willingness of the men to defer to rank, its orders and its prerogatives, served soldiers well when, in one of the war's sternest ordeals, survival often hinged on the preservation of military cohesiveness.

By comparison, the Americans had a less good track record. Behaviour that is often depicted as 'cool' or 'off-hand' in films was in fact a symptom of the absence of that *Innere Führung* which the Germans considered to be so important, the predictable, correct conduct under all circumstances that connects the individual to a larger community. The fragility of American discipline is evident from countless cases where officers lost all control over their men. This extremely disturbing feature has rarely been the subject of American research, because such conduct by enlisted men also seems to be an expression of typically American rugged individualism. American morale was, unlike that of the Germans and British, generally low. After all, it was not their war but a European conflict, and men wanted to avoid becoming casualties of it. The same attitude began to be seen on the British side as the war progressed: risk-avoidance began to appear, as well as a tendency to leave things to the artillery and the air force. Ultimately, victory was indeed made possible in this way, by what the German Chief of Staff General Halder termed the 'American historical material superiority'.

So how did the Germans lose a war with an army that was superior in all respects? Perhaps it can all be explained by this anecdote from Colonel David H. Hackford about his encounter with a German prisoner of war:

I remember a German lieutenant captured at Salerno who I was guarding in 1946 in a prisoners-of-war camp. He was a real tough looking Kraut and I was a young punk; a pimply-faced kid. He could speak perfect English, and I was riding him. I said, 'Well, if you are so tough, if you're all supermen, how come you're here captured and I am guarding you?' And he looked at me and said, 'Well, it's like this. I was on this hill as a battery commander with six 88-millimeter anti-tank guns, and the Americans kept sending tanks down the road. We kept knocking them out. Every time they sent a tank we knocked it out. Finally we ran out of ammunition and the Americans didn't run out of tanks. And that's it in a nutshell.' (15:294)

CHAPTER NINE

Epilogue

When I started writing this book I was able fall back on material that I have used for my other books in recent years. I knew something of the considerable differences between the Prussian/German Army and the British and Americans. I already had a good picture of the British, and I suspected that they themselves also realized that there was something fundamentally wrong in their system. I was shocked to observe the differences between the British and German trenches at the Bovington Tank Museum in Dorset, England. While the British trenches looked like a diminutive version of Dante's hell, the German ones were more like a series of interconnected rooms, provided with sturdy wooden walls and decorated with care. Everyone who sees them must wonder why one side was able to offer its men good shelter, while the other had little more than sloppily constructed, muddy holes. It is one thing to start with a simple trench, but to stick with such a thing for four years indicates a pathological lack of interest in the well-being of your men. The same goes for the tactics the British used.

When I delved deeper into the American Army, I initially thought that my earlier findings would be modified. The opposite was true. As I gained further insight into the psychological and sociological dimensions of the American Army, the picture emerged of an organization that, in this respect, made almost every mistake imaginable – and that during four years of war in which a lot could have been learned. In fact, the American Army persists in the same mistakes to this day. Many Dutch veterans, whether members of UN missions in the Middle East or of fighting units in Afghanistan, have confirmed my image in recent years: that the American Army still operates in line with the picture given in this book. In two aspects, however, my interlocutors praised the Americans: their logistics are excellent, and they do everything in their power to bring back their wounded and dead.

What about *Auftragstaktik*? Firstly, more than 18 million men were trained in this command concept, or in business terms this 'management concept', on the German side during the Second World War. I cannot imagine that this did not play a major role in the resurrection of Germany after the war. In a world where improvisation was the only way to survive and move forward, where people had been socialized into units and networks, where deep personal and emotional relationships had been developed, *Auftragstaktik* could have played an important connecting role in working and dealing with other people. It would be interesting to enquire in more detail whether this was the case.

In military organizations *Auftragstaktik* has continued to exist, but under a different name to avoid any 'infection' that might be suggested by its previous associations. US Army Field Manual FM 100-5 of the 1970s and 1980s contains passages that could have come straight from von Moltke:

> Agility – the ability of friendly forces to act faster than the enemy – is the first prerequisite for seizing and holding the initiative. Such greater quickness permits the rapid concentration of friendly strength against enemy vulnerabilities. This must be done repeatedly so that by the time the enemy reacts to one action, another has already taken its place, disrupting his plans and leading to late, uncoordinated, and piecemeal enemy responses. It is this process of successive concentration against locally weaker or unprepared enemy forces which enables smaller forces to disorient, fragment, and eventually defeat much larger opposing formations.

This text indicates that the core elements of modern *Auftragstaktik* apply more than ever to battlefields that are now much more fragmented than in the Second World War. In certain circumstances, fleeting opportunities, fluid situations and the chaos of battle force units to make rapid decisions. Speed of action is necessary for a smaller fighting force to eliminate a larger one, and speed can only be achieved by decentralized decision making along the lines of *Auftragstaktik*. American practice, however, was and is often different, as is clear from the following:

> In previous wars, officials in Washington, including the president, trusted military commanders in the field to make decisions. During the Vietnam War, their approach was dramatically different. Targets were selected and approved by a process that involved the Joint

Chiefs of Staff, the State Department and President Johnson . . .
The level of control was so comprehensive that even the number of
aircraft and the types of weapons used were dictated from officials
in Washington. This frustrated military commanders and pilots,
including those on board *Intrepid*, who often felt that politicians
prevented them from achieving military success in Vietnam.
(Intrepid Museum, New York)

The Gulf Wars and the war in Afghanistan also provide a picture of
technology which enabled centralized control of the fine detail of all sorts
of operations.

Advice from the sky

The American Army has been struggling for decades with two
opposing mindsets: on the one hand, decentralized decision-
making is important on a fragmented battlefield; on the other hand,
technology makes it possible for central command to follow the
fighting at the level of the individual soldier and be involved in
decision making. In Vietnam, it was the helicopter that made a
supervisory role possible:

> In the final analysis, the helicopter's most pernicious
> contribution to the fighting in Vietnam may have been its
> undermining of the influence and initiative of small unit
> commanders. By providing a fast, efficient airborne command
> post, the helicopter all too often turned supervisors into
> 'oversupervisors'. Since rarely was there more than one clash
> in any given area at any given time, the company commander
> on the ground attempting to fight his battle could usually
> observe orbiting in tiers above him his battalion commander,
> brigade commander, assistant division commander, division
> commander, and even his field force commander. With all
> that advice from the sky, it was easy to imagine how much
> individual initiative and control the company commander
> himself could exert on the ground, until nightfall sent the
> choppers to roost.

This image was confirmed in the 1980s by experiments at the National Training Center which showed that many non-commissioned officers had not learned to think independently and assumed that their superiors would think for them. Since they were conditioned to follow detailed plans, they did not dare to make decisions on the spot; officers, moreover, often found themselves doing things that they knew were unsound. In a survey of 12,000 officers from lieutenant to colonel, 49 per cent agreed that 'the bold, original, creative officer cannot survive in today's Army.'

Yet decentralized decision-making, at least at the higher levels, is not an unknown phenomenon in the US Army; that is, if you go far enough back in time. Grant's instruction to Sherman during the Civil War had as its premise: 'I do not propose to lay down for you a plan of campaign ... but simply to lay down the work it is desirable to have done and leave you free to execute it in your own way.' As the Civil War progressed, the need for decentralized decision-making grew, but its importance seems to have been subsequently forgotten. Another proponent of *Auftragstaktik* of a later date was, of course, Patton, who said, 'Tell them what to do and they will surprise you with their ingenuity.'

Against this background, we should also look at the popularity of the term 'mission command' in the US Army, a style of command that seems directly derived from *Auftragstaktik*. Mission command is combined with the concept of 'commander's intent': knowledge of the higher goal that the commander has in mind. It is unclear, however, whether in an organization that has for two centuries made centralization its highest goal, this 'dangerous form of modernism' can get a foothold. We have seen how many variables play a role in this concept of mission command and commander's intent, and what psychological and sociological dimensions these two simple terms encompass. And if the army's culture is not adapted to it, the chances of success will be small. The question is whether the Americans are capable of understanding concepts that are so far removed from their own culture. Past cases have already shown that 'Even after studying the Prussian and German armies for decades, the US military showed "difficulty interpreting" the concept of *Auftragstaktik* and most officers would not come closer to it even when they attended the next higher military education institute.'

How does this apply to the modern German Army? With the establishment of the Bundeswehr in 1955, the question of a command concept was again discussed, and *Auftragstaktik* remained the core of the doctrine, especially given the experience of the Second World War, when its superiority was so clearly demonstrated. The guiding principle of the new Bundeswehr, as represented in the Himmeroder Denkschrift, its founding document, was the deep interconnection of the army with society. Historical sensitivities in Germany meant that debate focused on the relationship between the societal or constitutional responsibilities of conscript soldiers and the military orders that they might receive. The concept of *Innere Führung* was redefined as placing orders in the broader context of political decisions: the soldier should decide if his actions were in accordance with the law, with the constitution in particular, with what should be expected of a citizen in uniform, and with human values, rights and obligations.

In 1998 *Auftragstaktik* returned in full: the Zentrale Dienstvorschrift (Central Regulation) C1-100/0-1001 'Truppenführung von Landstreit-kräften' (Command of Land Forces) runs as follows:

> *Auftragstaktik* is the overarching command concept of the Bundeswehr. It is based on common trust and requires an unwavering commitment from every soldier to fulfil his duty . . . The military commander indicates what his intent is, formulates clear and realistic goals and ensures that the required manpower and resources are available. He will only go into more details when certain actions aimed at the same goal must be coordinated.

The document also mentions seven conditions:

- Trust your people
- Accept mistakes
- Formulate realistic goals
- Give room to manoeuvre
- Make sure your subordinates assume responsibility with pleasure
- There can only be one leader
- Make sure that there is a common vision and focus on cooperation

This could be von Moltke speaking of *Auftragstaktik*. And so this book has come full circle.

APPENDIX

Absolute and Relative
Battlefield Performance

The Historical Evaluation and Research Organization (HERO) has built up a database of more than a hundred battles from the First and Second World War, supplemented with data from the Korean War and wars in the Middle East. This database is then used to map the combat effectiveness of the various armies. In his book *A Genius for War: the German Army and the General Staff*, T. N. Dupuy gives a detailed list of the battles that comprise the database, and from these he has calculated the battlefield performance of the combatants involved.

The distinction between absolute and relative battlefield performance is important. The first is based on a calculation of the losses on two sides of equal strength; the second takes into account a number of other circumstances and links them to a factor in which operating from a defensive posture is the central theme:

- Hasty defence, a factor of 1.2 advantage
- Prepared defence, a factor 1.5 advantage
- Reinforced defence, a factor of 1.6 advantage

All kinds of combinations are of course possible: for example, fighting from a prepared defence line in the first instance, followed by hasty defence during a subsequent retreat. These are further elaborated below. It is striking that the Germans are always in a minority, yet never fail to record a higher absolute and relative battlefield performance.

A. Overview of German versus Allied units in the First World War

	Allied Forces	German Forces
Battle strength of the units involved	6,896,000	5,090,000
Number of casualties	2,349.000	1,866.000
Losses with equal combat strength	3,241.620	1,866.000
Absolute battlefield performance per man	1.0	1.73
Relative battlefield performance per man	1.0	1.44

Explanation

These ten battles involved a total of 6,896,000 men on the Allied side against 5,090,000 Germans: a difference factor of 1.36. If there had been as many Germans as Allies, i.e. sides of equal strength, the Allied losses would have been correspondingly higher (factor 1.36). The numbers of losses yield an absolute battlefield performance of 1.73; in other words, 1.73 Allied victims per fallen German. The relative battlefield performance is a factor of 1.2 lower because the Germans fought partly from defensive positions and thus had a relative advantage.

B. Overview of German versus Allied units in the Second World War, June 1944 to May 1945

	Allied Forces	German Forces
Battle strength of the units involved	1,783,237	940,198
Number of casualties	47,743	48,585
Losses with equal combat strength	89,838	48,585
Absolute battlefield performance per man	1.0	1.84
Relative battlefield performance per man	1.0	1.53

Explanation

The numbers involved in the seventy-eight battles here represent a difference factor of 1.8. If there had been as many Germans as Allies, i.e. forces of equal strength, the losses on Allied side would have been correspondingly higher (factor 1.8). The number of losses yields an absolute battlefield performance of 1.84, or 1.84 Allied victims per fallen German. The relative battlefield performance is a factor 1.2 lower because the Germans fought partly from defensive positions and thus enjoyed a relative advantage. Incidentally, this does not take into account the air superiority and predominance in materiel on the Allied side. It is unclear how this should be calculated, but it should probably be a factor of at least 1.5; we would therefore be left with a relative battlefield performance of 2.25.

C. The Battle of Kursk

	Soviet Forces	German Forces
Battle strength of the units involved	98,000	62,000
Number of casualties	22,000	13,600
Losses with equal combat strength	34,750	13,600
Absolute battlefield performance per man	1.0	2.55
Relative battlefield performance per man	1.0	4.08

Explanation

In the fighting at Kursk there was a difference factor of 1.58 in numbers. If there had been as many Germans as Soviets, i.e. forces of equal strength, the losses on the Soviet side would have been correspondingly higher (factor 1.58). The number of losses resulted in an absolute battlefield performance of 2.55, i.e. 2.55 Soviets were killed per fallen German. The relative battlefield performance is a factor of 1.6 higher because the Soviets were in entrenched positions and thus enjoyed an advantage, so the relative battlefield performance is 4.08.

D. Overview of German versus Soviet units in 1944

	Soviet Forces	German Forces
Battle strength of the units involved	6,100,000	3,500,000
Number of casualties	5,000,000	1,100,000
Losses with equal combat strength	8,714,000	1,100,000
Absolute battlefield performance per man	1.0	7.9
Relative battlefield performance per man	1.0	6.07

Explanation

At the beginning of 1944, the difference factor in numbers was 1.74. The Soviets were able to maintain their strength during the course of the year through bringing up of new units, but the Germans were not. As a result, the Germans' strength fell to around 2,500,000 men. If there had been as many Germans as Soviets, i.e. forces of equal strength, the losses on the Soviet side would have been correspondingly higher (factor 1.74). The numbers of losses yield an absolute battlefield performance of 7.9, i.e. 7.9 Soviets were killed per fallen German. The relative battlefield performance is a factor 1.3 lower because the Germans had the opportunity to build reinforcements and therefore had a relative advantage of 6.07. This does not take into account the fact that during the course of the year the combat strength on the German side fell from 3,500,000 to 2,500,000 men. If the average is set at 3,000,000, then the ratios are 2.03, 9.22 and 7.09 respectively.

E. The Battle of El Alamein

	Allied Forces	German/ Italian Forces
Battle strength of the units involved	195,000	82,000
Number of casualties	2,400	1,100/1,200
Losses with equal combat strength	5,520	1,100/1,200
Absolute battlefield performance per man	1.0	2.4
Relative battlefield performance per man	1.0	1.6

Explanation

The fighting at El Alamein started with a difference factor of 2.3. If the forces had been equal, the losses on the British side would have been correspondingly higher (factor 2.3). The number of losses provides an absolute battlefield performance of 2.4, i.e. 2.4 British victims compared to every German or Italian. The relative battlefield performance is 1.5 lower because the Germans and Italians had the advantage of being in defensive positions, thus it becomes 1.6.

An incidental point here: the Italians had a lower battlefield performance, so if only German units had participated in the fighting, the Axis battlefield performance would have been higher.

Glossary

German	English
Abteilung	Battalion
Auftragstaktik	Decentralized command concept that clearly defines a goal, but leaves freedom in the way it should be reached
Aussere Führung	Enforced discipline
Befehlstaktik	Centralized command concept that leaves no room for own initiative; a team has to follow strict orders or act only according to a plan
Beweglichkeit	Manoeuvrability
Bewegungskrieg	War of manoeuvre and movement
Einheit	Unit, but also unity
Erfahrungsberichte	Feedback report
Ersatz Bataillon	Replacement battalion
Ersatzheer	Reserve Army
Fähnrichsexamen	Ensign exam
Fallschirmjäger	Paratrooper
Feldersatz Battalion	Replacement battalion at the front
Feldgendarmerie	Military police
Feldheer	Field Army
Feldwebel	Non-commissioned officer
Flak	Anti-aircraft gun
Führen durch Aufträge	*see* Auftragstaktik
Führung und Gefecht der Verbundenen Waffen	Leading and fighting with combined armed forces

German	English
Führen unter der Hand	Leading behind a superior's back
General Stab	General Staff
Grundlagen der Erziehung des Heeres	Basic principles of military education
Heer	German Army
Hörsaalleiter	Teacher
Innere Führung	Internalized discipline, self discipline
Instandsetzungsabteilung	Logistics battalion
Kadettenschule	Cadet school
Kaiser Heer	Army of the Kaiser
Kampfgemeinschaft	Unity/community in battle
Kampfgruppe	Combat group
Kampfstaffel	Mobile combat unit protecting a divisional commander
Kriegsakademie	Military Academy
Kriegsspiel	Wargame
Krisenfest	Stress-resistant
Kriegsschule	Military school
Landser	Private
Oberkommando des Heeres (OKH)	Supreme Command of the Army
Oberkommando des Wehrmacht (OKW)	Supreme Command of the Armed Forces
Panzerjäger	Anti-tank units
Panzergrenadiere	Armoured infantry
Panzer Kampfwagen (Pz.KPfw.)	Tank
Propaganda Kompagnie	Propaganda company
Reichsarbeitsdienst (RAD)	German state labour force
Reichswehr	Army of the Republic

German	English
Schnelle Kombinationen	Fast combinations
Sonder Kraftfahrzeug (Sd.Kfz.)	Special vehicle, often a halftrack
Schwerpunkt	Focal point of an attack
Stosstrupp	Shock troop
StuG (Sturmgeschütz)	Assault gun
Truppe	Troops, units
Truppenamt	Troop office
Verbundene Waffen	Combined arms
Wehrkreis	Military district
Wehrkreis Prüfung	Examination in the military district
Wehrmacht	Nazi Army, Air Force and Marines

Bibliography/References

1. Alger, J. I. (1982), *The Quest for Victory*, Westport: Greenwood Press
2. *Command Magazine* (1988), 'Hitler's armies, the evolution and structure of German armed Forces, 1993–1945', New York: Combined Books, Inc.
3. Batailles & Blinder no. 10 (2009), 'Les "chauds" en Normande', Aix en Provence: CaraTerre
4. Batailles & Blinder no. 22 (2012), 1944: 'Duels dans le bocage', Aix en Provence: CaraTerre
5. Batailles & Blinder no. 43 (2013), 'La "Panzer Lehr" face au debarquement', Aix en Provence: CaraTerre
6. Batailles & Blinder no. 53 (2013), 'Baptême du feu de la "Hitlerjugend"', Aix en Provence: CaraTerre
7. Batailles & Blinder no. 56 (2014), 'Echec à la "Das Reich"', Aix en Provence: CaraTerre
8. Batailles & Blinder no. 64 (2015), 'Panzer Grenadier 1939/1945', Aix en Provence: CaraTerre
9. Batailles & Blinder no. 65 (2015), 'Stug Abteilungen', Aix en Provence: CaraTerre
10. Carver, M. (1986), *Dilemmas of the Desert War*, London: B. T. Batsford Ltd
11. Creveld, M. van (1974), *Fighting Power*, Westport: Greenwood Press
12. Creveld, M. van (1977), *Supplying War: Logistics from Wallenstein to Patton*, Cambridge: Cambridge University Press
13. Creveld, M. van (1986), 'On learning from the Wehrmacht and other things', *Military Review*, January 1986
14. Dunigan, J. F. (ed.) (1978), *The Russian Front, Germany's War in the East 1941–1945*, London: Arms and Armour Press
15. Dupuy, T. N. (1977), *A Genius for War. The German Army and the General Staff*, London: MacDonald and Jane's
16. Ellis, J. E. (1990), *Brute Force, Allied Strategy and Tactics in the Second World War*, New York: Penguin Group

17. Esebeck, H. G. von (1943), *Helden der Wüste*, Berlin: Verlag der Heimbücherei
18. Franz, P. (1984), 'Operational concepts', *Military Review*, July 1984
19. Forty, G. (1977), *The Armies of Rommel*, London: Arms and Armour Press
20. Fussell, P. (2003), *The Boys' Crusade. American G.I.s in Europe*, London: Orion House
21. Griffith. R. (1992), *Forward into Battle*, Navato (Ca): Presidio Press
22. Guderian, H. (1952/2000), *Panzer Leader*, London: Penguin Group
23. *Guerre Mondial* no. 19 (2013), 'Le Panzer Division Herman Göring', Coaraze: Editions Astrolab
24. *Guerre Mondial* no. 19 (2015), 'La Wehrmacht face au débarquement d'Anzio', Coaraze: Editions Astrolab
25. Heckman W. (transl. S. Saego) (1981), *Rommel's War*, Garden City (NY): Doubleday and Company, Inc.
26. Held, W. and Obermaier, E. (1992), *The Luftwaffe in the North African Campaign 1941–1943*, West Chester (PA): Schiffer Military History
27. Holden Reid, B. (2000), *A Doctrinal Perspective, 1988–1998*, London: Strategic and Combat Studies Institute
28. Irving, D. (1977), *Rommel: the Trail of the Fox*, London: Wordsworth Editions
29. Jentz, T. J. (1998), *Tank Combat in North Africa*, Atgien (PA): Schiffer Military History
30. Kershaw, R. J. (1990), *It Never Snows in September: The German view on Market Garden and the Battle of Arnhem*, London: Ian Allen Publishing Ltd
31. Kurowski, F. (1985), *Der Afrikafeldzug*, Holzminden: Volker Hennig Verlagsbuchhandlung
32. Laffin, J. (1965), *Jackboot: the story of the German soldier*, New York: Cassell
33. Lewin, R. (ed.) (1984), *The War on Land 1939–1945*, London: Random House
34. Lewis, S. J. (1988), 'Reflections on German military reform', *Military Review*, August
35. Linderman, G. F. (2003), *The World within War: Americans' combat experience in World War II*, New York: The Free Press
36. Lucas, J. (1982), *War in the Desert*, London: Arms and Armour Press

37. Luftwaffen-Kriegsberichter-Kompagnie (1943), *Balkenkreuz über Wüstensand*, Oldenburg: Gerhard Stalling Verlag
38. MacGregor Knox, A. (2000), *Hitler's Italian Allies*, Cambridge: Cambridge University Press
39. Mackenzie, J. J. G. and Holden Reid, B. (eds.) (1989), *The British Army and the Operational Level of War*, London: Tri-Service Press Limited
40. Mantoux S. (2013), 'Le Raid sur Hammelburg', *Guerre Mondial*, Oct–Dec 2012/13
41. Messenger, C. (1976), *The Art of Blitzkrieg*, Shepperton (Surrey): Ian Allen Ltd
42. Millett, A. R. and Murray, W. (eds.) (1988), *Military Effectiveness, Volume III, The Second World War*, Boston: Mershon Centre, The Ohio State University
43. Montgomery B. (1958/2008), *The Memoirs of Field Marshal Montgomery*, London: Warwick Press
44. Moorehead, A. (1965), *The Desert War*, London: Hamish Hamilton Ltd
45. Murray, W. (1990), 'Force strategy, Blitzkrieg strategy and the economic difficulties: Nazi grand strategy in the 1930s', *RUSI Journal*
46. Murray, W. (1992), *German Military Effectiveness*, New York: The Nautical & Aviation Publishing Company of America
47. Murray, W. and Millet, A. R. (eds.) (1996), *Military Innovation in the Interwar Period*, Cambridge: Cambridge University Press
48. Muth, J. (2011), *Command Culture: officers' education in the U.S. Army and the German armed forces, 1901–1940*, Denton: University of Texas Press
49. Oeting, D. W. (1993), *Auftragstaktik,* Frankfurt am Main/Bonn: Report Verlag GmbH
50. Ogilvie, R. (1995), *Krijgen is een Kunst*, Amsterdam: Addison Wesley Publishing Company Inc
51. Perrett, B. (1986/97), *Knights of the Black Cross*, London: Wordsworth Editions Limited
52. Pimlott, J. (ed) (1994), *Rommel in his own Words*, London: Greenhill books
53. Playfair, I. S. O. (1956/74), *The History of the Second World War: The Mediterranean and Middle East II*, London: Her Majesty's Stationery Office

BIBLIOGRAPHY/REFERENCES

54. Posen, B.R. (1984), *The Sources of Military Doctrine: France, Britain and Germany between the two World Wars*, New York: Cornell Studies in Security Affairs
55. Richey, S. W. (1984), 'The philosophical basis of the AirLand Battle', *Military Review*, May, 51–52
56. Rosinski, H. and Craig, G. A. (ed.) (1966), *The German Army*, London: Pall Mall Press
57. Samuels, M. (1992), *Doctrine and Dogma: German and British infantry tactics in the First World War*, New York: Greenwood Press
58. Starren, H. (1998), *Grootmeester in Management*, Amsterdam: Teleac/NOT
59. Strachan, H. (1997), *The Politics of the British Army*, Oxford: Clarendon press
60. Strawson, J. (1969), *The Battle for North Africa*, New York, Bonanza Books
61. Toppe, A. (1991), *Desert Warfare: German Experiences in World War II*, Fort Leavenworth (Kansas): Combat Studies Institute, U.S. Army Command and General Staff College
62. Tsouras, P. G. (2002), *Panzers on the Eastern Front: General Ehrard Raus and his panzer divisions in Russia. 1941–1945.* London: Greenhill Books.
63. Warner, P. (1981), *Auchinleck, the Lonely Soldier*, London: Buchan and Enright Ltd
64. Watson, B. A. (1995), *Desert Battle*, Westport: Praeger Publishers
65. Wilt, A. F. (1990), *War from the Top: German and British military decision making during World War II*, London: Tauris and Co

Index

INDEX